CW00337825

ISBN 978-0-259-19183-4
PIBN 10808635

FB &c Ltd, Dalton House, 60 Windsor Avenue, London, SW19 2RR.
Company number 08720141. Registered in England and Wales.

For support please visit www.forgottenbooks.com

LIFE AND LABO

OF

JOHN ASHWO

AUTHOR OF "STRANGE TALES,"

BY

A. L CALMAN.

*** *The Profits to be devoted to the Chapel for t*

SECOND EDITION.

MANCHESTER:
TUBBS AND BROOK, 11, MARKET
LONDON:
SIMPKIN, MARSHALL & CO.; HAMILTON, AD
MORGAN & SCOTT.

1875.

TO THE READER.

MANY friends by whom the subject of this Memoir was held in high esteem for his work's sake, having expressed a great desire for a sketch of his remarkable life, I have compiled from his manuscripts and diaries some of the leading incidents, together with a brief account of the origin and progress of the Chapel for the Destitute, and other abundant labours in the Churches at home and abroad.

The only inducement to undertake the somewhat painful, yet pleasing task was, that any profit that might accrue from the sale of the book will be appropriated towards the support of the work in connection with the Chapel for the Destitute.

That the humble effort may commend itself to the Christian public, be owned of God, and result in the continued support and prosperity of the Chapel for the Destitute is the earnest prayer of

Yours very truly,

A. L. CALMAN.

CONTENTS.

—o—

CHAPTER I.—1813—1832.

Birthplace—Character of the Inhabitants—Jane Clough, Niff, Nudger Races—Early Surroundings—His First Sunday-school—Bamford School: its Associations—Sketch by Sir J. K. Shuttleworth—His First Prize—Removal to Catches, Simpson Clough—Johnny's Sorrow —His Father's Conversion—Scenery at Simpson Clough—His Apprenticeship as a Painter. - - - - Page 5—21

CHAPTER II.—1832—1837.

Falling in Love—Courtship and Marriage—His Second Birth—Persecution by his Fellow-workmen—Imbibing Sceptical Views—His Restoration—Joining the Church—Trial Sermon—Taken on the Plan as a Local Preacher—Reproved. - - - 22—36

CHAPTER III.—1837—1850.

Early Struggles—Out of Work—Shop-keeping—Debt—"Dark Night" —Visit to his Debtors—Empty Cupboard—The Sabbath—The Sanctuary—Precious Promise—Deliverance—Joy—The Old Packman—Commencing Business as a Master Painter—Difficulties—Family Afflictions—Sufferings and Happy Death of his Wife—Drowning of his Eldest Son—Heavy Trials. - - - - 37—52

CHAPTER IV.—1851—1858.

Phrenological Examination—Life-Work—Visit to the London Exhibition—Thoughts Suggested—Broken Vow—Sanctified Affliction—Origin of the Chapel for the Destitute. - - - 53—63

CHAPTER V.—1859—1863.

First Year's Report—Success—Second Report—First Narrative—Home for Fallen Women—Interview with Mr. Finney—Third Report—Cases—The Man who Sold the Donkey and Cart—Proposal to Present him with his Portrait—Cotton Famine of 1862—Relief of the Operatives—Collapse of Rochdale Saving's Bank—Consecration, 1863—Marriage of his only Daughter—"The Two Old Men." 64—77

CHAPTER VI.—1864-1865.

Visit to Birmingham, Guest of Mrs. Sturge—Society of Friends—Painful Experience—Popularity Irksome—Night at Home—Annual Report—"Julia"—"Young Ragged Friends"—1865, Dedication—Seventh Report—Penitents at the Destitute—"Sick Friends"—Fear of becoming Hard-hearted—Tramps at the Destitute—Deaths—Places Visited—Thoughts of Giving up Business—Closing Reflections. - - - - - - - - - 78—94

CHAPTER VII.—1866.

Annual Report—Village Labours—Widow Afflicted with Cancer—Diary for the Year—Interview with Mr. John Bright—Painting—Preaching—Lecturing—Writing. - - - - - 95—122

CHAPTER VIII.—1867.

Annual Statement—Matthew Henry—"William the Tutor"—Letters—Low Lodging-houses—Prayer—Dedication—Family Gathering—Jealousy at the Destitute—Retires from Business—Manchester Exchange—Old Scholars' Tea-meeting at Bamford—Quiet Saturdays. - - - - - - - - - 123—137

CHAPTER IX.—1868.

Tenth Report—Drink—Sad Cases—Visit to Palestine—Arrival at Jerusalem—Feelings—Letter—"At Jericho"—Return—Welcome—Help to Poor Churches—Candidate for Stockport—Sunday Closing Question—Reverence for the Sabbath—Appeal to Sunday Scholars—Deputation to Belper—Casualty—Sympathy with Sufferers. - - - - - - - - - - 138—159

CHAPTER X.—1869.

Sunday Schools—Letters from Adult Scholars—Letter from Miss Bright—Visit to Belle-Vue Prison; to Newcastle—Mothers' Meeting—Visit to London—Drinking Toasts at Dinner—Death of Sister Peggy, and Rachel Jackson—Visit to Edinburgh—Sketch—Grey *Friar's Bobby.* - - - - - - - - 160—176

CONTENTS.

CHAPTER XI.—1871.

Self-Consecration—Extract from Diary—Heartless Work—Visit to Cornwall--At Oxford—Annual Report—Liverpool Police Court—The Three Beds—Blind Friends—Sketch of Matlock—Master of Riber—A Good Wife—Tickling Noses—Ford Hall. - 177—196

CHAPTER XII.—1872-1873.

Reports—Cases—Balance Sheet—Receipts—"My Sick Friends"—Letters—One that Returned to Give Thanks—Visit to Bristol—Death of his Only Daughter—Matthew Henry's Return—Annual Assembly—Visit to the Isle of Man. - - - 197—220

CHAPTER XIII.—VISIT TO AMERICA, 1873.

Appointed Representative to New York Conference—Letter from Mr. John Bright—Preparation for the Voyage—Embarks on Board the *Minnesota*—Reminiscences—Emigrants—Down amongst the Stokers—Children's Prayers—Grecian Bend—Steward's Story—One-eyed Jack. - - - - - - - - 221-239

CHAPTER XIV.—OUTWARD PASSAGE.

Current Indicator—Sketch of Captain Freeman—Ocean Letter—St. John the Aged—Vicissitudes of Life—Banks of Newfoundland—Aurora Borealis—Columbus—May Flower—Arrival, New York—Letters to his Flock, Teachers, and Scholars. - - 240—255

CHAPTER XV.—RAMBLES IN THE NEW WORLD.

First Impressions of New York—The Bible House—Gramercy Hotel—English Sparrows—Their Houses—Origin of Fulton Street Daily Prayer-Meeting—Reception of Delegates to the Evangelical Alliance—The Converted Brahmin...Sunday Schools—Newman Hall, and "Come to Jesus"—Visit to the Central Park and Institutions—Speeches of Boys and Girl—Runaway English Boy—Mother's Letter—Gold Market. - - - - - - - - 256—270

CHAPTER XVI.—RAMBLES *(Continued)*.

Visit to Philadelphia and Washington—Addresses—The Capitol—Treasury—Senate House—The Mint—Normal Training School—Women's Congress—Irish Beggars—Hair Cutting—Falls of Niagara—Indian Settlement—Reception by Dr. Evans and his Staff—Visit to

CONTENTS.

Newhaven, Plymouth, and Boston—Pilgrim Rock—Grand Scenery—Snug Harbour—Farewell Meeting—Homeward Passage—Sailors' Omens—Storm—Floating Wreck--Sabbath Morn Reflections—Arrival at Home. - - - - - - - - 271—288

CHAPTER XVII.—JOHN ASHWORTH AS AN AUTHOR.

His Writings—The Late Mrs. Barrett—Prediction Fulfilled—Poem—Prize Essay—His First Book—First Productions—Women's Lodges—Publication of "Strange Tales"—Her Majesty the Queen accepts a Copy—Vouchers—Walks in Canaan—Simple Records—Criticism—Tracts on War—Offered Apartments at Cheadle Asylum. - 289—310

CHAPTER XVIII.—LECTURER AND PREACHER.

Popularity as a Lecturer—Lectures—Extracts—Young Women, Wives and Mothers—Young Men, Husbands and Fathers -Style of Preaching—Outlines of Sermons. - - - - - 311—328

CHAPTER XIX.—1874.

Renewed Consecration—Prayer—Widow's Tea Meeting—Death of a Dear Friend—Rochdale Town Mission—Symptoms of Failing Health—Visit to London—Conversation with Young Men—James Burrows—Chartists and Parsons—Heavy Work—Last Service—Reading about Hezekiah—At Matlock—Annual Report—Consults Physicians—Hope Gone—Farewell Letter to His Flock—Stockport Sunday School—Painful Sufferings—Peaceful Death. - - 329—344

CHAPTER XX.—FUNERAL.

Funeral Hymn—Music—Inscription for Tomb Stone—Dying Bequest—Letters of Sympathy—Touching Scene at Bury—Tribute of Affection—Funeral Sermons—Circular Letter—His Successor at the Destitute—Services at Chapel and Mission Room. - 345—364

CHAPTER I.

1813—1832.

AT the foot of a range of hills, forming part of what is called the back-bone of England, is Rochdale, situated on the banks of the river Roche, from whence it derives its name.

It has long been noted for its manufacture of flannel and other woollen goods.

Amongst the many illustrious names associated with the history of Rochdale will be recorded in the annals of fame those of two distinguished and great men: John Bright, the Christian statesman, and John Ashworth, the founder of "The Chapel for the Destitute," and author of "Strange Tales from Humble Life," &c.

Many of the great and good whose memories we love to embalm, have issued not from lordly halls or stately mansions; but, as if to defy circumstances, from the lowly cot of some secluded hamlet, or quiet country village: these have, not unfrequently, sent forth grand muscular men, giants of the earth, capable of wielding with extraordinary power the natural gifts of a Beneficent Creator, so as to move the world by their voice or pen; from such an one came the subject of this memoir.

Two miles north-west of Rochdale lies the hamlet of Cutgate, bordering the margin of the road leading to Haslingden; on the right stand a few humble cottages, in one of which, on July 8th, 1813, John

Ashworth was born; and in speaking of that memorable event, he was accustomed humorously to repeat the story, that on the day he was born an old woman took him up in her arms, kissed him, and looking him in the face, said, "Aye bless thee, thou'rt a fine lad, but thou'rt one too many."

This "fine lad," however, lived to prove that what seemed to the old nurse a useless incumbrance was not "one too many," an encouraging fact for struggling parents with large families. He was the second son and eighth child of John and Alice Ashworth, natives of the neighbourhood, and by trade woollen weavers.

Many of the villages and hamlets in Lancashire were notorious in those days for the rude manners and degrading sports of their inhabitants, but none more so than those of Cutgate and Bagslate. Bull-baits, cock-battles, dog-fights, trail-hunts, drinking and gambling had been for half a century their popular amusements, in which even the female portion of the community would engage with as much zest and delight as the men, and amongst the foremost of her sex was a powerful masculine woman, a brick-maker, named Jane Clough, who was chosen to lay the foundation stone of the Grand Stand of what were called the Nudger Races,* on Bagslate Common. (See "Contest," "Simple Records," page 149.) We may also here state that Nathaniel Kershaw, the subject of the narrative entitled "Niff and his Dogs," was a resident at Cutgate, and a ringleader amongst the men, and Mr. Ashworth used to say, that when a boy there was no man in the village he feared so much as

* So named from Nudger, a favourite race dog.

Niff. On walking over the ground with him the other day, he showed me the Green where the bull-baits were held—the same spot occupied by the preacher on that memorable Sunday, Sept. 11th 1853, when his quick eye caught sight of Niff standing at his door on the opposite side of the road, shaved and washed, with clean shirt on, and followed him as he drew near, and stood peeping and listening behind the holly bush. Nathaniel remarked, "He never took his eye off me; and yonder's the very spot; and it was a happy day for poor Niff, bless the Lord."

Amidst all these unfavourable surroundings John Ashworth spent his early days, and it would have been no wonder if he had, to some extent, acquired a taste for such objectionable amusements as were indulged in at that time. He had, however, two more powerful and counteracting influences, to which, under God, he attributed his preservation in youth, and the formation of his religious character in after life—a pious, praying mother, and the Sunday-school; and when speaking of the latter he used to say, "Thank God for Sunday-schools; the Sabbath-school has been a blessing to millions, but to none more than myself."

The first Sunday-school he attended was at Bagslate, about a mile distant from his home, and was held in the body of the old Wesleyan Methodist Chapel. Most readers will be familiar with the story of the wool-sheet pinafore, so touchingly given by Mr. Ashworth, showing his poverty while a scholar at Bagslate.

"One Saturday evening I was playing with my companions, when my mother gently laid her hand on my head and requested me to go with her into the house. I took up my marbles and quietly followed her.

"'What do you want me for, mother? It is not time to go to bed yet; let me play a little longer, will you?'

"'I know it is soon to call you from your play; but I cannot help it. Your trousers want mending; and I want to wash your shirt; for though we are poor we ought to be clean. I intended to get you a pair of clogs, but I am not able. I am making you a pinafore out of part of a wool-sheet; it will cover your ragged clothes, and you will then look a little better.'

"The quiet way in which she spoke, and the sad look which accompanied her words subdued all my objections. I silently walked upstairs to allow her to begin washing and patching; and while my playfellows were still laughing and shouting in the street, I crept naked into my humble bed;—not to sleep, but to think and to weep. My mind wandered far into the future that night. What air-castles I did build! I thought I grew to be a man, entered into business, made money, built a new house with a white door and brass knocker to it, planted trees around it, and had a lawn and a garden; bought myself new clothes, and twenty shirts;—bought my mother a new crimson cloak and a new bonnet, and gave her plenty of money to buy clothes for my brothers and sisters, and to get a set of mahogany drawers, an eight-day clock, and muslin curtains to the window,—I then fell asleep a man of great importance, and awoke in the morning without a shirt!

"Sunday morning ever found my mother doing all she could to get us in time for school. She rose the first and lighted the fire, got ready the breakfast, dressed the younger children, and helped us all. This Sunday morning I was going to have on my new "bishop," to cover my patched garments. I shall never forget that new pinafore. The wool-sheets had at that time stamped on them, in large black letters, the word WOOL. My mother had got one of these old sheets as a gift from the warehouse; but it was so far worn that she could not make my pinafore without either putting on a patch or cutting through the letters. She chose the lesser evil, thinking she could wash out the letters; but though she washed, and washed, and washed again, she could not wash out the remaining half of the

BIRTHPLACE OF JOHN ASHWORTH.

word. I put my arms down the sleeves and was stretching the front when I saw the letters. My little spirit sank within me in bitter sorrow. I looked into my mother's face, but when I saw the tears in her eyes I instantly said,—

"'Never mind, mother; never mind. It will do very well. It covers my patches; and when I get to school I will sit on the letters, and then no one will see them. Don't cry, mother; we shall be better off yet.'

"Away I went to the Sunday-school, with bare feet, and a pack-sheet pinafore, with half the letters WOOL down one side, to take my place in the third Bible class, among boys who were much better dressed, and who did not like to sit beside me on that account.

"I well remember the place where I sat that day;—how I put my bare feet under the form to prevent my proud class-mates from treading on my toes; the feeling that I was poor distressed me."

In his diary for 1870, under date July 14th, he records,—"Took one service at the opening of a new Wesleyan chapel at Bagslate, built on the site of the old school in which I was a barefooted boy. The Lord be praised for His goodness to me from that time to this moment."

When the old chapel was being taken down, having a distinct recollection of the form under which he put his bare feet, as well as the place where he sat *that day*, he went and bargained with one of the stewards for it. The form itself is of no intrinsic value, but it was of value in the estimation of him who had sat on it fifty years before a poor boy, with wool-sheet pinafore. He gave one guinea to be possessed of it, had it brought home, put into his study, where it still remains; and scores of times has prayer been offered up at that form, imploring God's blessing upon the work in which he was engaged.

At Bagslate Sunday school, where he received

his first lessons, he had the advantage and disadvantage of two teachers, apparently very different in temperament and disposition, his early impressions of whom he gives as follows:—

"We had two teachers, attending each alternate Sunday. One of them was a tall, patient, red-cheeked man, with soft hands, kind words, and a loving heart. We called him Old James, and we all loved him. The other was a stern, bad-tempered man, with a stick, which he took care to make us all well acquainted with. Some people say that you may flog a lad any time, for he is always either going into mischief or just coming out. Our stern teacher seemed to be one of this class of thinkers, for he laid on, right and left. Perhaps we deserved it; if so, we got it, but none of us liked it.

"One Sunday morning Old James was talking to us about heaven. We had been reading the twenty-first chapter of Revelation, and the old man seemed almost in paradise while he was reading and talking with us about it. Never before that day had I such a view of that happy place. Old James saw we were all affected, and he laid his soft hands on our heads, one by one, and besought us to be good lads, and keep holy the Sabbath-day, and then we should go to that glorious place of which we had been reading.

"Most of us had taken our dinners to the school, for nearly all in that class resided two or three miles from the place. At noon we gathered round the large, warm stove, in the bottom of the chapel, and began to untie our small linen handkerchiefs, to see what we had brought for dinner. I well remember mine was an apple-cake, the half of a circle, with the widest *selvedge* of any apple-cake I had ever seen. But it is a queer cake a hungry lad will turn his back upon, so I began digging my teeth into the selvedge, wondering when I should get to the apples. But when I remembered that the cake was as good as my poor dear mother could afford to make, and that she had made the best of what she had to do with, that settled all my questions, and I finished it without a murmur.

"As we sat round the stove, we began to talk about heaven, our morning lesson. Edmund, another scholar, said to me,—

"'Johnny, does thou think thou will ever get to heaven?'

"'I hope I shall, Edmund,' I replied.

"'And where will thou sit in heaven: with Old James, or with him with the stick?' Edmund asked.

"'With Old James, to be sure,' was my answer.

"'So will I, and so will I,' said the other lads, all round.

"That day we were all very good, and made a bargain that we would always go to the school, and keep the Sabbath-day holy, as Old James had requested us."

He left Bagslate and went to Bamford Sunday school, where he received his "first prize." Bamford is a pleasant rural village, about a mile from Cutgate, on the road leading to Heywood and Manchester. The chapel and school-house, surrounded with oaks and poplars, stand a little to the right of the old highway from Rochdale to Bury.

The chapel, school, and chapel-yard have their associations, which made the spot a very sacred one to Mr. Ashworth in after years. In the school he had sat a poor, barefooted boy; in it he had received his first prize. In the chapel one eventful circumstance took place, which we give in his own words:—

"A circumstance that took place about twelve years after. I was then grown into a young man, and the church had determined that I should take a very important place among them. Though the incidents in my mother's life already related produced a lasting impression on me, yet I never saw her weep as she did on the following occasion. My memory will ever retain the scenes and feelings of that eventful hour. It was one Sabbath evening, my mother, as usual, was seated in her pew in the house of God. The congregation was very large, and all were silently waiting for the appearance of the preacher. He, poor man, was on his knees in the vestry, praying for Divine help, and trembling with fear. One of the deacons opened the vestry door, and the young preacher rose from his knees and ascended to the pulpit. There was an elderly female among the congregation whose face was covered with her hands, and whose head was bowed in deep reverence. Large tears streamed down her pale cheeks, and her whole soul was greatly affected. That woman was my own dear mother! —and the young, trembling, timid preacher was myself!—her once little barefooted, ragged boy;—her own dear child. When I gave out the first line of the hymn, and the congregation rose to join in celebrating God's praises, my mother's head was still bowed down. Poor, dear mother; how she loved me; and yet she feared on my account. The sight of her made the tears run down my face and drop upon the Bible; it was a moment of intense emotion, and I greatly feared my strength would fail me. The events of the past came vividly up in my memory. I saw the corner where I sat on the morning I had on my pinafore made from the old pack-sheet, and the form under which I put my bare feet. But now we had met again in the sanctuary;—she to weep for joy; and I, her son,—a sinner saved by grace, and a preacher of the gospel of peace."

In the chapel-yard rest the remains of his father and mother, Rachel Jackson, the subject of "Trials," and many others that were near and dear unto him. Several times a year he was accustomed to visit his mother's grave, and in spirit hold converse with her he loved, and to whom he owed so much, and used to say, "Sacred is that place to me, and never do I stand beside that hallowed spot but I thank God for a meek, patient, and praying mother."

I have been favoured with the following sketch from the pen of Sir James P. Kay Shuttleworth, who was the Superintendent of Bamford Sunday school at the time when Mr. Ashworth received his first prize:—

"During the Cotton Famine, in 1861-2, I visited

Rochdale (Oct. 21, 1862) with Mr. A. Kinnaird, who was then my guest, for the purpose of inspecting the relief stores, the sewing schools, the day schools for young men, and generally making ourselves acquainted with the details of the system of relief. We were accompanied by the late Mr. George Leach Ashworth. While in the relief stores witnessing the distribution of flour and meal, I was in conversation with two of the distributors. After some time, one of them said,—'You do not remember me?' I looked into his face: I saw healthy features, lighted by bright eyes, and a quiet, kindly expression. 'No,' I said, after I had perused the face; 'if I ought to remember you, I am sorry that my memory fails.' 'Forty years have passed since you gave me my first prize in the Bamford Sunday-school: you can scarcely call to mind John Ashworth.' I was obliged to confess that I could not. I inquired whether he belonged to the family of handloom weavers—the Ashworth's of Bagslate—one of whom was, I think, a deacon at Bamford. My impression is that he was connected with that family. I asked him what he was doing. He replied with great feeling and earnestness, 'I never lost the impulse which I got in the Sunday-school at Bamford. I was never happy till I became a minister to the destitute. Have you not received some tracts from me?' 'I have received some remarkable tracts from John Ashworth, but I did not know who he was.' 'Here he is; the Sunday scholar who received his first prize at Bamford.' We had then much conversation. We revived the remembrance of the humble congregation at Bamford chapel, of the Sunday-school and its associations, and I heard from his own lips his subsequent biography, and an account of his work as a minister to the destitute. The duties of the day separated us, but we have been since then occasionally in correspondence. (I have all his tracts, and he has regularly sent me the Reports of his chapel.) The best service which I can render you is to describe the school in which he won his prize.

"Bamford Chapel was a very plain stone building, about a quarter of a mile from Bamford Hall. The estate had been purchased by my uncle, Mr. Joseph Fenton, then banker and woollen manufacturer. I was resident for about two years in this old mansion, and afterwards for a year at Meadowcroft with my father; in all, three years, I think from the age of fifteen to that of eighteen, in 1822, when I went to the University of Edinburgh. My aunt, Mrs. Fenton, was a lady of the old Puritan type. She was in opinion, in tone of character, and in all her habits, an Independent after the fashion of the ladies of the Commonwealth. The church and congregation at Bamford were, therefore, objects of great interest to her. The minister was a disciple of the late William Roby of Manchester. He lived in a simple two-storied house, built at one end of the chapel, while the Sunday school was at the other end. He was a simple-minded man, naturally so good and gentle as to give the polish of inborn courtesy to manners otherwise differing little from those of intelligent working men. His wife was living, and he had two sons, both learning the craft of shoemaking.

"The school was in charge of Robert Porter, a

deacon of the congregation. I taught every Sunday in the boys' school, and after a time became its superintendent. Here, no doubt, occurred my early association with John Ashworth.

"The congregation consisted chiefly of handloom weavers, and a few of the neighbouring tenants of small dairy farms. The only typical man who remains indelibly impressed on my memory is John Crabtree. I knew him best because I sometimes accompanied him when he went on Sundays, as often as his health and strength would permit, among the neighbouring highlands as a missionary to scattered congregations, gathered in the homesteads or cottages. I scarcely know what instinct it was which attracted me to this simple, earnest, grave man. Certainly not by his stern dogmatism, nor by his dreary wayside conversations, as we walked in the early morning many miles to some far distant meeting. I rather suppose that the example of his self-devotion excited my wonder.

"The most remarkable person, however, connected with the school was Thomas Jackson (father of the subject of 'Trials'), the minister's son, who, as I have said, was learning shoemaking. He was of slender frame and feeble health, but with two bright eyes, sparkling with energy and fun. He had a fiddle, and was indefatigable in his efforts to acquire skill in its use. Though gifted only with a poor voice, he trained the school in singing, led the chapel choir, and, after prolonged discipline and instruction, enabled the Sunday scholars to sing an oratorio. Moreover, he was an energetic teacher, conducting his class with spirit and intelligence, not without an occasional outburst of the humour of which his genial temperament was brimful.

"That which is most in my mind is his enthusiasm and earnestness, and the zeal with which he and some of his fellow-teachers inspired many of the youths who were their pupils.

"Thomas Jackson became, when I was far away from those scenes, a missionary teacher in the surrounding uplands and villages. He trod in the steps of John Crabtree, with equal earnestness, but with far more instruction, and with considerably greater ability. He married, lived in a cottage, which he built near the chapel, worked at his trade of shoemaking, brought up a large family respectably, and continued to the last faithful to his convictions and sense of duty. These are the associations in which John Ashworth won his prize as a scholar at Bamford school.

(Signed) "J. P. KAY.

"March 15th, 1875."

The circumstance, as narrated by Mr. Ashworth is as follows:—

"It was the custom in our Sunday school to give the boy who was first in the class, when the bell rang for closing in the afternoon, a round ticket of merit, bearing a figure one. These tickets were collected once each year, and the boy having the largest number had the most valuable prize presented to him. Teachers, scholars, parents, friends, and members of the congregation, assembled in the large school-room on Whit-Friday to have tea, and to witness the distribution of prizes. One year I had just one more ticket than any other boy in the school; and, in consequence, I was entitled to receive the highest honours. The evening before that memorable day on which I was to *receive* my prize, I was very uuhappy on account of still being without shoes or clogs, and I said to my mother, as gently as I could,—

"'Mother, do you think you could get me a second-hand pair of clogs for to-morrow? I am going to have the highest prize, and I shall have to go up the steps on to the platform, and I shall be ashamed to go with my bare feet.' . . . .

"The following day I washed my feet for a long time. I was determined that if I could not get anything to cover my ten toes, I would make them look clean. I was at the school before the time, and sat in one corner alone. Soon the people began to gather. On the platform there stood a large table, covered with a white cloth. On the cloth the prizes were arranged with as much display as possible. Books, penknives, pocketknives, inkstands, a small writing desk, and other valuables, arrested the attention of all who entered the room. The ceremony was opened by singing a hymn. Then one of the superintendents (the present Sir James Kay Shuttleworth) mounted the platform, and made a speech,—eulogizing the scholars for their good conduct during the year, and holding up to view the various rewards while speaking. When he came to the first prize he called out my name, and invited me on to the platform amidst a loud clapping of hands. O, how my heart did beat! I felt at that moment as though I would have given twenty pounds, if I had possessed it, for something with which to cover my feet. I arose from my corner, and threading my way through the people as softly as though I were a cat, I walked blushingly on to the platform, and received my reward of merit, amidst the repeated clapping of the audience. But when I got back to my place I sat down and cried as though my heart would break, because I was such a poor, poor boy, and because I thought some of the other boys sneered at my poverty."

Towards the close of the 15th century, a rather eccentric school master, named John Trebonius, who conducted a school after his own fashion, while he treated the rude nobility and ignorant priesthood of his time with little or no ceremony, had the profoundest reverence and respect for his scholars. "Who can tell," said he, "what may rise up from amidst these youths; there may be among them those who shall guide the destinies of the empire:" and one of those boys was Martin Luther, at that time a begging alms boy, who became the great hero of the Reformation. The teachers at Bagslate and Bamford schools little knew what energies were slumbering beneath that wool-sheet pinafore,—that the little, ragged, barefooted boy was to exercise such an influence for the good of his fellow-men. Labourers, Sunday-school teachers, may learn from this to respect poor children.

As a boy, his companions say he was full of fun, frolicsome, but thoughtful. Very early he acquired a taste for reading, and would stand for hours with his bare feet reading to the other members of the family out of "Fox's Book of Martyrs," and "Tales of the Covenanters," till they were all in tears. These influences, no doubt, had such an effect upon his mind, that they made him the avowed and unflinching opponent and antagonist of oppression and tyranny of every description, whether political, civil, or religious.

When about ten years of age, the family removed from Cutgate to a row of houses called "Catches," a few hundred yards nearer Rochdale. Here John began to learn his father's trade, that of weaving, in the room over the house; and the touching incident recorded in the tale of "My Mother" occurred about this time, when he says:

"One hot summer day, a poor woman was seen toiling up the hill called Fletcher Round, with a flannel 'piece' on her back. A little boy was walking by her side. On reaching the Milkstone, she laid down her heavy burden, and leaning on the 'piece' for support, she wiped the sweat from her face with her check apron. With a look of affection, the boy gazed into the face of his mother, and said, 'Mother, when I get a little bigger you shall never carry another 'piece.' I will carry them all, and you shall walk by my side.'

"On that very day the painful fact flashed into the mind of that little boy that he was the poor child of poor parents—the young son of a humble, toiling, kind, and affectionate mother. But as he grew bigger and stronger he redeemed his promise, and carried the 'pieces' up Fletcher Round, and on to Mr. Whitworth's warehouse at Sparth, without calling at the Milkstone to rest."

When about sixteen, he removed with his parents to the neighbourhood of Simpson Clough, near Bamford, residing part of a year at a place called "Top o' the Wood," occupying the middle one of three brick houses, near the "Bird in Hand," then down at Simpson Clough, where the family remained till the death of their father. His father died April 5th, 1849, aged 75, and his mother Dec. 4th, 1851, aged 77.

At the former residence took place the incidents related by Mr. Ashworth in a tract published by the British Temperance League, entitled, "Johnny's Sorrow." It is well known that the family suffered much from the intemperate habits of their father, but it was to them a source of gratification and thankfulness that before he died he became a changed man. On one of the fortnightly visits which Mr. Ashworth paid to his parents in subsequent years, enquiring for his father, his mother informed him that he was gone into a neighbouring wood. There the son, who had so frequently witnessed him in his debasement, found him engaged in prayer, in the same wood in which "Johnny," on that dark night of his sorrow, prayed for him that he might become a good father, and not get drunk any more. Without disturbing him, he ran home with joy to tell his mother. The good woman smiled through her tears as she responded, "Our prayers are heard at last, and my sun is now setting in a clear sky." Mr. Ashworth's life-long hatred to the "accursed thing," as he termed it, and his unflagging efforts and advocacy in the cause of temperance, may, doubtless, be attributed to the remembrance of what he, and others dear to him, suffered in consequence of his father's besetment.

Simpson Clough, where commenced another era in this eventful life, is beautifully situated between Heywood and Bamford, on the old road leading from Rochdale to Bury and Manchester. The house occupied by the family is on the margin of a deep ravine, very much frequented by visitors going to and from Ashworth Wood. The country around is picturesque, and in every respect calculated to inspire a youthful, energetic, and poetic mind like John Ashworth's, with the highest and noblest aspirations. In the front of the house is a plantation sloping down to the river Roche, which flows past its base. At the back is Ashworth Wood, one of the most romantic spots in the neighbourhood, where the young aspirant was accustomed to spend many hours, and where some of his earliest productions in poetry were composed.

His admiration of God's works and the beauties of nature were no doubt, to some extent, acquired by the scenery around. Not having any particular liking for the weaving trade, he had a desire to change, and accordingly engaged himself to a painter in Heywood, named Harrison. Before completing his apprenticeship, or having learned much of the business, his master failed, a circumstance which led him to seek employment in Rochdale—which he found—and although he could neither paper nor grain, he was determined no one should know it but himself; and such was his power and energy of mind to overcome difficulties and make the best of circumstances, that he undertook to do them, and soon became master of both. He said he watched the other men, saw how they did, and by this means was soon competent for any kind of work.

CHAPTER II.

1832—1837.

THAT most interesting of all periods to young people now came, when, as he has told us, he "fell in love," and "could not help it."

The person who became his wife was the only daughter of William and Jane Thornber, a respectable, godly farmer and his wife, who came from the neighbourhood of Clitheroe to a farm at Balderstone; from thence they removed to Cutlane farm, a short distance on the other side of Cutgate from Rochdale; and it was on the day of their removal, and when the Ashworth family resided at Catches, that he first saw her with whom he "fell in love;" but it was when they settled at Simpson Clough that their love was consummated in marriage. Mr. Thornber was a very useful and rather popular local preacher.

We now give Mr. Ashworth's courtship and marriage in his own words:—

"One fine summer evening, about seven o'clock, when returning from my day's work, and about one hundred yards from home, I met a tall young woman, with a small basket in one hand, and a little flower-pot containing a geranium in the other. I had never seen her before, and the moment we met I stood still, intending to speak to her, but could not. My sudden stopping caused her to stop also. She blushed and passed on; not one word was spoken, for it was all done in a second. I was grieved at my want of manners, and feared I had offended her; but I felt what I had never felt before, and what made me hasten home to change my coat and hat, that I might track her steps at a respectful distance, and see where her dwelling was; for I had made up my mind to follow her, if she went to Jerusalem. But on arriving at home my fears were calmed by my sister informing me that the daughter of the new farmer, coming to be our neighbours, had just gone past, with a beautiful flower in her hand. This to me was real good news; I did not tell her that I too had seen the farmer's daughter, but I was very glad that she would be living within a mile, and I should often have an opportunity of seeing her again. After washing and making myself as tidy as possible, I set out to see the farm house. I had seen and passed it hundreds of times, during the period the former tenant resided there; but what I had regarded with indifference, I now looked at with the deepest interest. The whole place was changed. The house stood about fifty yards back from the highway. I passed several times, intensely anxious to see her again, to be certain she did now live in that very house, but I saw her not. The flower-pot was in the window, however, and this was to me a pleasing circumstantial evidence that certain hands had placed it there. Some young men, when they fall in love, prudently keep their own counsel, and wisely avoid speaking or writing to the loved one until they have instituted a minute investigation; and they often find it is as well they did so, for discoveries are sometimes made that completely extinguish the flame, and no one is the worse. Others rush on without thought—all fire and no judgment—propose at once, are accepted, and made miserable for life. 'A prudent man foreseeth the evil, and hideth himself; but the simple pass on, and are punished.' In nothing is there more prudence required than in choosing a wife; for the greatest blessing a man can have in this world, next to the salvation of his soul, is a good wife; and the greatest earthly curse a bad one. I had fallen deeply in love; and, with the little reason I had left, began to enquire into the character of the object. I found she was a modest, clean, industrious, worthy young woman, kind and affectionate to her father and mother, the oldest child of religious parents, and herself a member of a Christian church. When I learned all this, I began to think she was too good for me, and almost despaired of success. When the family came into chapel, the first Sunday morning after their arrival, many eyes were fixed on the strangers, but none with so deep an interest as my own. She was there; yes, she was there—I think a true worshipper; and, oh, how beautiful! how neatly attired! I had never seen so nice a bonnet: it was a real bonnet, not a patch stuck on the top of the head, as bonnets are now, but a modest, sensible bonnet—a bonnet I well remember to this day. I felt I *must* propose, accepted or not. I wrote a letter; read it; it would not do;—wrote another, and another, before I got one I thought suitable. I posted it prepaid; it was returned; I sent a second; it also was returned. Through a female friend I sent her a choice book; it was sent back unopened. I got an old woman, friendly with the family, to speak for me; but she managed badly, and my case seemed hopeless. I frequently passed the farm-house close to the door, wishing to say good morning, or good day, or something good, and felt anxious to speak to her parents on the question, but all seemed hopeless. One day, the father quietly, but in a serious tone, said to his beloved child,—'Jane, there is a young man passes this door very often, though I think it is rather out of his way, and I have felt some concern about you. Is your father's and mother's teaching worth anything, child?' 'Yes, father, more than I can tell you; I never felt so thankful as I do now for you having taught me not to take any step involving my welfare without first consulting you.' 'Have you given him any encouragement?' 'No, father; he has sent letters and books, and tried other influences, but I am in no way committed.' 'I am glad to hear that; I have spoken to your mother on the subject, and we both think you are in trouble about the matter.' Jane made no answer, but her eyes filled with tears, and she went into the dairy to hide her emotion. I heard of this conversation with great joy, and planned to meet the father on his return from the market, and request permission to visit the house. He spoke to me civilly, but seemed perplexed; nevertheless he requested me to call about eight o'clock on the Thursday evening in the following week. Thursday came, and eight o'clock came; but how I got into the house I cannot tell. I did get in, however, and found the farmer sitting on one side of the hearth, with one leg over the other, swinging his foot, and looking thoughtfully into the fire. The mother was near him, darning stockings, with a very white face; and Jane was beside her, sewing, with a very red face. None of them seemed to notice my entrance, so I took a chair as near to them as I durst, and we all sat and sat and sat in silence like a Quaker's meeting. When *he* would speak I could not tell, and I dare not. At last he began to ask a number of questions; putting the very worst question first, he said,—'How old are you?' I told him. 'What's your trade?' I told him. 'How much can you earn?' I told him. 'Do you attend any place of worship?' 'Yes, sir, I am a member of a church.' 'Do you ever go into a public-house?' 'No, sir, never; and I hope I never shall.' 'When you bring home your wages, do you give your mother what you like, and put the rest in your pocket?' Here was a deep question, and a question intended to fetch out my true character; for he knew—and who does not know—that there is many a lad put by his parents, at considerable sacrifice, to as good a trade as they can get him, who, during his apprenticeship, brings home very little money, and is all the time a burden to them; but the moment he gets full wage, when he might greatly help his struggling mother, just gives her what he thinks proper,—as little as he can,—puts the rest in his pocket, and struts through the streets like a dandy-cock—a big man. God never did bless a son like that, and never will. My answer to the question was,—'That I never kept one penny from my mother, for I could never give her enough.' Again he was silent, undoubtedly contending with his feelings, and I was anxiously waiting for the verdict. At last he said,—'Well, my young man, I like your answers, and we think our child has done right in not encouraging you, until we had a better knowledge of your character; but we are not blind to her thoughts. Respect yourself, and respect my daughter; she is a good child. Let everything be honourable between you, and may the God of her father and mother bless you both!' The last sentence was said with a trembling, choking utterance, and amidst heavy sobs and heaving breasts from all present.

"There are some who would make merry with the gravity of this night's interview, but to me it was felt to be a serious matter. Births, marriages, and deaths are no trifles. Our union in this world often determines how we shall go through and out of it. As one who said,—

'My success in life
Is due to my wife,'

words that can be adopted and with truth repeated by thousands. My own parents approving of my choice, in due time we were married."

The ceremony took place at Rochdale Parish Church, on the 15th October, 1832.

Four years after his marriage, a greater and still more important event took place, which gave a bias to Mr. Ashworth's future life, viz.: his second birth.

In a memorandum he records, "I was born again, Oct. 3rd, 1836." This great change may be traced to the combined influences of the Sabbath school and a godly mother; but was now brought about and developed through the piety and prayers of her who had become his wife. Early in life, he had what he called "a name and a place amongst God's people," but was destitute of saving faith: "the form of godliness he had, the power he never knew."

On coming to reside in Rochdale, through the influence of his fellow-workmen, he was induced to join a debating club, and to some extent imbibed their sceptical principles.

This was a source of great trouble to his wife, for she thought she was marrying a godly young man. She was importunate in her prayers and unceasing in her efforts for his conversion. At last her prayers and his mother's were answered: the happy day came; both rejoiced together; and from that moment, a great change came over their home. A family altar was erected, the Bible was read, and they knelt together at the throne of grace.

What so valuable to a young couple setting out in life as to feel that they are the children of God by faith in Jesus Christ, having God's Book for their guide, and His love in their hearts. Like a ship leaving port and fully equipped for the voyage, they are now prepared to battle with the storms of life, bear each other's burdens, and share in each other's joys, till at last they reach the haven of eternal repose.

Mr. Ashworth details his conversion as follows:

"An event took place for which I can never be sufficiently thankful. I had always been regarded by my family, friends, and neighbours, as a steady young man; I had a deep regard for the Sabbath, and a reverence for the name and honour of God, and felt pained to hear any one swear. Drunkenness I abhorred with a depth of hatred I cannot express; and, in the eyes of the world, I was considered a good young man. I was a regular attendant at the house of God, and had a name and a place amongst His people; but I had an inward consciousness that I was not really and truly a child of God; that, like the five foolish virgins, I had no oil in my vessel with my lamp. Though I was pretending to go out to meet the Bridegroom, I could not join in singing psalms or hymns of Christian experience, but stood sad and silent, with the book in my hand, while others sang. I knew that Christ's words,—'Except ye are born again (of the Spirit) ye cannot see the kingdom of God,'—were spoken to me as much as to Nicodemus; and that without holiness of heart, I could never enter that kingdom. I felt that I had only a profession of religion; a form of godliness without the power; a name to live, and was dead. Oh, how I longed for the inward witness—the witness of the Spirit that I was a child of God—to know and feel that my name was, not in the church book only, but in the Lamb's Book of Life! I was at that time a teacher in a country Sunday-school. One Sunday morning, the superintendent—a good, old Christian—rang the bell for silence, put on his spectacles, and rose to give out the opening hymn. The words were—

'Behold, a Stranger at the door,
He gently knocks, has knocked before;
Has waited long, is waiting still,
You use no other friend so ill.'

The words so melted the soft heart of the venerable servant of Christ, that he could not give out the last line, but stood speechless. We were all waiting, and looking at him with surprise, for we had sung the two first lines. His lips quivered with emotion; he struggled to finish the line, but could not, and was forced to sit down, covering his face with his hands, another teacher taking his place.

"I could never describe my own feelings at that moment. I was on the point of crying out, but by an effort kept back both the feeling and the words. I was ashamed to confess Christ before men, and weakened that day the striving of the Spirit. The following day was to me a day of intense spiritual conflict. In the workshop I had a small room to myself; nineteen times during that day did I fall on my knees with the cry,—'God be merciful to me a sinner,' or 'what must I do to be saved?' and began to think the Lord ought to pardon me for so many prayers. In the evening I set out to see my parents, residing about three miles distant; as I was returning home it was dark and windy, but I cared little about the weather. When about a mile from my home, I stopped under an old oak tree, and kneeling down, besought the Lord, for Christ's sake, to speak peace to my troubled soul. Oh, what a moment was that! my mental vision of Christ crucified for sinners—*for me*—was so powerful, that it seemed taking place just then before my eyes. I saw that my debt was paid on that cross—paid in mercy, but paid in full, and paid in blood; this I believed from the deepest depths of my soul. I believed on the Lord Jesus Christ, and was saved. I did not shout, I did not weep; but an overwhelming flood of joy came over my soul. I was now justified, not for praying nineteen times, not by works, but by believing; justified by faith, and had peace with God through our Lord Jesus Christ. On arriving at home, I told my wife of the great change,—of my peace and joy,—of my real conversion; and we rejoiced together. I could now sing the hymns of Christian experience, and I felt my name was written in the Lamb's Book of Life. I was happy, and immediately had a strong desire to labour more earnestly in some way for the glory of God, and the good of others; I felt, I believe, as Paul felt when he said, 'Lord, what would'st Thou have me to do?'

"My decision and firmness on religious things often brought me considerable persecution from my fellow-workmen, but I only mention one circumstance. Up to this time I had seen much drunkenness, and heard much swearing and obscene language amongst them. I had not often reproved them before, but now I saw it to be my duty, and prayed for prudence to do it rightly, and to speak the truth to them in love. I knew the importance of my own conduct being right,—of letting my light shine before them,—to give me greater power. Being one day altogether in the shop waiting for wages, one of them said, mockingly, 'Let us have a prayer-meeting.' This brought a loud laugh from the others. The same man then went to the top of a short step-ladder, turned up his eyes, put his hands together, and tried to begin; but, letting fall his hands, and looking round on the company, said, 'What must we pray for?' 'A barrel of ale,' said one; 'A good fat pig,' said a second; 'Roast-beef and plum-pudding,' said a third. Again they burst into roars of laughter, all looking at me, but I could not laugh. I was much pained, and mentally sought aid from Him who was crowned with thorns, spat upon, mocked, and smitten, and saw how little I had to bear compared with His suffering. The man that stood on the top of the ladder, began to feel and look very foolish, and came down ashamed of himself, and the day after showed what he really thought of me, by asking me to go and see his sick mother. Out of the eleven present at the mock prayer-meeting, only one is now alive; all have died of drink, and very poor, and nearly all have sent for me in their last hours to read and pray with them. But a worse trial awaited me than being scorned, mocked, and laughed at. I had been reading 'Dick's Christian Philosopher,' 'Herschel's Architecture of the Heavens,' 'The Stellar Worlds,' and several other works on astronomy, and was greatly amazed while passing, in thought, through illimitable worlds, measureless expanse, countless orbs of heaven,—suns, moons, stars, comets, planets, nebulæ, galaxy after galaxy, systems, and centres of systems, eternal fields of light, stretching out into infinite heights and depths, far out beyond the reach of thought, making the mind stagger and tremble with the profoundest awe! The question came unbidden,—'Did the great Omnipotent Creator and Builder of this vast universe care so much for this little world of ours—so little, that if it was to drop from its orbit, it would be no more missed than the falling of a leaf in a dense forest of trees;—Did this great Being ever clothe Himself in man's form, and, for man, groan and die?' This question troubled me, and caused my faith to reel. For six weeks I never mentioned the name of Christ, and I do not think I ever smiled during that time. My veneration for the great Deity was increased; but His incarnation and humanity I doubted. In this state of mind, one night I stood gazing up into the heavens; the stellar worlds were shining in their full glory. As I stood in silent and deep emotion, thought after thought arose, following each other in rapid succession. What are these worlds? Are they mind? Have they souls? Can they think? Do they hope, or fear, or joy, or sorrow? Is not the immortal soul—that thinks, loves, hopes, fears, rejoices, and sorrows—worth more than a ball of dead, unintelligent matter? Behold yon numerous worlds! The gloomy doubts, that for six weeks had oppressed my mind, fled in a moment, and I then saw the unspeakable love of God, displayed in the redemption of infinitely precious never-dying souls, through Christ, who, though He was rich beyond our conception,—the Proprietor of the whole universe,—yet for our sakes became poor, that we, through His poverty, might become rich; thus teaching, that in value, a world is not to be compared to a single soul. Oh, my soul—

> 'The stars shall fade away, the sun himself
> Grow dim with age, and nature sink in years,
> But thou shalt flourish in immortal youth.'

"Since then I have never doubted the divinity of Christ, and in proportion as I look at and love Him as my Redeemer, the more heart and energy I feel in all my labours. For it ever was, and ever will be, the love of Christ that constraineth us. He is the great living, moving, abiding principle that nerves His servants for any and every work."

Mr. Ashworth joined the church, became a Sunday-school teacher and local preacher, which duties he continued to discharge till his death.

In the memorandum recording his conversion he says,—

"I first prayed in public in Smallbridge Sunday-school, Sept. 18th, 1836."

"I first prayed in my class, Oct. 7th, 1836."

"O Lord, help me to persevere."

"I tried to preach the first time on the 30th April, 1837, in the house of Thomas Brierley, at Brickfield, Smallbridge, near Rochdale, at seven o'clock in the morning, from Psalm cxxvi. 3."

"I preached my trial sermon on the 8th Oct., 1837, in the School-room of Baillie-street Chapel, from Isaiah xxviii. 16. My dear brethren, the local preachers, were unanimous in their vote that I should be put on the Plan on trial. This greatly encouraged me, as more than twenty of them heard me; also about forty painters, who had gone to see me break down."

Mr. Ashworth frequently related to me another circumstance not recorded, connected with that memorable occasion. Mr. Molineux, who was then in the Rochdale Circuit, waited upon him, to convey the verdict of the leader's meeting, and said, "Well, brother Ashworth, we are unanimous in our vote that you should be taken on the Plan upon trial, but the brethren wished me to say that, while they do so, they at the same time think that if you had less of 'Young' and 'Pollok' in your sermons, and more of Jesus Christ, you would be more useful."

The necessity for this kind rebuke was occasioned by the young preacher having been to a neighbouring village, and delivering what he thought a most magnificent sermon from the text, "All thy works shall praise thee, O Lord, and thy saints shall bless thee." He opened out his discourse in grand style, quoting from Young, "Morning stars, exulting, shouting, o'er the rising ball;" from Shakespeare, "The cloud-capp'd towers, the gorgeous palaces," and that sublime piece from Pollok's "Course of Time," beginning,—

> "Whose garments were the clouds;
> Whose mintrels, books; whose lamps, the moon and stars;
> Whose angel-choirs, the voice of many waters;
> Whose bouquets, morning dews; whose heroes, storms;
> Whose warriors, mighty winds; whose lovers, flowers;
> Whose orators, the thunderbolts of God;
> Whose palaces, the everlasting hills;
> Whose ceiling heaven's unfathomable blue."

Mounting up still higher, amongst what he called the stellar worlds, he expatiated on the satellites of Saturn, Uranus, and Jupiter, finishing his aerial flight in the milky way. An aged servant of God, at whose house he went to tea, after the repast was over took him into the front parlour, and when both were seated said, "Well, my young man, thou hast been flying thy kite high this afternoon, very high, and if thou does not mind the string will break, and it will come wibble wabble down; thou hast been walking over the stars in stilts, cloud-capp'd towers, shouting o'er the rising ball, satellites, Jupiter, and milky way, indeed!

It is thin milk in the pulpit. Thou got so high up, thou never saw Calvary, where the Maker of all died for those gospel-hardened sinners that were staring at thee; thou never told us that the work of God that praises Him most was the work of redemption, shedding His blood for a guilty world. My dear young friend, do come down before thou tumbles down; keep at the foot of the cross; it is he, and only he, that humbleth himself that shall be exalted, either in the pulpit or out."

Give instruction to a wise man, and he will be yet wiser. The kind and seasonable reproof of the old man, and the recommendation of his brethren, had its effect. He said he felt his feet that day, and was cured of cloud-capp'd towers.

CHAPTER III.

1837—1850.

IF anything in this world will test a man's true character, and develop his mental capabilities, it is his early struggles in life, especially his married life. For a man with a keen sense of honour, a spirit of independence, a deep affection for his wife, and a desire to make her home happy, to meet with reverses at the very threshold, is enough to destroy all his bright hopes, and drive him, as it has done thousands, to despair; but not so the subject of this memoir.

> "As hours of pain have yielded good,
> That days of ease refused;
> As herbs, tho' scentless when entire,
> Spread fragrance when they're bruised,"

and as the mighty oak, driven by the furious blasts, strikes deeper its roots, so these early struggles seemed to call forth all the latent powers of body and mind, to which, without doubt, may be attributed, to a great extent, his self-reliance and success in after life, also his deep sympathy with young people in similar circumstances. Thus he records:—

"My wife and I began the up-hill journey together, but neither of us had any idea when we set out, how steep our road was to be. At the time of marriage, I was earning about twenty shillings per week, but in a short time work unexpectedly fell off. I shall never forget the morning when all the hands were told that business was to stop, and all work to be suspended till spring. A sensation of numbness came over my whole body, and I felt it difficult to stand on my feet. I knew it would be all but impossible to get a single day's employment elsewhere. How was I to face my young wife?—how carry her the fearful intelligence? My pride received a great shock, for I was anxious to appear respectable and stand well amongst my new connections. Not wishing to return home during working hours, I called to see a provision dealer, who had two shops about a mile apart. Seeing I was rather dejected, and learning the cause, he offered me one of his shops at a valuation. He knew I had not four pounds in the world, yet he was willing to trust me, and introduce me to some of his customers, and also to the wholesale factors.

"On returning home in the evening, I informed my dear wife of the events of the day,—my loss of work and the offer of the shop. She left it with me, to do as I thought best, and in a few days I stood behind a counter, a shopkeeper, in appearance a little up in the world. When I began shopkeeping, the credit system being general in that district, I was, or thought I was, forced to adopt the same plan. Customers began to flock in, especially those who had lost credit at other shops,—for bad payers are sure to find new shopkeepers. Paying for old and taking the new on credit was the understanding; but I soon found it was only the understanding, not the practice. I had again got employment (painting), my wife attending to the shop, but on taking stock we found that we were fast sinking to ruin, and we determined to give it up.

"A neighbour, thinking he could mend our work, agreed to take the shop and fixtures, for little more was left, and pay for all in four quarterly payments. I saw all my creditors and obtained time, agreeing to pay all in full. [Mr. A. had gone behind sixty pounds.] For this purpose I entered into a money club, and now began the most painful struggle for very existence, that lasted for several years. Oh, debt, debt! Talk about the nightmare!—why, debt, to the honest man, is both night and day-mare. The borrower is indeed servant to the lender, and this he is made to feel with a vengeance. Take two men of equal height, to begin with, I think the man out of debt would be two inches taller than the man in debt. It has a depressing, crushing, paralyzing effect, and hangs like a dead weight on the mind. It acts on the liver, makes the skin yellow, and bushels of Parr's Pills have been taken by bilious people, made so by debt. The bilious man seldom sees the sun shine; clouds, clouds, nought but clouds, and I think a man may die of debt. The payments into the money club, which when drawn were to meet all my liabilities, swallowed up a large portion of my weekly wages. This kept us very poor, and the winter setting in, work again fell away, and we were reduced to the greatest straits. One Saturday we had not one copper in the house, nor one pennyworth of bread, nor one hatful of coal. It was the day on which the man that succeeded me in the shop was to pay the second quarter's instalment. In the evening of that day I set out, expecting to receive it, and gather a few shillings from some other of the villagers that owed me money. The night was very dark, but I had travelled that way so often I could have found the way blindfold. On arriving at the shop, I found the door fast and all in darkness. Almost frantic with fear, lest he had run away, I knocked louder and louder. At last an old woman, named Taylor, who resided in the next house, came to the door with a candle in her hand. Holding it over her head, and seeing who it was, she said, 'Why, is that you? Have you not heard?' 'Heard what?' I replied, almost choking. 'Why Lee is dead and buried. He dropped down dead last week, and somebody came and took all there was in the shop, and sold it. Will you come in and sit down a bit?' 'No, thank you,' I replied, my heart beating like a drum. I left the house of double desolation, and began groping my way towards a place called Crown-point, a few hundred yards higher up, to the house of another of my debtors. There I expected to receive ten shillings, towards several pounds owing to me. The moment I opened the door, the wife screamed out,—'Oh dear! oh dear! my husband is just dead; he has this moment drawn away. Oh dear! I wish you had been a little sooner; he wanted some one to pray with him. Oh dear! oh dear! how to bury him I cannot tell, for there is not a shilling in the house.' Without speaking one word, I gently closed the door, and set off towards home, feeling quite sick. But remembering that I must get a little money somewhere, I called at the house of a person that owed me two pounds twelve shillings, for meal supplied for baking oat-bread. The old woman was crying and rocking herself in a rickety chair by the fireside as I entered. On seeing me, she moaned out,—'Oh! I am fain you have come; eawr Joe is deein'; he cannot last long. Do go up stairs an' read th' Bible an' pray wi' him, do; an' as for brass, win no brass for ye; nay, indeed us noather.'

"I left the moaning old woman, and her aged dying husband, and again plunged into the pitch darkness. The deep gloom of the night was a true reflex of the gloom of my sad soul. Had it thundered and lightened, or had there been a howling, roaring storm, the terrors without would not have exceeded the miseries within. One had fallen down lifeless, and ere I knew, he was buried, and part of my little property swept away. Another lay dead in the house, and, instead of receiving the few shillings I expected, I had the wild wail of his stricken widow. And a third lay dying, and his sorrowing wife entreated me to read the Word of God and pray with him.

"I durst not call at another house, but set out towards home, greatly depressed in spirit, and miserable indeed. On arriving near the town (for I was then residing near Rochdale) the very gas light seemed to mock my misery. I was faint and weary, and going to a home where there was not one bit of bread. My case was truly deplorable, for I knew that my credit was done at the grocer's, my landlord had threatened to take my little furniture for arrears of rent. Before reaching home, I met a friend in the street, who lent me two shillings. Eighteen pence of this my wife took to the grocer's, and with the sixpence I fetched a barrow of coal. The Sabbath came. Thank God for the Sabbath! for though we were poor, we had a name and a place in Zion; and, oh, how often have earth's cares been rolled back by the sublime melodies of the sanctuary, and the waves of trouble been stilled by the voice of Him who still speaks in His Holy Word; and to none are the promises so sweet and so well understood as those who need them most. God is always nearest to those who lie the lowest. When, after that night of darkness, the Sabbath morning dawned, we were truly glad to go into the house of the Lord; and as the minister read out those dear words of the Saviour, 'Behold the fowls of the air: for they sow not, neither do they reap, nor gather into barns, yet your heavenly Father feedeth them; are ye not much better than they?' my wife gently turned her head and looked at me through her tears. That look said, He will take care of us.

"The day following I tried hard to get work,—tried at various places, for I would have done anything honest,—but all to no purpose. In the evening we sat by the fire talking matters over. We had just blown out our only candle to save it, when a man opened the door to ask if I resided there. I again lighted the candle, and requested him to take a chair, and inform me why he was seeking me. Handing me a small book, he said, 'I want you to look at that book. We are thinking of having our club-room decorated. A few figures and foliage will be required illustrating our Order, and we wish you to say how much you will do it for.' Though I made no pretension to be an artist, yet I saw instantly what was required, knew I could do it, and made out the estimate—twelve pounds. He accepted the offer, urged me to get the work done as quickly as possible, and closed the door, bidding me good night. The moment he was gone, I began, like a madman, to dance and sing, 'Oh, let us be joyful, joyful, joyful, joyful! God has sent deliverance, praise His holy name.' My wife had few words; her feelings and gratitude were too deep for utterance. She gently said, 'I knew we should have help, but *how* I could not tell.' At six the following morning, with a little bread and butter in my pocket, I set out for Manchester, to see a room that would greatly assist me in thought, and one recommended to me by the person that brought me the book. It was a cold winter morning, but I walked the twelve miles, took a sketch of the work, walked home again, saw a neighbouring draper and told him my case. He trusted me with the canvas required. The cottage in which I then resided had three stories, the top room being just what I required. My wife cut out the canvas according to the drawing, we fixed it up, and I was soon at work, coating the canvas and preparing my colours. The canvas being ready, and the outlines completed, very soon from the magical combination of colour in tints, lights, and shadows, came forth the high priest of the Druids, with his flowing beard, his long white robe, cutting down, with his golden axe, the sacred mistletoe from the forest oak; the aboriginal Briton, half-naked, with his tatooed skin and implements of war; the hunter with his spear, his dog, his wallet, &c. I was working like a man inspired with his subject, and with nobler emotions and higher feelings than came from the canvas. My wife sat beside the stove, sewing and watching with deep interest the work of my pencil; and we sang together,—sang the praises of Him who redeemed us both by His most precious blood,—sang in strains of thankfulness,

'When passing through the watery deep,
I ask in faith His promised aid,
The waves their ordered distance keep,
And shrink from my devoted head:
Fearless their violence I dare,
They cannot harm, for God is there.'

The scenery was finished in three weeks; I took it to the club-room, fixed it up, and received my twelve pounds. I called on the grocer and draper, settled my accounts with them, paid my landlord the arrears of rent, bought a load of coal, gave my wife the few pounds remaining, and again sang, 'Oh, let us be joyful.'

"When I think of this time I feel joyful yet. To dwell on the happy hours of the past, and to recall to memory departed days of gladness, to the rightly constituted mind doubles the felicities of life. Pleasure and pain are mingled in the cup of most, but it is ingratitude to think only of the gloomy and forget the bright. I know that what makes the strongest impression on the mind is likely to be the most lasting, but it is not wise to deepen the furrows of grief by useless repining, and one of the best antidotes to our miseries is to count our mercies. He that marks the mercies of God, shall never want a mercy to mark. There was a period in the history of this country when the merchandise was carried on the backs of pack horses from city to city. A good old packman, speaking his experience amongst his Christian brethren, once said, 'My dear friends, you all know my two old horses, the black one and the white one. The white one walks very steadily, with or without a burden; but the black one runs through every gap in the road side except he be well weighted; but when he is well weighted he walks quite steadily, and never looks at the gaps at all. Now, I think I am like my old black horse, for I walk the most steadily when I carry the greatest burdens to keep me in the right way.'

"I have not always thought so, but think now that I am like both the old packman and his black horse; and that He who loves me, and knows me better than I know myself, has seen it necessary to keep me low by frequent and varied trials, of which my trials in business have not been the least, because so long protracted.

"One of the masters in town came to my employer, requesting he would lend me for a few days, to help him to finish some urgent work. The few days extended to several years, and I ultimately became his foreman; and at last he, wishing to retire from business, offered me his entire stock at a valuation, and promised to introduce and recommend me to all his customers. 'How am I to pay you the valuation?' I asked; 'you know I have not five pounds in the world.' 'I will trust you, for I think you are honest,' was his reply. 'How long?' I asked. 'Well, I will give you three years; longer if you require it, you paying interest,' was his answer.

"With much fear and anxiety I accepted the offer, and thus found myself, instead of a journeyman, *a master*—but a master on credit and without means. My name was in large letters, but my earnings were in few figures. What I gained in honor and importance, I more than lost in sleep and peace of mind. Little know some men how much they have to be thankful for. If workmen knew the difficulties many masters have daily to struggle with, in finding them employment and money for their wages, there would be much less envy in the world than there is. To contend with severe, and often reckless competition; to give long credit or lose your customers; to take in bill after bill, and be told to 'call again,' though you are at your wit's end for money; to be as afraid of a traveller calling, or Saturday coming, as if you were going to be hanged, is not much to be envied. Hundreds of times on a Saturday have I been utterly unable to tell how I was to get wages for the men, and have had to try the patience of my friends. I am thankful that not one of my men ever went home short of what was his due, but it has often been at the expense of fearful struggles of brain and body. I well remember one Saturday anxiously waiting for an account promised, that would just meet my requirements. As it did not come I went for it, thinking I had been forgotten, and found my debtor had gone on pleasure to Scarborough, but had left no money. And here I would say to all those going to watering places or on pleasure trips,—Settle your poor tradesman's bills before you go; you will prevent much trouble, and increase your own peace of mind.

"My greatest mortification about money matters arose from the conduct of my old master. When I took his stock, payment was to be made at periods agreed upon; but as soon as I had a tolerable account to draw, he was at my heels. He was a perfect torment, and would walk into my house, telling me that he could not and would not wait; that he had made me what I was, and I ought to pay him, and thank him. Often have I found my wife in tears, and on asking the reason, the answer was, 'He has been again.' I well knew who *he* was. Dreams may or may not come to pass, but this I know, that I never saw that man in dreams, but I knew trouble was coming; and my wife and I had frequently agreed that on the day we paid him the last pound, we should have an extra cup of tea.

"But it may be asked, Did not I bring all this upon myself? Why not remain on weekly wages? Why become a master without means? What else could I expect? This is easily said; we can all prophesy for yesterday. I did what I thought best at the time, and few men have worked harder to succeed. We lived very carefully, made no show, and I never entered a public house, and am thankful to say never lost my credit. The long-looked-for day came at last, the day on which I was able to pay my relentless creditor; and so glad was I, that I determined not to put the settled paper in my pocket until I had shown it to my wife. In this happy state of mind I walked through the shop into the sitting room with the paper in my hand. But I soon found that troubles are great or small only relatively. What seemed a great trouble yesterday may sink into insignificance, compared with the one we have to-day. On entering the room I found three doctors there, who had just finished a consultation, and had agreed that the immediate amputation of my dear wife's foot was necessary to save her life. The poor sufferer had heard the decision, and sat in the chair with her face covered to hide her tears and agony. I need not say that, on the doctors retiring, we wept together. Our three children were called into the room and gently told what was coming. They all threw their arms round our necks, frantic with grief, and begged that, if possible, it might not be, but were told it must be or mother would die. It was the rapid softening of the ankle bone that required this extreme remedy. For several months she had felt great pain in walking, and we had our own medical man calling almost daily. He, not willing to take the responsibility upon himself, called in other two surgeons, and they urged immediate action.

"After a sleepless night, the morning of the operation came, and as there is no possible condition of Christian experience which the love of God cannot meet, my wife was calm, and ready at the moment fixed. An affectionate and tried female friend, ever ready for every good work, came to be with her during the operation. She was a woman of strong faith but few words. She knelt down in one corner of the room, in silent prayer, and rose with the words, 'All things work together for good to them that love God.' The truth of this we both proved, for though we were both members of a Christian church, and myself holding a high office in the church, yet we were over-anxious about the world, and both could date our deeper work of grace after the last trial, which brought us nearer to God.

"She gradually declined in health, until she was entirely confined to her room, and then to her bed. And here again, I say, bless God for religion. The trying time for my dear suffering wife was again come; the last foe was approaching, not to take a foot, but her body to the tomb. As a rule, people die as they have lived. When I first saw my wife, young as she was, she was then a Christian; and now, after many years of happy married life, as she droops by my side, she is still a Christian; and the rapturous felicity, the joys unspeakable, of the last few weeks of her life, can never be told. Anything more truly glorious I never saw, heard, or read of. A short time before breathing her last, she was very desirous of hearing her aged father pray once more before she died. Hear this, ye praying fathers! Here is a dying child requesting, in her last moments, to hear *once again* the well-known, well-remembered voice, which, in her childhood, she first heard in prayer. I went to tell the old man of his daughter's request. With quivering lips and swimming eyes he put on his broad-brimmed hat, took hold of my arm, and, in silence, we walked on to witness the last sad scene.

"She received him with a smile. Poor man, how he loved his child. He tried to speak to her, but could not. He walked about the room struggling with his feelings, but every time he turned towards the bed, to look on the pale but sweet face of his only daughter, knowing that in a short time her bright eyes would be closed in death, he seemed overwhelmed. In this state he knelt down—knelt long ere he uttered a word. At last utterance came, and, oh, what a prayer! We rose from our knees in tears, but the dying one had no tears. She was too happy for that, being on the verge of that place where tears are never shed. She smiled and whispered, 'It sounds like old times, father. Fa-re-well!'"

Mr. Ashworth, by his integrity, attention to business, and indomitable perseverance, ultimately succeeded in establishing a good business and forming a respectable connection; but he was not without his trials. Besides the care and anxiety of business, he had to contend with heavy affliction in his family, in addition to what has already been referred to, and he often said and wondered how it was, that while he was doing all he could for the good of others, and devoting much of his time in trying to alleviate the sufferings of others, that God should lay such weights upon him by family affliction. "For years and years," he says, "I have never been beyond the reach of anxiety, but always on the brink of it; I have had great sickness in my house." But he always solved the problem by saying, "God knows; there must be a 'need be' for it; shall not the Judge of all the earth do right?"

Two children died in infancy, John and William: the first when about a year old, very suddenly; the second when four years of age was scalded, and after lingering a short time died; both lie with their mother in St. Stephen's church yard. His eldest son, Felix, a very clever, promising young man, who had emigrated to Melbourne, was drowned while going a journey on horseback. The following notice of his melancholy death is from *The Albury Border Post*, of which he was some time one of the Proprietors.

"It is our melancholy province, in our present issue, to chronicle the untimely fate of Mr. Felix Ashworth, late one of the proprietors of this journal. Mr. Ashworth left Albury on Thursday, the 27th ult. (September, 1860), for Deniliquin and Moulamein, for the purpose of transacting business, and intending to reach home on Monday or Tuesday next. The deceased was the son of Mr. John Ashworth, of Rochdale, in the county of Lancashire, in England, and arrived in the colony about three years ago. He has been resident for two years and a half in Albury, during two years of which period he has been connected as proprietor with the 'Border Post'; and, until recently, with the 'Chittern Standard' since its commencement on the 13th of June, not quite four months since. Mr. Ashworth's marriage was chronicled in these columns, which now records his decease. But eight short days since he parted from his wife in high health and spirits, and within that brief space is hurried from this world, with all its mingled joys and sorrows, to that other land 'where the wicked cease from troubling, and the weary are at rest.' 'May he rest in peace.'

"The circumstances connected with the sad death of Mr. Ashworth have at length transpired. About one o'clock on Thursday, the 4th instant (October, 1860), Mr. Ashworth, in company with Messrs. Thomas Henty and W. Sherwin, left Deniliquin intending to make Conargo, a distance of about twenty-five miles, the same evening. About half a mile from that place they turned off the road to look at a dam that was in course of erection. Messrs. Henty and Sherwin rode on to where the men were at work. Mr. Ashworth proceeding about two hundred yards farther with the intention of watering his horse. At the spot he selected for the purpose the bank is almost perpendicular, and the depth of water about fifteen feet. The horse must have fallen in, throwing its rider at the same time; and it is singular both stirrup leathers were torn from the saddle in his fall. The men at the dam heard a cry, and immediately ran to his assistance, and a black fellow plunged in the moment he saw him in the water. He, however, could not find the body, and it was not till two hours and a half afterwards that, with the assistance of three more, the remains were recovered. The body was removed to McKenzie's hotel, Conargo. Mr. Ashworth's remains were interred in the cemetery at Deniliquin at three o'clock on Sunday last. Very great regret is felt at the unhappy accident, and a considerable number of the residents, including all the printers here, followed the body to the cemetery; the coroner being also present in the church while the Rev. R. Barker read the funeral service; and the horse of the deceased, the cause of so much sorrow, was led in the procession."

His second son, and only surviving child, also emigrated to Queensland after the death of his brother.

His only daughter, Mary Jane, the late wife of Amos Barraclough, was always delicate from a child, but for many years previous to her death was a confirmed invalid, and a great, but patient sufferer. A particular attachment existed between father and daughter, and their affection for each other was strong; the great deference with which they regarded each others opinions on various subjects was very striking. Mrs. Barraclough died March 21st, 1873, and was interred at the Rochdale Cemetery, where both now lie side by side till the morning of the resurrection.

Mr. Ashworth married for his second wife Hannah, daughter of the late Mr. Joseph Wood, of Rochdale, who still survives him, a step for which he ever felt truly thankful.

CHAPTER IV.

1851—1858.

BEFORE entering into what may be termed Mr. Ashworth's real "Life-work," that the reader may be better able to understand the secret of his success, how he accomplished so much, and from such a humble origin and opposing circumstances rose step by step in the social scale, until he occupied a position not only of credit and comfort to himself, but one that caused him to be loved, honoured, and respected by thousands of people in nearly all parts of the world, it may be interesting, as well as instructive, to give what may be called an analysis of the natural organisation of those superior powers of body and mind with which he was so richly endowed. The following is the result of a Phrenological examination by Professor Fowler, and which Mr. Ashworth considered on the whole very correct.

"You have by nature a strong and powerful organisation and character. You are equal to almost any amount of trial, discipline, or culture, and can make smaller organs quite influential, should the circumstances be favourable to their action. You have an unusual degree of life, vital power, and health ; and can go through more labour, both of body and mind, than the majority of men. In fact, few individuals have so much strength and hold on life as you have. You possess muscular power ; can bear burdens and endure physical exercises and fatigues, and sustain yourself where others would fail.

"Your mental temperament is favourably developed. You are very susceptible to mental emotions, and to high states of mental action. Your thoughts and feelings are of the intense kind. You also are excitable; still not so excitable as you are intense and high-toned. Your brain is rather large, giving comprehensiveness and vigour to your mind. You grasp the whole of a subject, and are conscious of all its bearings and consequences.

"Your phrenological developments are immense; some of the faculties being quite large, while others are less so. Your love of nature is strong, and you possess a full development of conjugal love, parental feeling, and interest in home and place; but your attachment to friends appears to be the strongest, giving you a deep affection for those to whom you once become drawn. You are equally distinct in your likes and dislikes. Your executive brain is large. You do not stop because there are impediments in the way, but appear to be inclined to put forth strong and vigorous efforts to accomplish an end. Your destructiveness causes you to be capable of enduring and able to bear much pain, and exert an influence where much energy of body and mind is required. Your sense of property is good. You value pounds, shillings, and pence; and although you may spend and give much, yet you economise in the use of your money, and make it tell to as good an advantage as possible. You have not that amount of cautiousness that gives fear and timidity; in fact, you are, by nature, rather venturesome, and have none too much restraining power. You are rather defective in the qualities that give ambition, display, politeness, affability, and disposition to cater to public opinion. You find it necessary to curb your radical remarks with reference to the customs and fashions of society. You are liable to take strong ground, to come square out and out and do what is to be done, and leave all the rest undone. The ceremony you care little for. Your self-esteem, especially that part that gives independence, is very marked, giving you pride, self-reliance, independence, and willingness to take the responsibilities of your own life and actions upon yourself. You ask no human being to back *you up in* anything. You seldom quote from others, but give your statement for what it is worth. You are remarkable for your firmness, perseverance, and determination of mind. At times the manifestation of firmness amounts almost to obstinacy.

"Your moral organization is most peculiar in development. Benevolence is very large and influential. You cannot live carelessly and recklessly of the happiness of others. You are instinctively inclined to shape your own course so as to be adapted more or less to other people. This is the ruling feature of your mind, and your influence over other persons is based on your sympathy, as much as any other quality. Spirituality is large, introducing you to a spiritual life, giving you a consciousness of spiritual affinities, inclining you to prayer and belief, and opening up channels to the spiritual life. You are disposed to commune with spirits, and have more belief in spiritual existence and influence than ninety-nine in a hundred. Hope is rather large, giving regard for the future, and consciousness of immortality. Veneration, especially the fore part of it, as applied to man, is weak, hence you have but a limited degree of respect for persons, except as human beings, and this only as they live properly, and sustain a good moral character. Name, rank, titles, dignities have no weight with you. Your regard for sacred things is a matter of culture, gained by giving your attention to religion and spiritual things. From the aid of the organ of spirituality you may have high views and feelings as applied to the character of God. Consciousness is not naturally strong, and you have had to contend with the effects of its deficiency. You have been tempted to extremes, to use extravagant measures to accomplish an end, and you are liable to make excesses of what you say and do. This, and the deficiency of veneration, are the two most important defects in your mind; hence you should guard against all kinds of intemperance in speech as much as possible; and bear in mind that you are liable to start a point for present effect, and say things in too extravagant a manner. Your ideas of abstract right and wrong, morally speaking, are stronger than your prudence and circumspection.

"Intellectually your special gifts are, great power of observation, great capacity to accumulate knowledge, uncommon intuition of mind, and ability to see more in a given space of time than the majority of men can. You remember what you see, and places you visit, very accurately. You have power to understand the laws of gravity, to perceive colours and enjoy them, to appreciate numbers, and to arrange and systematise; but your memory of disconnected facts and events is not great, save by association. You enjoy music; are very punctual in keeping your engagements. You have fair command of language, above the average, but not so much as to talk when you have nothing to say.

"Comparison is very large, giving you unusual powers of illustration, description, and ability to study the bearing of one subject on another. You see everything in the light of contrast or comparison. You are fond of studying human motives and character; are shrewd in your judgment in reference to others; and your first impressions are about as correct as any you have; in fact you are able to look right through people. You are given to reasoning, studying the relation of cause and effect, inquiring into how and why things are. You are usually agreeable, pliable, playful, and much interested in subjects of an amusing character. You have a very active sense of fun and art. You enjoy a joke highly, and can make about as much fun as any other man, if you set yourself about it. You have imagination and scope of mind, and you take extravagant views of subjects. You are much interested in everything that pertains to oratory, poetry, beauty, art, or extravagant thought. You enjoy the sublime and grand in nature, and can take in the whole scenery without any difficulty. The power of your organization mentally and physically is such that you can accomplish more than most persons; and you are in consequence under greater obligations than men generally are to your Creator for the gifts you have under your control."

We now come to the period when Mr. Ashworth entered upon his great *Life Work*,—when those special gifts, with which he was so richly endowed, found their proper sphere of usefulness and development. There are circumstances in the lives of most men who have made their mark in the world, that call out those special gifts into active and vigorous operation, and lead them to follow that course for which, in the providence of God, their physical, mental, and moral capabilities are particularly adapted and designed.

When the late Dr. Chalmers was minister of the quiet, country, Fifeshire village of Kilmany, he was comparatively little known; but when, in the course of providence, he was called upon to labour in the city of Glasgow, then the entire man became changed—then he began to realize his great work; and that mighty intellect, and those latent energies that had been slumbering for years, burst forth in all their full vigour, with a power and eloquence that not only moved the masses, but astonished the world. It is a common saying that "we are creatures of circumstances," but, thank God, these very circumstances are to many a ladder wherewith to rise.

"Who breaks his birth's invidious bar,
Who grasps the skirts of happy chance,
Who breasts the blows of circumstance,
And grapples with his evil star."

We might refer to many illustrious names to whom these lines apply, but at present we have only to do with one. We have spoken of *A Work*, but the subject of this biography, while he had one purpose in life, one aim, one object, was not a man of one idea; neither were his labours confined within the narrow limits of sect or party; his full soul and capacious mind could only find vent in such a multiplicity of work, and various spheres of usefulness, that few men could accomplish; and after several years' experience he says,

"I find the more work a man does in the cause of God, the more he wishes to do;" and with regard to the catholicity of his labours, when asked by the late Dr. Guthrie, of Edinburgh, if he did not belong to the Methodist Free Church, some of his friends exclaimed, "He belongs to humanity at large." But in speaking of his work, we speak of it as a whole; and the particular branch of it to which we would now refer is that in connection with and arising out of the "Chapel for the Destitute."

The *circumstance* which suggested the thought of it was a visit to London, during the Great Exhibition of 1851, when people from all parts of the world visited the Metropolis. Never was there seen before such a gathering "out of all nations." To the minds of the people thus assembled, many new ideas would be suggested by what they witnessed, in reference to mechanics, science, philosophy, and art, and they would return to their homes with enlarged conceptions of trade, and thoughts of new schemes, which would doubtless be of immense advantage to the commercial prosperity and social well-being of the various communities to which they might belong. But in that vast multitude were many good people, speaking different languages, children of the same great Father, and loving the same Lord Jesus Christ, whose thoughts were not confined to the magnificent works of art and science within the spacious building. Accordingly Mr. Ashworth informs us,—

"It was during a visit to London, in 1851, that the thought was suggested. I had seen its palaces of glass, brick, and stone, visited its museums, galleries, and other splendid places of attraction, also its prisons, penitentiaries, hospitals, houses of refuge, &c., but the Home for the Destitute interested me more than all beside. What I saw and felt on visiting this place produced a degree of anguish from which I have never wholly recovered. Hardened villainy, misery, wretchedness, and hopeless despair were evident on every side; all the woes of the apocalypse seemed to have overtaken the miserable inmates. I felt they were all my brothers and sisters, and I felt that sin had done it all; and I also felt a degree of veneration for the men whose Christian philanthropy had reared this shelter for the truly destitute. Infidelity, I knew, had not done it. That the Gospel of Christ, applied by the Spirit, could reclaim these miserable beings, I had not the slightest doubt.

"In all towns hundreds of such are to be found, who never hear the gospel, and who never attend either our churches or chapels. Is it not the duty of every man, whose heart God has touched, to do all he can for the redemption of such? and if they will not come to us, then we must go to them—meet them on their own terms, and provide them with places of worship adapted to their own condition;—in the spirit of love trying to gather in the outcast, and tell them the tale of the cross.

"These reflections induced me to make a vow, that on my return to Rochdale I would at once open a 'Chapel for the Destitute.' I consulted my friends, and endeavoured to enlist them in the undertaking. 'What!' says one, 'are you going to teach the poor that our churches are not open to them? We have plenty of room; why do they not come?' 'What!' says another, 'are you going to widen the distance betwixt the rich and the poor, by opening for them separate places of worship?—you will do more harm than good.' 'What!' said a third, 'do you expect to get a congregation from amongst the degraded? If you will tap a barrel of ale every Sunday you will, but not otherwise.'

"I am now ashamed to say that, meeting with the above objections, and finding none to help me, I gave up the undertaking."

An interval of seven years passed away, during which Mr. Ashworth was by no means idle; while "diligent in business," he was also "fervent in spirit, serving the Lord," being actively engaged as a Sunday-school teacher, class leader, local preacher, and discharging various other duties in connection with the church; but there was other and special work, which he was under a solemn obligation to do, that had been left undone.

Christians are often prompted, and feel that God is calling them, to do a particular kind of work; but as the doing of it would entail upon them a considerable amount of responsibility, expose them to criticism, and require a good deal of self-denial in carrying it out, they shrink from it, and, like Jonah when commissioned to go and preach to the Ninevites, do all they can to evade it, until God lays His afflicting hand upon them, brings them low, and then, like Jonah, they are glad to say, "I will sacrifice unto thee with the voice of thanksgiving: I will pay *that* that I have vowed." So with His servant: he was brought low by affliction, and had to say, "All thy waves and thy billows are gone over me." Then it was he remembered his *vow*, and, like David, he now longed to go into God's house to perform it.

Some years after, during an address referring to the time when this vow was made, Mr. Ashworth stated that in early life he had some conviction that God had work for him to do. He was about twelve years of age when he first heard William Dawson preach, and it was while the sermon was being delivered that he particularly felt that he had some work to do for God. That about ten years ago he had a conviction the church was doing *nothing*, and remembered very well making a vow that if God Almighty would make him more useful, he would obey Him, even if He asked him to go through fire. He could tell them that that vow was made while he lay on his face in his bedroom. He lay on his face for three or four hours, and vowed that if God would only make him more useful, or found it necessary that he was to know deeper sorrow or more trouble, he would take it meekly whatever it was. He wrote the promise down, and very shortly afterwards one of the greatest sorrows that ever took place in the whole course of his life occurred, and that was the death by drowning of his eldest son. After this he felt such strength as he had never felt in all his life. From that consecration to God sprang the "Chapel for the Destitute." He saw his work at once: he felt he must go and labour for Him amongst the lowest of the low.

How many vows and good resolutions made on beds of sickness and suffering have been forgotten! How many have promised God in their distress, that if He would restore them they would consecrate themselves to His service, whose goodness has been like the "morning cloud," which soon passeth away! "Were there not ten cleansed, but where are the nine?" His servant felt, as thousands have done, it was good to be afflicted. Accordingly he says,—

"While labouring under affliction I remembered my broken vow, and again resolved that if the Lord would deliver me, I would do all I could to bring sinners from the highways and hedges. I prayed earnestly that He would give me grace and firmness of purpose to endure any amount of ridicule, abuse, misrepresentation, opposition, or imposition; that He would take money matters entirely into His own hands, and send pecuniary help as it might be required. Believing that God would bless the undertaking, I determined not to consult any human being, but go at once to work, dependent upon God's help and blessing. I took a small room, and got two thousand bills printed as follows :—

CHAPEL FOR THE

DESTITUTE,

(Near the Bank steps,)

Baillie-street, Rochdale.

Ye houseless, homeless, friendless, pennyless, outcasts, Come!
In rags, and tatters, ... Come!
Ye poor, and maim'd, and halt, and blind, ... Come!
Of whatever colour or nation, creed or no creed, ... Come!

Jesus loves you,
And died to save you.

'Come, then, to Him, all ye wretched,
Lost and ruin'd by the fall;
If you tarry till you're better,
You will never come at all.'

NO COLLECTIONS.

All we seek is your welfare, both body and soul.

Service every Sunday evening at a quarter-past Six.

Come, poor sinners; come, and welcome!

"Fifty of these bills were fixed on blue pasteboard, with a small loop of red tape at the top. With nails in one pocket, and a hammer in the other, I went to all the barber's shops and lodging-houses in the town, requesting permission to hang up the cards. In no place was I refused, and I returned home late in the evening, rejoicing *over my success.*

"One Sunday morning—and to me a memorable Sunday morning—with about five hundred bills in my pocket, I began to walk through the back streets and low places; and where I saw either man or woman in dirt and rags, I offered them a bill, and respectfully requested them to come to the service. If they could not read the bill, I read it for them. Some made merry with it, others stared at me, but very few promised to come."

The result of that day's labours, with an account of the opening and subsequent services in connection with the "Chapel for the Destitute," is given in Mr. Ashworth's characteristic style in the three parts of the narrative entitled, "My New Friends," Nos. 11, 12, and 13 of the First Series of "Strange Tales," the reading of which is deeply interesting and somewhat amusing. The building was originally erected for the Young Men's Christian Association, having a large Lecture Hall, with several small rooms underneath. It was in one of the latter Mr. Ashworth met his first congregation on that memorable Sunday, October 4th, 1858, and in which they continued to meet till March 6th of the following year, when it was found necessary to remove to the larger room upstairs, where, with a slight interval, the services have been conducted ever since.

CHAPTER V.

1859—1863.

REPORTS have been issued from year to year, which show the growth of the work, and the extent of the operations carried on. The first was in October, 1859, the preface to which is as follows:

THE CHAPEL FOR THE DESTITUTE.

"In presenting the first account connected with the above place, I wish to say a few words on its origin; I wish also to say, that had I been able to support the place myself, I should not have thought it necessary to give any report at all; but as several friends have kindly sent me money, unsolicited, I feel bound to inform them how it has been expended. I believe that the work in which I am engaged, is the work of God, and that He will open my way, and send pecuniary help to any amount, or any extent, that may be required, without either anniversary sermons, public collections, or my troubling myself in the matter. I believe in answers to prayer, and have good reason for so doing; pleading the promises, as I find them in the Scriptures, is my stronghold; my greatest difficulty is to keep *self* out of the undertaking, and to seek the glory of God only. How desirable it is to reach this blessed state in all we do.

Our strength......................the Grace of God;
Our rule..........................the Word of God;
Our object........................the Glory of God."

Soon after the opening of the Chapel for the

CHAPEL FOR THE DESTITUTE.

Destitute, Mr. Ashworth began to publish, from incidents arising out of and in connection with his work, a series of touching narratives, entitled, "Strange Tales from Humble Life," to which we shall afterwards refer. The immense circulation and popularity of these, while it increased the already abundant labours of the Author by demands upon his services, also contributed very much to the success, support, and prosperity of the Destitute. The first, entitled "The Dark Hour," was issued with the second year's Report, the preface of which is as follows:—

CHAPEL FOR THE DESTITUTE.

SECOND REPORT.

"During the last year, my connection with the CHAPEL FOR THE DESTITUTE, and what has directly or indirectly grown out of it, has brought me in contact with a large number of cases presenting almost every variety of character: tramps, confirmed beggars, clever impostors, ruined tradesmen, gamblers and cripples; invalids, in every state; real misfortune and unavoidable poverty; thankfulness for small help and cold ingratitude for considerable assistance; hopeful cases painfully relapsing; the most unlikely becoming the most promising; sick beds and death-beds many—some awful beyond expression, and others cheering to reflect upon.

"Our congregations on the Sunday, range from one to two hundred: and the attendance at the Thursday-evening meeting has gradually increased. Some cases of real conversion, and many of considerable reformation, have taken place. I am greatly encouraged by seeing numbers of the really poor so regularly attending the preaching of the Gospel; their orderly conduct and respectful demeanour during service have been uniformly pleasing.

"I have during the year seen much of the dark side of fallen humanity; have had to sound deeper the depths of depravity; and am more than ever convinced that the Gospel of Christ is the only power that can fathom these depths, and bring countless millions from the verge of hell, as trophies of its power. These convictions bind me to one purpose and one object—to point to the Lamb of God, that taketh away the sin of the world.

"I have kept a diary of some of the principal incidents that have fallen under my notice. The 'Dark Hour' is one of them. My only object in giving it publicity is, that the reading of it may be made a blessing to others, such as the witnessing and recording of it has been to myself."

Mr. Ashworth, in conjunction with Miss E. Ormerod and two other ladies, made an effort this year to establish a Refuge in Rochdale for fallen females, from which class many sad cases came under their notice and sought their help, one in particular that died in the workhouse. The following Report, issued by the Secretary, shows with what success.

"March 20, 1860.—It is only known to a few individuals that an attempt has been made in our own town, during the last few weeks, to rescue from the haunts of vice and misery, such young women as were truly penitent, and who needed and earnestly desired the proffered aid, to enable them to effect their escape. Four have been rescued, and have proved their sincerity, and their gratitude is unbounded. Two were placed in lodgings, and are now in situations, giving satisfaction to those who, actuated by tender compassion and a principle of large-hearted benevolence, ventured to employ them.

"It is thought desirable, as others are anxious to escape from their degradation, to raise a fund for the support of this object, in the maintenance of a 'Female Refuge,' where they could be removed at once without delay.

"This report is presented by request."

A great desire was felt by Mr. Ashworth and other good men for a revival of God's work in Rochdale. Mr. Finney, an American, was on a visit to this country, whose labours in various churches, especially the Methodist Societies, were being graciously blessed, and consequently in great demand. Mr. Ashworth and one of the ministers in town were deputed to wait upon Mr. Finney, who was at that time (March 20, 1860) the guest of Mr. Barlow of Bolton, and if possible secure his services. The following account of their interview is given by Mr. Ashworth :—

"Being shown into the library, we had only to wait a few minutes, when he made his appearance in a printed morning dress. After a mutual introduction all sat down.

"'What is your errand, gentlemen?' asked Mr. Finney.

"'We come from Rochdale,' was the reply, 'and the friends are anxious to have you a few nights with them. We have a very large chapel, and no doubt it will be crowded to hear you.'

"'Is your chapel well ventilated?'

"'Yes, very,' we reply.

"'The Manchester people are urging me to give them three nights in the Corn Exchange, before I return to America, which will be in a few days.'

"'We understand you are wanted there,' we observed.

"'But I cannot come to you and go to Manchester?'

"'Well, perhaps you will give us the preference.'

"'Indeed! indeed! Let us kneel down and pray about this matter,' said Mr. Finney.

"We knelt down, and I do not think either of us will ever forget that moment.

"Mr. Finney began first, and said,—

"'Lord, here are two selfish men come from Rochdale to request me to go to that town to preach; they say they know I am requested to go to Manchester. I cannot go to both, and they want me to give Rochdale the preference; they care nothing about Manchester souls, only about Rochdale souls; but, Lord, souls are souls, equal in value everywhere: teach these two men that souls are souls.'

"Then laying his hand on my shoulder, he said, 'Pray, brother.'

"What I said I cannot tell, but I know I was very short. He then laid his hand on my companion, saying, 'Pray, brother.'

"He also was very brief, and we arose from our knees with no little confusion.

"After a considerable pause Mr. Finney rose up, paced quickly about the room, and abruptly said, 'I feel I have nothing to do at Rochdale.'

"Just then Mrs. Finney came in from a morning's meeting, and looking at her, he observed,—'You are looking pale, my dear; have you had all the meeting to yourself? I fear you have. Do you know since you went out the doctor called, and thinks I ought not, in my state of health, to take the service in the Manchester Exchange; that

I am exhausted, and may die in the pulpit. If I do, what will you say, dear?'

"Mrs. Finney placed both hands on his shoulders, looked him right in the face, and in a solemn, impressive tone replied, 'I shall say, Rest, warrior, rest, thy warfare's ended!'"

CHAPEL FOR THE DESTITUTE.

THIRD REPORT.

"This has been a year of sorrow and joy; many trials and much encouragement. Much more than in either of the preceding years have I stood in need of *faith* and *patience*. None but those engaged in similar work can tell the many trying circumstances daily arising, and the extreme difficulty of deciding which is the best course to adopt. During this year, I have had to deal with many hundreds of painful cases,—some of real destitution, and others of gross imposition. How to tell where charity will be a good or an evil, succour the needy, or encourage the idle, is often perplexing in the extreme; but I have confidence in Divine guidance, where it is earnestly sought, and believe that, in many cases, real good has been effected.

"Given R. G., for lodgings, 2s., also a shirt and pair of shoes. This young man was formerly a teller in a bank, well-educated, of good parentage, and married an educated lady of respectable family. Drink had ruined him. I had him under care for several weeks, during which time I received from his sorrowing wife the following letter:—

"'Dear Sir,—I thank you for your kindness to my poor erring husband. A few years since he was regarded by every one as a gentleman, held high trust, and was much respected. His ruin has been rapid and complete; drink and expensive company have been the cause. I and our two children are now with my father, but on the condition I never see my husband. I sometimes hear from him, and I hope he will keep near you, for I understand he is better off in Rochdale than he has been for some time. The Lord bless you for your kindness to him.'

"M. J. came to the Chapel in a dreadful state of wretchedness and rags, the consequence of a very sinful life. Got her lodgings, clothed her, and my Scripture-reader got her employment; she had to be maintained until she could learn; part of the money she has paid back. I take this opportunity of thanking one or two of the mill-owners for kindly helping me in these cases. This girl is much altered, and is still attending the Chapel and meetings.

"Paid for lodgings for thirteen persons, 3s. 3d. One of these persons was formerly the proprietor of a boarding-school, and had possessed a considerable income. He could speak and write three languages, was very gentlemanly in his deportment. Drink had ruined him. After our service, I had some conversation with him. He stated that he believed his case hopeless; that if a quart of brandy stood before him, and the loss of his soul depended on drinking it, that he should drink it. Another was a sea-captain, formerly owner of two coasting vessels. Both were lost in one month, and uninsured. His wife had died of grief. He was on his way to Hull, to seek employment. He simply asked for one night's lodgings. He was very clean and decently dressed. I found him provision for the following day (Sunday). At the Chapel he wept much. He stated that since he was brought to poverty, he had thought more of God in one hour, than in the whole twelve years he was getting riches.—For providing a widow, with five children, goods to commence hawking, which became a great help, 9s.—For a few clothes, to improve a miserable bed, for a woman that wished to reform her life, 5s. 5d."

Mr. Ashworth speaks of this year as one in which he was much tried, and stood in need of *faith* and *patience.* One of the grossest cases of imposition he had to deal with was the one mentioned in No. 12 of "My New Friends," whom he calls Thomas, to save him from exposure. The following is a copy of the letter given by Mr. Ashworth to this man to try and collect the *required sum:*

"Drake Street, April 30, 1861.

"J—— D——, the bearer of this note, has been a striker for the blacksmiths, but in consequence of affliction he is unable to do hard work.

"We think a donkey and cart may perhaps do well for him. Six pounds is the price asked for one, and I have promised if he can raise one half, to help him with the other. So he is trying to raise three pounds.

"He has a small family of children, and only one worker; I think him a person worthy of help.

"JOHN ASHWORTH."

Then follow twenty names of well-known charitable ladies and gentlemen in town, who had contributed sums varying from one shilling to five, amounting altogether to £3 1s., Mr. Ashworth becoming responsible for the entire cost. The reader will know, from the perusal of the narrative above named, that this "New Friend" sold the donkey and cart while on a drunken spree, and then threatened, if Mr. Ashworth said a word to him about the money, to run a knife through him. No wonder we find such records in his Diary as,—"A day of sorrow, on account of the deep deception and ingratitude of the poor, amongst whom I have to labour."—"Lost my temper: Lord help me!"—"Much grieved from causing a woman to shed tears; prayed for pardon." Mr. Ashworth was also for several weeks suffering much from physical prostration, as well as mental anxiety; and was still more pained by his congregation proposing to present him with a full-length portrait of himself, also related in Narrative No. 12.

1862.—Has been one of the most eventful years.

The terrible civil war in America, producing what is called the *Cotton Famine*, and as a consequence, untold misery and privation, of which the operatives in Rochdale had a heavy share, which was borne with amazing patience. When the great crisis came, Mr. Ashworth (as on other occasions) was equal to the emergency, and was one of the first to take steps to organize a system of relief for mitigating the sufferings of the working classes. He, along with Mr. W. A. Scott, convened a private meeting by circular on the 8th, and then a public meeting followed on the 13th of January, when a committee was formed, with the late lamented Mr. George Leach Ashworth as chairman, into the work of which Mr. Ashworth threw all his energies, and, with the other gentlemen, spared no time or labour in administering relief and comfort to the distressed operatives.

The reader will remember, it was while engaged in one of the relief stores, distributing meal and flour, that Sir J. P. Kay Shuttleworth made the acquaintance of his old Bamford Scholar, who introduced himself as the bare-footed boy to whom he had given his first prize forty years before.

Mr. Ashworth preserved, as a memento of the liberality of our American friends during the cotton famine, one of the barrels sent over by them with flour for the relief of the Lancashire operatives. He had it varnished and placed in his study, along with the form on which he sat in Bagslate Sunday-school. It has on it the following inscription:—

"I am one of the thousands
that were filled with flour,
and sent by the
Free States of America,
in the ship George Griswold,
to the starving people of Lancashire,
whose miseries were caused
by the aggressive and civil war
of the slave-owners
in 1862-3-4."

In addition to Mr. Ashworth's indefatigable labours in connection with the Relief Committee, he was unremitting in his efforts at the Chapel for the Destitute. To the poor the Gospel was preached; and while ministering to them the bread of life, he was also able, through the kindness and liberality of his friends, to do much to alleviate their sufferings. When God's judgments are abroad in the earth, the people learn righteousness. Poverty causes many to bow their knees in prayer, and seek the Lord in their distress. So it brought many to the Chapel for the Destitute. The congregation increased so much that the room, which seats several hundreds, became too small, and, for a time, the services were conducted in the Public Hall. As may be supposed, large numbers came for relief; but many found the Pearl of Great Price; some of them have gone home to heaven, who dated their conversion to that time, and, like the man in the parable, when reduced to want, not only said, "I will arise, and go to my Father;" but could sing,—

"I came to Jesus as I was,
Weary, and worn, and sad,
I found in Him a resting-place,
And He has made me glad."

So, many who came in their poverty and destitution, were made rich in faith, and heirs of the kingdom of heaven.

Previous to the Cotton Panic an event took place (1848) which had already brought distress and ruin into hundreds of families,—the collapse of the Rochdale Savings Bank,—by which 2,965 depositors sustained a loss of £38,287. Amongst them widows, servants, miners, labourers, sick-clubs, and trust accounts, and all chiefly through one man. Mr. Ashworth, along with other gentlemen, did all he could to obtain some compensation from government (but in vain) for the sufferers in this disaster, and was one of a deputation who went to London to obtain an interview with Mr. Gladstone, then Chancellor of the Exchequer, on the subject, on July 23rd, 1862, and were introduced by the late Mr. Richard Cobden.

1863.—Jan. 1st.—Mr. Ashworth records, "On the last night of the year I entirely dedicated myself to God, body and soul: felt much liberty in prayer. Confined at home in consequence of an inflammation in the eye. I am always a gainer by affliction; it makes the soul mellower and humbler." Several times during the year he was subject to bilious attacks. On one occasion he writes, "Still confined to my room. I think my heavenly Father is putting me under discipline. He knows best what will do for me, and I feel I am in His blessed hands. How precious to be a child of God!" Mr. Ashworth's mind was exercised in various ways during the year. He had his temptations, trials, disappointments; but had also many manifestations of God's love and mercy, for which he expresses his deep gratitude, mourns over his indifference at times for perishing souls, and too much anxiety about the world and business, and frequently implores, "Lord, help me." On the 8th Oct., his only daughter was married, when he writes, "This day is a day of days; my dear daughter married to A. B. My heart feels more than I can express. The Lord bless them."

In connection with the "Destitute," "This year," he says, "has been the most prosperous in regard to the attendance of the poor people at all the services, both Sunday and week-day, and for several weeks hundreds were not able to gain admittance. This gave me much sorrow, and caused me to wish we had a large and settled place of our own, for the poor and destitute in Rochdale to worship in." A female Scripture reader was engaged, whose valuable assistance Mr. Ashworth often speaks of, and who continued to labour with much success amongst the poor, till failing health compelled her to give it up; and after several years of painful, protracted affliction, she passed away, and is now reaping her reward.

In the Preface to this year's Report, Mr. Ashworth writes as follows:—

"We have lost, amongst other deaths, LAWRENCE HOYLE and JOSEPH TAYLOR, (Pinder,) the two persons that constituted the subject of the narrative called 'The Wonder! or the Two Old Men,' in the last year's report. I visited them both in their sickness. To them Christ was indeed precious. They held fast their confidence, and died in peace. The body of Old Lawrence now lies in Haslingden Church-yard, and Pinder's in Heywood Cemetery. I preached the funeral sermon of both on one night, from the words 'The sting of death is sin.' Let none despair, since these two old men found mercy. Their conversion was indeed marvellous.

"The narratives ('The Dark Hour'! 'Mary, a Tale of Sorrow'! and 'The Wonder'!) contained in the three last reports, and the last of the ten narratives now published, called 'My New Friends,' have had an amazing circulation; and as one result my friends, and the friends of the poor, have sent me larger means than in any former year. This has greatly strengthened my hands, it gives me greater power of doing good; and during the dreary distressing cotton famine it has been doubly welcome. By having a Scripture-reader to assist me in visiting the homes of the poor, I get acquainted with real cases of need, and feel better satisfied that the money is well spent.

"Few persons living have more cause for gratitude than myself. Judging from the numerous letters almost daily received, our reports and narratives are being read from hundreds of pulpits, and are spreading throughout the length and breadth of the land, stirring up many to seek the temporal and spiritual welfare of the long-neglected outcasts of society. I have been present at the opening of three chapels for the destitute during the year. God has wonderfully answered my prayers. Once again, I consecrate myself to His service, believing that He will still give me all the help I require, in body, mind, and means. In Him, is all my trust; and my prayer still is, HOLD THOU ME UP, AND I SHALL BE SAFE."

And in the monthly statement of cases relieved, the following, amongst others, are recorded:—

"Late one evening, a poor woman wished to speak to me. On going to the door, I found her weeping. I knew the woman to be a decent, respectable person, and on inquiring her errand, she informed me that herself, her husband and children had been without food all day; that her eldest girl had persuaded her to come and see me, as the only person they could think of to help them in their distress. I gave the woman 2s., for which she was truly thankful. Many, very many such cases have I had during this terrible cotton famine.

"For providing food and a night's lodging for a young

woman, and restoring her to her sorrowing family, 2s. 6d. These are amongst my most painful cases. They often reveal early depravity or cruel neglect. Many such, in their moments of penitence or despair, apply to me for help or counsel. I have this day helped one on her way to her relations at Leeds; and got another into Hollingworth workhouse. She informed me that she was without parents, but had an uncle called Bell, residing at Northwich. I wrote, requesting him to have pity on his sister's child; but the answer was he could do nothing for her. I gave the letter to the girl; and while she read it, tears rolled down her ragged shawl. For six days I had charge of her, but not being able to get her work, she very willingly went to the workhouse.

"An old man, called Lawrence Cocker, eighty-six years of age, came to ask my help in getting him a few clothes, to 'prevent him being starved to death.' He informed me that he 'remembered the first Sunday-school in Rochdale, and the first long chimney; but now,' said he, 'they are both as common as mushrooms, and I think commoner: folks are more learnt than they were; young ones know more than old ones did, un I think they're better.'

"Gave a Testament to a man who pawned it, along with one of my hymn-books he had taken from the chapel, to raise more drink. The pawnbroker, seeing the following inscription in it, returned it:—'Edward Turnbull; a present from John Ashworth.'"

CHAPTER VI.

1864—1865.

ON January 1st, 1864, Mr. Ashworth was the guest of Mrs. Sturge (widow of the late Joseph Sturge), Birmingham, where he spent several days in useful labour, visiting the Boys' Reformatory, Female Penitentiary, and addressing various meetings.

In this congenial family he met with many members of the Society of "Friends," to which they belong: a body of Christians he much admired, and for whom he always had the greatest respect,—so much so, that a lady one day jokingly told him "that he was half a 'Quaker' and half a 'Methodist.'" He certainly loved the consistent unworldly lives of the "Friends," but it needed the warmth of Methodism to satisfy the emotional part of his nature.

Mr. Ashworth was also much impressed with the comfort of their homes, as well as the purity, piety, and benevolence of their lives, of which the reader may judge by the following sketch :—

"The Society of Friends, though not very numerous, has, in many respects, always been powerful for good. Its members having the most profound regard for the Bible, as a revelation from heaven, and teaching the doctrine of a conscious salvation by faith in Jesus; the witness of the Spirit testifying to the reality of that salvation, and also a sure and divine guidance in the life; believing the precepts of the Scriptures to be imperative, and their practice the best evidence of a true obedience to Christ, showing their love to Him by keeping His commandments, they have calmly but firmly resolved to walk by these precepts, obey God rather than man, and peaceably take all consequences. They believe that Christ taught a universal brotherhood, and universal peace. They therefore condemn all slavery and all war: they contend that evil never destroyed evil, but that it must be overcome with good. They also believe that in matters of conscience we are responsible to God only, and that nothing—priest or power—ought to intermeddle. Their views have often subjected them to imprisonment, persecution, and the spoiling of their goods; but they have patiently endured all. No power could ever coerce them to a compliance contrary to their own convictions of duty: ritualism, ecclesiastical dignitaries, priestly assumption and pretension they quietly pass by; preferring in their simple worship to walk by faith and not by sight, and regarding the power of godliness as far more important than mere form. They teach and practice temperance, sobriety, honesty, industry, and commercial integrity. They are anxious to avoid worldly conformity; theatres, balls, cards, concerts, races, or other fashionable and questionable amusements they avoid; thinking it more their duty, and productive of far more true pleasure and happiness to encourage schools, attend to benevolent objects, conduct mothers' meetings, and visit the fatherless and widows in their affliction. The females refuse to be drawn into the interminable labyrinths of restless, frivolous, foolish fashion, or deck themselves in mantles, wimples, crisping-pins, gold, pearls, or useless and costly array; but adorn themselves in sensible, modest apparel. Some have recently deviated from this rule, and have entered the labyrinth, but without adding grace to the person or peace to the mind.

"They are well and carefully trained in domestic duties, and make good wives and mothers. They have excellent schools for giving all their children, rich and poor, a good education; the wealthy in all matters helping those that are less able, none of them are ever left to the mercy of the parish, or to die in the union workhouse. They are loyal subjects, worthy citizens, good neighbours, intelligent, respectable, and respected; and as philanthropists, conspicuous to the whole earth. Many of them are very rich, most of them are in comfortable circumstances. Their average life is twenty years more than the rest of the community: they are the 'meek that inherit the earth.' I never saw one of them drunk, or with a black eye, a cork arm, or a wooden leg. It is very strange and suggestive of a painful fact, that a people so anxious to walk by Christian rule should be considered singular in a professed Christian country, but so it is. That they have had amongst them some who have not been consistent they well know and deplore, but, as a rule, they have adorned their profession. Glory to God and good will to man has been a marked feature in their character. Some of their own rules have crippled their expansion, and they have perhaps not been sufficiently aggressive, but they have made their mark in England, and especially in America. Their peaceable, earnest benevolence, irrespective of creed or country, has taught the world a lesson; and they have sown seed which, if not developed in the form of Quakerism, will bless mankind with a less untrammelled and more vigorous Christianity. The 'Friends' are emphatically the friends of the down-trodden African, wherever he was in slavery and chains; and if his fetters are now broken, and the dark sons of Ham are free, it is mainly owing to the undying exertions of the 'Friends' on his behalf.

"Perhaps no part of their customs is more calculated to impress a stranger than their mode of burying their dead. They have no written or printed form of words; no officiating minister or priest. At the entrance of the cemetery is placed a form or bench, on which are laid crossways three or four strong linen bands of pure whiteness; over these the coffin is laid, and by these the bearers carry it to the side of the open grave. Around the place of sepulture is a low, wide platform, on which the friends and relatives of the deceased stand: the body is lowered in silence, and in silence they look on all that can be seen of the dead. When Mrs. M—, of Rochdale, was interred, that silence was broken by the clear but tremulous voice of her eldest daughter. Few persons then present will forget that impressive moment when she gave a testimony to the power of Divine grace in her dear mother's experience,—'How it had found her and saved her; and that grace, always sufficient, had long sustained her; that in her last days her Saviour was very precious to her, and faith in Him soothed her passage to the grave; and over that grave gave her the victory. Thanks be to God which giveth us the victory through our Lord Jesus Christ!'

"Strangers at the funeral expected that something would have been said about the many excellences the dear departed one possessed, for she had long been a friend to the poor, and many of them were there to pay their last sad tribute of respect to her memory; but there was no eulogium of the dead. With them "Christ is all, and in all."

"Amongst the many mourners assembled in the 'Friends' burying ground that day, was one whose feet stood on the very spot where her body was soon to be laid. The next that was marked to fall. Mrs. Y— was one of those unpretending, quiet creatures, that loved to do good by stealth, and was most beloved by those who knew her best. Often have I crossed her path, when on her errands of mercy, and often have the poor and needy, especially during the dreadful cotton famine (of 1862-3) received from her, and her other 'Friends' she interested on their behalf, sums of money to supply their needs; and when she came with her one, two, or five pounds for the poor, how happy she seemed to be. When in the winter she could carry any of them—and often in the night, for fear of being seen—some articles of clothing to keep them warm, or some little nourishment for the sick, she seemed truly thankful that she could lessen human suffering; and on these visits of mercy it gave her an opportunity to talk with them of what, to her, was the truest source of all real comfort.

"I was one day walking in my garden, when an invalid lady, drawn in a Bath chair, stopped near where I stood: this invalid was my sick friend. She reached out her hand over the low rail fence; I took hold of it with feelings of sadness, as I looked into her pale face. She saw I was surprised at her altered looks, and observed, 'Thou sees me much altered, John Ashworth; and I think thou sees me on my last journey, for my weakness is greater than I thought. I often think of thee and thy poor people at the Chapel for the Destitute, and the poor suffering creatures at the relief board. Thou sees if I am sick, I have bread; and I have also the Bread that cometh down from heaven, which makes my sickness easy to bear. How well it is when the lamp is trimmed, and we have oil in our vessels with our lamps; then the Bridegroom will be welcome.'

"'Yes,' I replied, 'and I do feel thankful to hear you speak with such confidence; the time for true testing seems with you near at hand.'

"'Yes, it is; but I have no fear. Our Saviour will be with me in the valley.' Then again giving me her clammy hand, she cheerfully said, 'Fare thee well, John Ashworth.'

"It was a farewell, as far as regards this world, for it was, as she predicted, her last journey. She lay down on her bed of sickness, and for several weeks passed through a very heavy affliction, but endured it with strong faith and patience."

This year, although it was to Mr. Ashworth in some respects one of prosperity, was also one of painful and bitter experiences, which at times ruffled his temper, saddened his heart, and caused great depression of spirit. Hence we find, "Altogether this has been to me one of the most unhappy days." "Still unhappy and sorrowful." "Still depressed in mind: Lord help me." "My temper this week has been anything but that of a Christian: I must watch and pray more, or fall." "Still in an unsatisfactory state of mind: Lord help me." "Lord, do help me, do help me, for I am very low." "Feel still in need of grace to help me in my trying circumstances." "What must I do, O my heavenly Father? Thou canst save, and I believe Thou wilt save; all Thy waves seem to go over me, but if Thou slay me, I will trust Thee, for Thou knowest I love Thee." "A very fine morning; all God's works praise Him. I do wish I could rejoice in the Lord at all times. The very birds, that know nothing of the goodness and love of God, seem to be happier than most Christians. I will try to joy in the God of my salvation."

The immense and increasing circulation of the Narratives, the number of which was greatly augmented during the year, had now brought an amount of popularity which he found rather inconvenient, and often irksome.

One Saturday evening, on returning from Manchester, he says,—"A very full meeting; hot and sweating, returned home through wet and cold at eleven o'clock. I find it a heavy tax to be a little popular." And again,—"Returned from Preston this morning, found many letters waiting, requesting me to go to other places. Lord guide me in these things; I wish to do all I can, but find it hard work." He also felt it becoming prejudicial to his own spirituality and peace of mind, and writes,—"I find that except I look well to my God and my own heart, these ovations will rob me of my humility and peace." "Sent home in private carriage late in the evening. The fuss and ovations I have from day to day, especially in the towns I visit, will ruin my peace with God. Lord help me to give all the glory to Thee."

The demand that was made from various quarters for his services, either to preach special sermons or to lecture, added to all his other labours, made the year one of incessant toil and activity; and so unusual was it to have an evening at home, that on one occasion he records thus, "A night at home!!! Wrote the piece of poetry called "Sympathy," ending with the words,

> "To wipe a tear from sorrow's eye,
> Ourselves will feel the greater joy."

So heavy had the work become, that for the first time Mr. Ashworth entertained the thought of giving up business, and on February 3rd he says, "Correspondence very heavy. I wish to be guided right, but I have this day been seriously thinking of giving up business, and working only for God." And again, on April 30th, "I think again of giving up business, and devoting all my time to good works."

"It is now six years since I first met my congregation of poor friends at our 'Chapel for the Destitute,' and when I compare our present circumstances with that day, I desire to feel very thankful for what the Lord has done for us. Year after year the poor of the town, in great numbers, have attended our various meetings for preaching the Gospel, reading the Scriptures, and Christian experience, and at no time have they been more attentive, earnest, and anxious for Spiritual food than at present. Our various gatherings are truly means of grace. Many new born souls are now walking in Him who is the Light of Life. Some have left us for the other world, having died joyfully. Others are drawing near to death full of hope. I have just left the sick chamber of one who called a few months since, in great joy, to tell me he had found the Saviour, and that Saviour is now to him unspeakably precious.

"But we have had many drawbacks during the year. Many sad failures. Many painful cases of blighted promise. Many things to make me sorrowful, and bow me to the dust. Many a 'Lord, help me!' has been wrung from a sad heart. Oh! how feeble is man at the best. We all need much grace, but none more than those who have to labour for souls amongst them whom sin has hardened. Yet I feel I *must* do it, for I am convinced that the tale of the cross is the most powerful influence for man's good in every way."

The work in connection with the Chapel for the Destitute was increasing and gradually extending. Under date July 25th, Mr. Ashworth records, "'Niff' called to talk about the wickedness of Bagslate; he seems much concerned about it." This suggested the idea of embracing the villages in his operations, and towards the close of the year two missionaries were added to the staff of agencies already employed, and were sent to labour, the one (Rev. Robert Taylor, now Missionary in New Zealand) in Bagslate, and the other in Smallbridge, while the Bible woman continued her work amongst the poor in town, of whose labours Mr. Ashworth records,—

"My Scripture-reader has visited 3,171 cases of the poor and sick, and 26 deathbeds. This visitor is a great help to me, for my rule is not to relieve any case until inquired into, thus saving me from much imposition."

Amongst the cases that came under notice during

the year are "Julia," the subject of the narrative No. 23, who was restored to her parents; Sarah McKenzie and Tommy Pollitt in No. 25, Second Series, "My Young Ragged Friends"; and amongst the items of expenditure two shillings and sixpence for "Johnny's Box," No. 17.

On October 19th, he writes, "Many cases of sorrow, deep poverty, and sin. My work is sad work, yet glorious. The Lord strengthen me."

1865, January 1.—"Bless the Lord for the mercies of last year; praise Him, O my soul. And now, at the beginning of another year, I again give myself to my dear Jesus, body, soul, and spirit; and earnestly beseech Thee, O my Father, to make me this year more useful than ever I have been, both with tongue and pen. O, my Lord, do help me to serve Thee with singleness of eye. May I have nothing of self in all my service for Thee; and, if it be Thy will, help me this year to write what Thou wilt again own and bless for the good of others. On my knees I beg of Thee to bless me and my family this year; may we all be Thine. Bless the Destitute this year. Oh prosper Thy work amongst the poor. Lord, hear my prayer. On the last moments of the old year and the first of this, on my knees, I again give myself to God."

It was not long before the prayer for the poor was answered. On Sunday the 22nd January, after preaching at the Destitute from Acts xvi. 30-31, it was evident the Spirit of God was at work. Many were in tears, and when those that were seeking mercy were asked to stand up, nineteen responded. This was the beginning of a very gracious work. The following is from the Annual Report:

"For the seventh time, I give to my friends, and the world, my yearly account of the 'Chapel for the Destitute;' what money I have received, what I have done with it; and a short sketch of our operations during the year.

"At present we have four agents. Two males and two females. The former labouring, one at Smallbridge, and the other at Bagslate. The latter, one a Bible woman, labouring principally amongst the poor families in town, and attending to the various services at the Destitute; the other is in Bamford, and though an invalid, yet is well-acquainted with her own district, and has been a safe medium, and of great service in feeding the hungry and clothing the naked. Her services are gratuitous, and she is thankful for the privilege.

"These agents have read the Bible in many homes, attended many of the sick and dying, held many meetings, and given timely relief, and useful clothing, to many really needy cases. Our books show that we have given relief to 4,024 cases during the year,—3,279 in money, 507 in clogs, and 238 in clothing. From reading my narratives, individuals and families in distress, from various quarters, have applied to me for help, many of whom I have felt it my duty to relieve, as in the case of 'The Widow.' It will be seen that our income is larger this year than in any former year, yet our expenditure a little exceeds it, but this gives me no concern; it is a small matter with Him whose servant I hope I am, to send by tens, hundreds, or by thousands. I often ask myself, '*What is the money value of a Soul?*'

"Our services at the Destitute are still very encouraging. I again say, that nowhere do I find a congregation more sincere and attentive; their love for the plain, simple Gospel of Christ is very great. I have not yet been able to get a site for a larger building, but hope soon to do so.

"I thank my friends, at home and abroad, for the help they have rendered to the poor and the destitute this year, and pray that our gracious God may bless and prosper them.

"JOHN ASHWORTH.

"October 1, 1865."

"Gave 1s. to a poor creature, about twenty-one years of

age. This fallen creature seemed utterly lost. She had come a long way to see me, thinking I might someway help her. These are to me the most painful cases.

"1s., with several other sums given to a very young woman. Word was brought to me that this poor creature was weeping day and night, in one of our lodging-houses. On visiting her, I found that she had been delivered of a still-born child. She had been in service in a public-house, ruined, and turned out, wandered to Rochdale, where she fell ill. When fit to remove, I got her into the Workhouse. She is now living with a respectable family who know all, and she bids fair for living a new life.

"Another similar case I handed over to Mr. Geldart, and received the following letter :—

'City Mission Offices,

'Manchester, March 31st, 1865.

'My dear Sir,

'I am truly glad to take charge of M— R—. The time of the day, &c., made it rather difficult to get her lodged safely, but I got her to come again at five o'clock this evening, and one of our female missionaries is gone up with her to the Penitentiary. I found it was not safe on her father's account, to have her lodging anywhere in the neighbourhood. I shall be able to write to you as to her reception at the Penitentiary.

'She seems truly sincere. Another blessed result of your prayers and labours. I trust she will prove a jewel in the Saviour's crown. She wept much at the thought of a loving Saviour waiting to receive her.

'Yours truly,

'THOMAS GELDART.

'Mr. John Ashworth.'

"An old man, 94 years of age, one of my regular pensioners, called one cold morning last winter to ask my advice about buying a blanket, and having one pennyworth more of stew daily. He told me he had saved forty-two shillings to pay for a good oak coffin for himself, and he was afraid to touch the money. I advised him to get warm in bed, and get his stew, and he would be sure to have a coffin when he required it.

"2s. 6d. for a pair of spectacles. The old man to whom this was given loved his Bible; to him it was a real treasure. He had lost his glasses, and was in great trouble about them. He was rich in faith, but poor in pocket, and it was a great pleasure to me to help my aged brother to retrieve his loss. He is now gone where spectacles are not required. His death was a glorious triumph, and he reigns a king and a priest unto God and the Lamb.

"Gave 10s. to a poor woman who is afflicted with weakness in the spine, and so utterly helpless that she has been unable to rise from her bed for 41 years. She is one of my many very dear friends. Nowhere do I see religion shine more brightly than it does from the afflicted ones, for though day and night, summer and winter, the body remains on the bed of sickness, they have peace and joy in the Holy Ghost.

"For a water bed, £6 1s. 6d. This bed was bought for a young woman who has been confined to her sick bed nine years, of an affection of the spine. During the first three years of her sickness she derived much pleasure from her Bible and other books, but blindness came over her, and for the last six years she has been in total darkness. She wept for joy when she was first placed on the new water bed. Her case is a sad one indeed : poor, sick, and blind; but she enjoys a peace which neither poverty, sickness, nor blindness can take away."

"2s., and many more small sums, to ——, a person I have known to be worth several thousand pounds, and move in respectable society, but now he is one of the most pitiable objects. Drink! drink! drink! has made him a miserable outcast. None of his relations will look at him. But no one thinks worse of him than he thinks of himself; he finds no fault with anyone; he knows that he has wearied them all out."

There were many other painful cases. Two girls just come out of prison; two from Staffordshire sent home to their parents. Feb. 1, he says, "Had many poor people at my door to-day; fear becoming hard-hearted; so many idle, dirty, ragged, drunken people calling on me, at least one hundred weekly." On Sunday, March 19,—"Bitter cold; thirty-one tramps at the Destitute. Text, 'The blessing of the Lord maketh rich.'" These sit at the back of the chapel, in one corner, near the stove, which they find very warm and comfortable. They generally brush up for the occasion, put on their best appearance and come clean; are very attentive during the service, and at the close Mr. Ashworth would *take stock*, enquire into the cause of their misfortune, give them good counsel and a little pecuniary help. Some terrible revelations were made during those searching enquiries. A few, with tearful eyes and throbbing hearts, would make a clean breast of it, tell the very worst of their case, and the cause of all their misery, blaming no one but themselves. These were the honest portion. Others would make it appear they were not to blame; that they were decent fellows, but the mill at which they worked was burned down, or their master had failed, and all hands thrown out of work; or, perhaps they had been in the Manchester Infirmary three months with rheumatic fever. Many of them gave indications of no ordinary mental powers, and of having seen better days. Mr. Ashworth's knowledge of, and insight into, human nature, gave him wonderful power and tact in dealing with such individuals —he had a remarkable discernment of character. At the same time he had a marvellous amount of patience and sympathy with these poor creatures, and when cases of imposition occurred, used to say, "Christ did not give over healing the lepers, because only one out of the ten returned to give glory." On one occasion, a friend was speaking to him of an orphan servant girl for whom she had found several places in quick succession, and remarked, "If she leaves this one, I shall not provide her with another;" he replied, "Then you can't say 'until seventy times seven.'" Several deaths took place during the year. "Tommy Pollitt," whose trousers—his only pillow—his mother took from under his aching head and sold for drink. Ben Hornbin, or "Little Ben," as he was called, the street sweeper, of whose death Mr. Ashworth records, June 6th, "Sent the Scripture reader at nine o'clock down to see Ben; found him dead. Feel very sad: he was one of the first-fruits, and a monument of the Destitute, and a worker amongst the outcast." Fourteen days previous, Ben was present at the prayer meeting in "John and Mary's" cellar, described in Narrative 34. Ben and Adams (another who found mercy at the Destitute, and is still one of the most regular attenders) went out visiting every Sabbath morning amongst the sick poor, the aged, and the outcast, distributing tracts and speaking to them of the love of Jesus to poor sinners. On August 17th, "Emmott," the subject of the Narrative (27), died this morning at five o'clock, in great peace of mind.—A "brand plucked from the burning."

In addition to conducting services in Rochdale and the villages in the neighbourhood, Mr. Ashworth also visited the following places during 1865, where he spent one or more days in preaching, lecturing, or addressing meetings: Leeds, Oldham, Blackpool, Sandbach, Lincoln, Colne, Settle, Nottingham, Ilkeston, Manchester, Bolton, Preston,

Hollinwood, Kendal, Todmorden, Birtle, Glossop, Bury, Middleton, Bradford, Stockport, Walsden, Cleckheaton, Halifax, Prestwich, Birstal, Rawtenstall, Liverpool, Scarborough, London, Blackburn, Macclesfield, Louth, Great Harwood, Staleybridge, Burnley, Padiham, Huddersfield, Keighley, Haslingden, Wakefield, Ashton, Darlington, &c. To many of these he had been more than once during the year, *viz.*, to sixteen meetings at Manchester, nine at Oldham, four at Bury, and four at Bolton. Very often he had three services on the Sabbath, and two on the week-day. At Ilkeston he records, "Went down a coalpit one hundred and twenty yards to preach to the colliers at their request. About one hundred of them. It was a solemn time."

The thought of giving up business still occupied his attention. Being so much from home, and not able to attend to it, made him very uneasy and perplexed what to do. On one occasion, he says, "Returned home this morning; found the foreman away drinking. I must either give up business or leaving home. Lord guide me." But when at home he was "diligent in business." A commercial traveller, who was staying at a Temperance hotel opposite to his paint shop in Drake-street, after enquiring of the hostess if she knew such a man as John Ashworth, and after assuring him she did, he remarked, "I suppose he is one of those men that go up and down preaching, praying, and neglecting his business." To which she replied, "Do you see that shop over there?" pointing to the place. "Yes," he said. "Well then, every morning, at a quarter to six o'clock, you will see John Ashworth there, sending his men to their work."

And in order to do this, if it were at all possible, he returned from his engagements the same evening, though it was often near midnight, and sometimes after, before he reached home; yet he was at his place in the morning.

December 31, Mr. Ashworth closes his diary as follows:—"With the deepest gratitude I would bow down before my God, and bless and thank and adore Him for all His mercies to me and mine during the year. He has given me strength for my labours. I have preached and lectured in many towns on moral duties; I have spoken, I hope, the word of truth to at least one hundred thousand persons this year, besides all my usual labours; yet my dear Lord has given me health and journeying mercies. O, Lord God, help me to praise Thee; do help me to praise Thee; now that the last moments are fleeing away, help me to praise and bless Thy Holy Name."

CHAPTER VII.

1866.

IN the eighth Annual Report of the Chapel for the Destitute Mr. Ashworth states,—

"We can still say, what was said eighteen hundred years since, that the common people hear the Gospel gladly.

"Our village-labours have been greatly blessed, and urgent requests come from many other places for a share of these labours; and I am hoping we shall soon be able to extend in this department, for it is much required.

"The wide circulation of the narratives, now reaching several millions, both in England, on the Continent, in Australia, and America, have not only increased our income, but induced others to work amongst the poor, and judging from many letters received, have been the means of leading sinners to Christ, for which I wish to be thankful; for to be an instrument of good, however feeble, is still my greatest desire; and if successful in the smallest degree, I would give all the honour to Him whose smile and approval is a great reward.

"Given to R., five shillings. This is one of those cases that makes me glad, and thankful that I am furnished with means to help the poor. Often, during this year, as in former years, have I been deceived and imposed upon, but very often have I had the joy of being the medium through which (as in the above case) the really decent, honest, deserving poor have been blessed; and it is worth something to know that many such have been relieved during this as in former years.

"Three shillings to a poor widow, who for upwards of four years has been a terrible sufferer from a cancer. It is remarkable to see the cheerfulness and patience, though the fatal disease is eating away her breast, and slowly but surely sinking her to the grave. Her pains are frequently dreadful; and her friends often weep to see her agony. But she never complains or murmurs, and she is another illustration of what religion can do in the hour of trial.

"One pound. This was given to one of my sick friends not mentioned before, who has been greatly afflicted, and confined to bed for thirteen years. I have never entered a neater, cleaner, little cottage. Her husband is master, nurse, housemaid, and cook, besides attending to his work. She has a small bell fixed to the bed-post, and a string hanging near her head, having no use in her hands; when she requires attendance, she rings the bell by pulling the string with her mouth. When telling me of her husband's kindness, she shed tears. He never speaks one unkind word to her, or gives her one unkind look. The religion of Christ has done much for both of them, for which they are thankful and happy.

"Two shillings and fourpence. This was paid for the schooling of one of my little ragged friends. I have, during the year, paid several sums to various schools for children that have been running wild in the streets, most if not all of them children of drunkards, who would not deny themselves of one pint of beer to send their children to school. There is nothing that needs our pity more than a drunkard's child, and I think the money paid for their education is well-spent.

"The total number of cases relieved during the year 3141."

The poor widow referred to, afflicted with cancer, resided in a neighbouring town, and is certainly one of those remarkable cases which illustrate what the grace and providence of God can do under circumstances of poverty and painful suffering. She survived two years longer, and for upwards of six years bore with the greatest patience and cheerful resignation her heavy affliction. The first symptom of the fatal malady made its appearance on her left breast in a brown spot about the size of a farthing, but before three years it had made such ravages that the doctor said her life then was a miracle, and she might expect death any moment. The doctor, whose services were gratuitous, was often much affected by what he heard and witnessed at that sufferer's bed side. Who can tell the lessons these meek, patient, afflicted ones teach to mankind. In her midnight waking hours she derived much comfort from singing, of which she was very fond. One night she was singing,—

"My God, the spring of all my joys,
The life of my delights,
The glory of my brightest days,
And comfort of my nights";

when a collier who resided next door heard her, which he had often done before, and to whom she had frequently spoken about his soul. But for the first time, on this occasion the thought entered his mind, that there must be some reality in religion that could make a poor suffering creature like her so happy that she could sing. He was sure nothing else in the world could do this. He became a seeker after salvation, found mercy, and from being a pigeon-flying, Sabbath-breaking, ungodly man, he became a new creature in Christ Jesus. Eventually the disease spread till it reached her arm, which mortified, and death soon followed. The day she died, she asked some friends that stood around her bed to sing a favourite hymn of hers, "My Jesus I love Thee," &c. When they came to the two last lines of the third verse, "And say when the death-dew lies cold on my brow," &c., and with the death-dew literally thick on her brow, her happy spirit took its flight to—

"Sing with the glittering crown on her brow,
If ever I loved Thee, my Jesus 'tis now."

January 1. On this the first day of another year I implore and beseech my Heavenly Father to take me under His special care, and guide me in all my ways. I pray that I may this year bring more glory to His name, than in any former year of my life.

In writing, Lord, guide my pen, so that many thousands may be blessed by reading what I write. In speaking in the various towns to which I may have to go, may I sow good seed amongst the people; but especially bless my labours at the Destitute and amongst the poor. O, my God, I again consecrate myself to Thy service, body, soul, and spirit; make me, O make me a burning and shining light; give me health of body, a firm resolve to do what is right, a heart full of tenderness and love to all, a spirit of kindness and forgiveness, humble and meek as a child; and if it please Thee, O Lord, bless my children, save them from sin, preserve their lives, and let all my house live before Thee. Amen, amen.

At Watch-night Service, Castlemere Chapel.

Went to Greenhill school Tea Party; crowded meeting; hope good was done.

Jan. 2. Many letters of invitation; writing replies.

Jan. 3. Reform meeting at theatre; went after my class. I never yet gave up a church engagement for a meeting on politics or any other question. A master speech from Mr. Bright.

Jan. 4. Restless about another narrative. A good service at the Destitute.

Friday, Jan5. Had a long conversation with Mr. John Bright on how to reach the poorer classes effectually. His opinion on "respectable" worshippers; gave me ten pounds for the Town Mission. Attended Baillie-street school committee.

Saturday, Jan. 6. Went to Macclesfield; met a supper party at the Mayor's.

Sunday, Jan. 7. Macclesfield school sermons; amazing gathering; had to lock the gate.

Monday, Jan. 8. Macclesfield; tea meeting and lecture. Visited the new ragged school. Two poor boys at 108 steps.

Tuesday, Jan. 9. Sunday closing meeting, Manchester.

Wednesday, Jan. 10. Class meeting—precious time.

Thursday, Jan. 11. Leeds. Addressed a meeting of Bible women and other friends at five, and a large gathering of poor people at eight o'clock.

Friday, Jan. 12. Leeds. Visited two of "My Sick Friends." Spoke to 42 young women in the "Home." At Farwell, met the workpeople belonging to Mr. A.'s Iron works in the church. Spoke two hours.

Saturday, Jan. 13. Returned from Leeds; found many letters.

Sunday, Jan. 14. Baillie-street school sermons. Had the ordinance of the Lord's Supper at the Destitute.

Monday, Jan. 15. Littleborough. Lecture, "Young Women," &c. Visited several sick before going.

Tuesday, Jan. 16. Huddersfield. Guest of Mr. R. (a Friend). Addressed a Band of Hope meeting at seven, and lectured to a very large audience at eight o'clock, on "Young Women," &c.

Wednesday, Jan. 17. Returned home: attended class.

Thursday, Jan. 18. Christened two 50 horse engines at John Mason's. Good service at the Destitute.

Friday, Jan. 19. Sent money to Elizabeth Hill, Bolton.

Saturday, Jan. 20. Pendleton; Manchester. Addressed two large gatherings. Returned home late and tired, Mr. C. with me. Looked into gin shops, dreadful sights.

Sunday, Jan. 21. Visited sick cases. Service at Destitute.

Monday, Jan. 22. Manchester. Many letters of invitation; do not know what to do with them.

Tuesday, Jan. 23. Tottington: lectured at re-opening of Wesleyan chapel; crowded out; large collection. Returned home late; cab broke down; not hurt.

Wednesday, Jan. 24. Worcester: addressed a large gathering at "Friends'" meeting house.

Thursday, Jan. 25. Leominster: Visited with Mr. N. many "Friends." Lectured in the Corn Exchange; quite full.

Friday, Jan. 26. Returned home. Spent a quiet evening at home reading and writing; what a privilege.

Saturday, Jan. 27. Attended the reading of a will; returned home late, concerned about my Sunday work.

Sunday, Jan. 28. Two addresses at Baillie-street. Service at Destitute.

Monday, Jan. 29. York: addressed Miss P's. men's class in the Merchants' Hall—spoke two hours—grand sight. O the power of love to God and man as shown by this gathering.

Tuesday, Jan. 30. York; visited the Retreat (asylum); strange sights. Spoke an hour at the "Friends'" adult class tea party. Spoke two hours in the Lecture Hall to a vast crowd.

Wednesday, Jan. 31. Returned home; hope my journey to York will be made a blessing to many. Seventy-six invitations this month.

Thursday, Feb. 1. Painting, preaching, lecturing, writing, and travelling hundreds of miles weekly, keep me very busy; hope to have a little rest. Service at Destitute.

Friday, Feb. 2. Had many poor persons seeking work. Wrote the first part of my new narrative; I pray that it may be made a blessing to many such thoughtless creatures.

Saturday, Feb. 3. Writing. "S." at the door in rags, with a black eye, asking me to look to her two boys. Sent one to school, and bought the other a shirt.

Sunday, Feb. 4. Gave address at Castlemere. Service at Destitute.

Monday, Feb. 5. Barnsley. Gave an address in the theatre—a perfect crush; church minister moved a vote of thanks. Visited the ragged school.

Tuesday, Feb. 6. Derby. Meeting in Mr. G.'s chapel; spoke two hours. Mayor in the chair.

Wednesday, Feb. 7. Conducted service at Derby railway station, about five hundred present—grand sight.

Thursday, Feb. 8. Smallbridge. Addressed a meeting of colliers at six, and conducted service at Destitute.

Friday, Feb. 9. Deluged with letters this week; do not know what to do. Finished the narrative; Lord bless it.

Saturday, Feb. 10. Female visitor poorly. Many letters of invitation from all parts.

Sunday, Feb. 11. Visiting the poor. Destitute in the evening.

Monday, Feb. 12. Work. Called at Bamford to see "Rachel."

Tuesday, Feb. 13. Heckmondwike. Large meeting. Three deputations.

Wednesday, Feb. 14. Returned home; many poor people.

Thursday, Feb. 15. Great many letters. God help me and guide me. Good service at the Destitute.

Friday, Feb. 16. Hamper of clothing from London.

Saturday, Feb. 17. Letter from H. Walked over the hills for health. Many poor to-day. Two deputations.

Sunday, Feb. 18. Destitute.

Monday, Feb. 19. Cullingworth: preached at three; lectured at seven.

Tuesday, Feb. 20. Returned home over eight miles of hills covered with snow in a cab; horse ran away; no harm. Attended meeting at Roby school, Manchester.

Wednesday, Feb. 21. Lancaster: met Miss D's "mothers" at three, spoke one and a-half hours. Searched the castle records, found the execution of "George." Arrived at Kendal at six. Spoke two hours; hundreds had to go away.

Thursday, Feb. 22. Windermere; went to see a sick man; was requested to preach; sent the bellman round; large gathering in the Wesleyan chapel. Returned to Kendal at five. Spoke to one thousand five hundred people in "Friends'" meeting house; visited six dying persons to-day.

Friday, Feb. 23. Returned home; found many letters, all calling out for help. Feel thankful for the kind advice given me by Mr. W. at Kendal; hope it will profit me.

Saturday, Feb. 24. Work; wages. Set out for York and Burythorpe; arrived at the latter about six, after being lost in the fields; guest of Mr. C., York.

Sunday, Feb. 25. Burythorpe; opening of a new chapel.

Monday, Feb. 26. Burythorpe; tea meeting in new chapel.

Tuesday, Feb. 27. Darlington; addressed the first half of the "Friends" school at three, the second half at six, and lectured in the Central Hall at eight to the largest audience ever known in the place. Guest of Mr. T.

Wednesday, Feb. 28. Returned home at two. Saw all the men at work. Many letters, nearly all invitations. Met my class.

Thursday, March 1. Manchester. Executive of Sunday closing meeting. Destitute in the evening.

Friday, March 2. Went to read over "Old Mary"; attended committee of Baillie-street school; elected again by ballot as one of the fifteen officers of the school for the eighteenth time.

Saturday, March 3. Bolton; called to see Elizabeth Hill, forty-three years in bed; her sister also in bed—great trial to her. Addressed Band of Hope meeting in Temperance Hall.

Sunday, March 4. Destitute; preached very badly from "one thing needful."

Monday, March 5. Boscough-bridge; opening a new Wesleyan place of worship: preached at two, lectured at six. Many had come a long distance and could not get in; cold night, sorry for them.

Tuesday, March 6. Returned home; attended to business.

Wednesday, March 7. Darwen; a large meeting of poor people. Called to see an old christian, confined to bed twenty years.

Thursday, March 8. Destitute—a good meeting.

Friday, March 9. Committee meeting Baillie-street.

Saturday, March 10. Left home for Bristol at ten; called at Manchester.

Sunday, March 11. Bristol; three services.

Monday, March 12. Bristol. Visited the Refuge and Retreat, spoke at both places. Called on George Muller. Three hours' walk on the Downs. Lectured in the evening; many could not get in.

Tuesday, March 13. Bristol. Visited many sick; the Orphan Houses; one thousand one hundred and fifty orphans; addressed them by request; teachers all knew me. Lectured in the evening to a vast crowd.

Wednesday, March 14. Returned home at eleven in the evening; think much of my visit; spoke eight times in public.

Thursday, March 15. Many letters. Men full time. Service at the Destitute; many tramps, weather cold, must help them.

Friday, March 16. Writing letters.

Saturday, March 17. This has been a remarkable week. I hope my visit to Bristol will be productive of good to myself and others. Glad to have a night at home.

Sunday, March 18. Preached at Bluepits for the Independents; Mr. H., of Leeds, at the Destitute.

Monday, March 19. Swinton: lectured on behalf of Sunday-school. Feel anxious about my Good Friday work.

Tuesday, March 20. Hadfield, Mottram; a painful mistake; strange day; saw several sick.

Wednesday, March 21. Much mortified about missing my engagement at Mottram. Quarterly meeting; attended class. B., distressed in mind, sent for me; prayed with him.

Thursday, March 22. Halifax: tea and public meeting; organising a visiting society; returned home.

Friday, March 23. B. in great distress; despairs of mercy; prayed.

Saturday, March 24. Walsden: annual tea meeting. Left for Bury.

Sunday, March 25. Bury christian church, morning. Walked home. Destitute in the evening.

Monday, March 26. Leaders' meeting. Anxious about my paper for Friday.

Tuesday, March 27. A day of anxiety; wrote part of paper on "Sunday-schools: their true object and hindrances."

Wednesday, March 28. Writing. Many poor people to-day. The tramp system requires some different measures to what we have.

Thursday, March 29. Destitute service—congregation not so good.

Friday, March 30. Meeting of Sunday-school Union in Baillie-street chapel; John Bright, M.P., in the chair. Read paper; well received; a memorable meeting.

Saturday, March 31. Mr. Bright laid corner stone of new Town Hall; vast concourse of people. Went to Wakefield; spoke at a Sunday-school tea meeting; guest of Mr. F.

Sunday, April 1. Wakefield; three services; Lord help me.

Monday, April 2. Cleckheaton; opening of new schools

Tuesday, April 3. Elland; addressed meeting; returned home. Six large meetings since Saturday.

Wednesday, April 4. Many letters, all invitations. Reform meeting in Mitchel Hey mill, Mr. Bright speaking. Attended my class.

Thursday, April 5. Stockport; Town Mission meeting. Returned home late.

Friday, April 6. Visited several sick. Feel fagged—want rest of body and mind. Sweet meeting with a Christian friend.

Saturday, April 7. Heavy this morning. Shop. Evening at home.

Sunday, April 8. Castlemere chapel; Destitute.

Monday, April 9. Feel a strong drawing of the Spirit; attended service at Baillie-street; leaders' meeting.

Tuesday, April 10. Thornton. Preached in the afternoon; lectured in the evening. Many from long distances had to go back, could not get in.

Wednesday, April 11. Returned home; business; much tired.

Thursday, April 12. O how foolish to neglect things eternal for a little more earth,—earth which we must so soon leave.

Friday, April 13. Conversation with Mrs. Bright.

Saturday, April 14. Home in quietness. The Lord greatly helped me in my thoughts about my Sunday work. O how delightful when the thoughts are calm and heavenly

—when we can look away from business and the world to spiritual things.

Sunday, April 15. Whitworth in the morning; Smallbridge Mission in the afternoon; Destitute in the evening.

Monday, April 16. Feel I want a few days' rest, but cannot get them. Leaders' meeting; unprofitable.

Tuesday, April 17. Manchester, Gravel-lane tea meeting; five hundred present; returned home.

Wednesday, April 18. Manchester, Militia Barracks; spoke to about six hundred of the men by request; dined with Mrs. W. Attended Alliance Meeting in Public Hall, Rochdale, same evening; moved the second resolution.

Thursday, April 19. Destitute; good meeting. Feel I ought to write several new narratives; do not care to write for mere writing's sake.

Friday, April 20. Writing "George," or consequence of idleness. Many letters. Do not feel well; could like a week away.

Saturday, April 21. Writing; preparing for Sunday.

Sunday, April 22. Higginshaw, school sermons. Mr. C. at Destitute.

Monday, April 23. Returned home. Deputations from Wakefield, Preston, Bury. Leaders' meeting.

Tuesday, April 24. With the men at six; went to Marland.

Wednesday, April 25. Mr. D.'s District Town Mission meeting. Class met for tickets.

Thursday, April 26. Took a garden at Bankhouse from first of May. Destitute—a good meeting.

Friday, April 27. Deputations, and many letters. Finished the narrative "George."

Saturday, April 28. At home preparing for Sabbath.

Sunday, April 29. Bury, Brunswick chapel, morning; walked both ways. Destitute at night.

Monday, April 30. Business. Wrote first part of "My Sick Friends." Pray that I may be guided, so that it may be a blessing to many.

Tuesday, May 1. Business. Went to Manchester. Evening at home, very tired; feel sad when thinking of Felix.

Wednesday, May 2. Writing. Class meeting.

Thursday, May 3. Got a young woman a place. Service at the Destitute.

Friday, May 4. Many letters to answer; visited several sad cases.

Saturday, May 5. Shop at six. Attended a tea meeting in the Public Hall of colliers and their wives; crowded; hope good will come.

Sunday, May 6. Heywood in the morning; Destitute at night.

Monday, May 7. Newton Heath—lecture on behalf of a poor Wesleyan chapel; fine gathering. Returned home.

Tuesday, May 8. Denby-Dale Wesleyan chapel; lectured and returned home same evening—arrived at one.

Wednesday, May 9. Assisted in opening of Bury bazaar. Met my class in the evening.

Thursday, May 10. Pendlebury; a lecture; crowded meeting; arrived home late; am thankful God owns my labours in any degree.

Friday, May 11. Went to Oldham on business.

Saturday, May 12. Went to Manchester; guest of Mr. S.

Sunday, May 13. Lever-street, Manchester; services morning, afternoon, and night.

Monday, May 14. Returned home; business, business all day. Reports about speculating gentlemen.

Tuesday, May 15. Went to Isle of Man with Mr. O.; fine sail; profitable conversation on the way.

Wednesday, May 16. Isle of Man; spent most of the day on Douglas Head and the sands.

Thursday, May 17. Isle of Man; rode to Laxey; spent some time at the mines; bathed. Much profitable conversation.

Friday, May 18. Returned home, I think better for the journey.

Saturday, May 19. Left home for Grimsby; arrived at five; visited the docks.

Sunday, May 20. Three services, Independent chapel.

Monday, May 21. Returned home; thankful.

Tuesday, May 22. Halifax Jubilee; 29,000 scholars, 20,000 spectators—a glorious sight; greatly assisted my conception of what heaven will be. Returned home much pleased and profited. Guest of Mr. S.

Wednesday, May 23. Business.

Thursday, May 24. Met my poor people at the Destitute; small company, but good meeting.

Friday (Whit), May 25. Fine day; all the schools turning out in great spirits,—flags, bands of music, and singing; walked with Baillie-street scholars.

Saturday, May 26. Writing "My Sick Friends;" feel I cannot do justice to my undertaking. I do hope I may be helped in this work.

Sunday, May 27. Bagslate, morning and afternoon. Destitute in the evening.

Monday, May 28. Very poorly this morning; did not go out.

Tuesday, May 29. Macclesfield, at opening of new Ragged Schools; spoke in two places; returned home same evening.

Wednesday, May 30. Want more men, but cannot get them. Attended my class.

Thursday, May 31. With the men early this morning. Wrote a letter to the "Observer" on behalf of our cabmen, to obtain for them a place of shelter. Service at the Destitute.

Friday, June 1. Walked through Crimble Vale to Heywood; many birds and flowers. Called to see R.; sister a little better.

Saturday, June 2. Heavy wages; money bad to get. Went to Halifax.

Sunday, June 3. Halifax; school sermons.

Monday, June 4. Returned home. Leaders' meeting. Poor Bagslate.

Tuesday, June 5. Went to Manchester, Bolton, and Edgeworth. Gave a lecture at the latter; General Neil Dow in the chair.

Wednesday, June 6. Bolton; guest of Mr. B. Went

out with N. D. in the fields; much talk about American affairs. Attended my class.

Thursday, June 7. Many poor people this week; need much patience. Attended Town Mission committee meeting, and Destitute in the evening.

Friday, June 8. Went to see two of "My Sick Friends" at Leeds.

Saturday, June 9. Manchester; large meeting at Red Bank, Ebenezer chapel; spoke one and a half hours.

Sunday, June 10. Castlemere chapel school sermons. Destitute: "Go home to thy friends," &c.

Monday, June 11. Writing. Sent sketch to Agnes Cooper, Settle, to be read.

Tuesday, June 12. Writing. A. B. of Kendal, subject to-day.

Wednesday, June 13. Letters from Leeds on behalf of "Sick Friends."

Thursday, June 14. Writing; feel I need God's help; I am anxious to be guided.

Friday, June 15. Glorious weather. Additional matter from Leeds.

Saturday, June 16. Finished writing "My Sick Friends;" pray the Lord will bless it. Went to Preston; guest of Mr. H.

Sunday, June 17. Preston; three services; addressed six thousand in Corn Exchange.

Monday, June 18. Returned home. Left for Todmorden; lectured on behalf of Wesleyan chapel; John Crossley, of Halifax, in the chair; returned home same night.

Tuesday, June 19. Bradford, in Yorkshire; hundreds not able to get in; returned home same night, or rather one o'clock next morning.

Wednesday, June 20. Quarterly meeting, Baillie-street; requested to be representative to the Annual Assembly; glad to get off by a defeat.

Thursday, June 21. Manchester. Destitute in the evening.

Friday, June 22. Business; fine morning. Teachers' meeting at Baillie-street.

Saturday, June 23. Went to Bradford, near Manchester. Walked from Miles Platting through Phillips Park. Full meeting.

Sunday, June 24. Bradford, school sermons; three services.

Monday, June 25. Returned home; M. J. poorly; been afflicted in my children; had to bow in the dust many a time.

Tuesday, June 26. Blackburn; lectured in the Independent chapel; guest of Mr. B. Ministry resigned.

Wednesday, June 27. Returned home. A good class meeting. A request for permission to translate "Strange Tales" into Welsh.

Thursday, June 28. Many sorrowful cases: S. from Wakefield; two men about their wives, one from prison and Lizzie. Destitute; many present.

Friday, June 29. Cannot get work done to please customers; think me not attentive, think them unreasonable.

Saturday, June 30. Went to Bacup by coach: a drunken load; a drunken, swearing coachman; got off at the top of the brow going down to Bacup; broke down a few minutes after, but no one hurt.

Sunday, July 1. Bacup school sermons; three services.

Monday, July 2. Walked home this morning. Went to Manchester; meeting in Wesleyan chapel, Cheetham Hill; returned home late.

Tuesday, July 3. Huddersfield; lecture on "Young Men," &c.; returned home, arrived at one; thankful my health holds out. God be praised.

Wednesday, July 4. Anniversary letters. Concerned about my work amongst the poor. Attended my class.

Thursday, July 5. Went to see N. Destitute.

Friday, July 6. Went with Mr. C. to Bankhouse gardens; had much talk about good things. Need these quiet country walks to strengthen body and mind.

Saturday, July 7. At home this evening, for a wonder. How sweet is retirement, and quiet thought, and communion with my God; need them much.

Sunday, July 8. Littleborough; opening a new chapel; "Precious seed." Destitute; "Be ye also ready."

Monday, July 9. Lectured in Temperance Hall, Rochdale, on behalf of the building fund; crowded meeting. Thankful my own town gives me as great a welcome as any other place.

Tuesday, July 10. Temperance Conference in "Friends'" chapel, Manchester. Meeting in Free Trade Hall, and lectured in Lever-street chapel. An infidel in great distress.

Wednesday, July 11. Left for Mansfield. Met by R. and G. W.

Thursday, July 12. Mansfield: meeting in the new Wesleyan chapel in the afternoon. Lectured in the Corn Exchange in the evening; retired hot and weary.

Friday, July 13. Mansfield: drove through Sherwood Forest; saw the large oaks. Lectured in Methodist church.

Saturday, July 14. Returned home; pic-nic with scholars at three to the gardens at Bankhouse; very orderly.

Sunday, July 15. Green Hill, morning. Destitute at night.

Monday, July 16. Took on two new men. Leaders' meeting.

Tuesday, July 17. Went to Edgeworth to see the men at work. This is a beautiful world. How every thing proclaims God's goodness—hills, dales, rocks and brooks, buds and flowers; all and every thing tell of His goodness. O that man would praise the Lord.

Wednesday, July 18. Feel poorly in body; class this evening. O how I require all these soul means of grace; we need them to check the world's influence.

Thursday, July 19. Very busy in painting, &c.; correcting proofs. Destitute, good service. Lord, do bless my labours amongst the poor. Reading "Oberlin"; may I be as humble and useful as he was.

Friday, July 20. "Blessed are the peacemakers, for they shall be called the children of God." Letter from America.

Saturday, July 21. Very hot day. Left for Bradford, near Clitheroe; found old C. still alive, glad to see him.

Sunday, July 22. Bradford; three services. Afternoon and evening in the open-air; not room inside. Largest collection since the chapel was built.

Monday, July 23. Clitheroe; lectured in the new Independent chapel. Mayor in the chair.

Tuesday, July 24. Returned home; went to "Friends'" meeting house to see Miss B. married. Many letters.

Wednesday, July 25. Writing to H. Mothers' meeting. A good class meeting. Intend to see Mr. S., and make peace.

Thursday, July 26. Destitute. I need patience.

Friday, July 27. Went to see Eliz. Hill; her sister dead. Sad, sad, case. Glorious triumphs of faith in both cases.

Saturday, July 28. Many cases of poverty and distress this morning. A quiet evening. Preparing for Sunday work.

Sunday, July 29. Heywood in the morning. Destitute at night.

Monday, July 30. Business; sent estimate for Baillie-street chapel.

Tuesday, July 31. Manchester, on business. Visited R.

Wednesday, August 1. Letter from a young enquirer. Class.

Thursday, August 2. Concerned about the work at Baillie-street chapel.

Friday, August 3. Lost the painting of Baillie-street chapel in consequence of declining to paint according to specification.

Saturday, August 4. Blacko. Laying corner stone of Independent Methodist chapel. Returned home about nine.

Sunday, August 5. Littleboro' in the morning. Destitute in the evening.

Monday, August 6. Feel thankful for a little rest, and being able to remain at home a few days, and I am thankful for a comfortable home. I have moments of great and deep distress about my dear, drowned Felix; and much anxiety about my child now from home.

Tuesday, August 7. The reading of "My Sick Friends" by a lady in Scotland brought me £10 to be divided amongst them. I feel thankful on their account.

Wednesday, August 8. A sad instance to-day of reaping what we sow.

Thursday, August 9. Much conversation with a prosperous worldly man about his soul, and allowing earthly things to engross all his time. I hope he will be converted.

Friday, August 10. Went to men at Edgeworth. Turton Fair—a wicked, drunken place. A quiet evening at home; thinking about good things.

Saturday, August 11. Huddersfield; attended meeting to raise funds for the chapel.

Sunday, August 12. Huddersfield; three services.

Monday, August 13. Huddersfield; visited model lodging house. "Brewing" magistrate. Went to Holmfirth. Lectured on "Young Women," &c.; dense meeting. Returned home at one in the morning.

Tuesday, August 14. Thinking about eighth report; do not know what to do about D.'s request. Lord, show me the way, for I am blind.

Wednesday, August 15. Good class meeting.

Thursday, August 16. Went to Bagslate, Ashworth, Bamford, Hooleybridge, and Heywood. Destitute in the evening.

Friday, August 17. Perplexed about the request to join M.'s works; do not know what to say.

Saturday, August 18. Many poor cases. Poor woman in lodging-house, the wife of a drunkard. Lodging-house life, a wicked life.

Sunday, August 19. Visiting the sick. Destitute; sermon on Sabbath observance.

Monday, August 20. Rushbearing. No rush-cart this year, for which I feel thankful; worked hard to obtain this, yet there are many drunken people in town—mostly strangers. Leaders' meeting, and a little quiet reading after.

Tuesday, August 21. Most of the schools gone on cheap trips. Wet morning.

Wednesday, August 22. Amongst the men. Did not go to class.

Thursday, August 23. Destitute this evening; large congregation. The Lord revive His work.

Friday, August 24. Much concerned about James Burrows, the young man sentenced to be hanged in the morning. Went to Manchester; sent my card to Mr. Wright in the prison; came immediately with Mr. Bagshawe the chaplain; they were glad to see me; received permission from the High Sheriff to visit the young man; was with him two hours. Never shall I forget the interview.

Saturday, August 25. Pendleton, Manchester. At the laying of corner stone by Mr. B.; spoke, and also in the Mechanics' Institution after. Poor Burrows, eight this morning.

Sunday, August 26. Baillie-street school address; spoke on James Burrows by request. Destitute at night; many could not get in.

Monday, August 27. Manchester; lectured in Hanover-street chapel; crowded. Pablo's circus girl. Called on the "Widow"; found her in trouble.

Tuesday, August 28. Still pressed to join M.'s works; don't know what to say. Lord, guide me in this matter.

Wednesday, August 29. Class meeting. Writing "Burrows"; do not like the subject; would rather write about better things.

Thursday, August 30. Writing narrative. The public very anxious about it.

Friday, August 31. Called to see several sick cases.

Saturday, Sept. 1. Left for York; guest of Mrs. R., a kind Christian lady; many things to think of. Lord, show me what to do, and guide me. Stood this day on the grave of James Burrows.

Sunday, Sept. 2. York; three services.

Monday, Sept. 3. Went with Miss P. to see her sick

cases; were ordered out of a house by a drunken man. Large meeting at Monk-bar chapel.

Tuesday, Sept. 4. Returned home; many letters of invitations; very much work to do. I again seriously think of giving up the painting business. Something must be given up. I cannot longer do as I am.

Wednesday, Sept. 5. Mottram; large meeting of mothers; guest of Mrs. M.; large and happy family.

Thursday, Sept. 6. Returned home; went to Manchester and Edgeworth. D. still away from his work; very wet; clothes saturated; went to bed early; very tired.

Friday, Sept. 7. Baillie-street school committee meeting.

Saturday, Sept. 8. Busy morning. Set out for Louth at twelve, via Hull.

Sunday, Sept. 9. Louth; school sermons.

Monday, Sept. 10. Louth; had a pleasant drive. School tea meeting in the evening; large crowd.

Tuesday, Sept. 11. Went to Cleckheaton; lectured in the Town Hall; fifteen hundred present.

Wednesday, Sept. 12. Returned from Louth; found many letters crying, come, come, come. Attended district Town Mission tea meeting; Mr. K. leaving; much weeping. Went to my class.

Thursday, Sept. 13. Narrative out; enormous demand; hope it will do good.

Friday, Sept. 14. Work much wanted in painting; do not see my way about giving it up. Local Preachers' quarterly meeting; all peace of mind; pleasant meeting.

Saturday, Sept. 15. A very busy day. Bagslate Band of Hope meeting in Wesleyan school-room; hope good will be the result.

Sunday, Sept. 16. Destitute. Subject: "And they made light of it."

Monday, Sept. 17. Liverpool; lectured in F. M. C. Cholera in the neighbourhood; no wonder; full of drunkenness.

Tuesday, Sept. 18. Liverpool; visited "Home" for the

fallen; spoke to them an hour. The ragged school, reformatory; lectured in the evening.

Wednesday, Sept. 19. Liverpool; addressed about seven hundred boys and girls in "Friends'" schools this morning. Returned home; attended Town Mission committee at three; and quarterly meeting.

Thursday, Sept. 20. Many letters; do not know what to do with them. Good meeting at the Destitute.

Friday, Sept. 21. Letter from H. about finding him a wife; dare not meddle in the matter. Many letters from poor widows in various places wishing help.

Saturday, Sept. 22. Nottingham; lectured in Alfred-street chapel on "Young Women," &c.; vast crowd. Many came ten miles.

Sunday, Sept. 23. Nottingham; three services.

Monday, Sept. 24. Nottingham; dined with local preacher. Mothers' meeting at three. Lectured in Mission Hall at seven; fearful crush.

Tuesday, Sept. 25. Returned home; thankful; a pile of letters, come! come!

Wednesday, Sept. 26. Town Mission committee meeting. Selected Mr. W. in place of Mr. K. Class this evening.

Thursday, Sept. 27. Preparing report. Good attendance at the Destitute. M. S. from Cincinnatti, America, called.

Friday, Sept. 28. Writing preface to report. Deputation from Red Lumb about school. Teachers' tea meeting, Baillie-street.

Saturday, Sept. 29. Money, money, wages bad to get; never had so much money owing in my life, and never had so much difficulty in getting it. Quiet evening at home; great privilege.

Sunday, Sept. 30. Littleboro' in the morning. Destitute at night; anniversary service.

Monday, Oct. 1. Heywood Town Mission meeting. Sent three boys to the ragged school this morning; had their likenesses taken. I begin to think that a compulsory education will yet have to be given to these poor ragged children of drunken parents. Day of humiliation for *our* churches.

Tuesday, Oct. 2. Darwen; lectured on behalf of chapel debt.

Wednesday, Oct. 3. Returned home; letters, letters, all crying come; wish to do all I can, but cannot comply with one in twenty. All Baillie-street classes united this evening.

Thursday, Oct. 4. Manchester; meeting of Sunday School Union in Free Trade Hall. Lord Shaftesbury in the chair. The Earl wished me to present him with my second vol. of Strange Tales. Spoke; a good meeting.

Friday, Oct. 5. Writing "John and Mary" for eighth year's report. The Lord guide me; very anxious work.

Saturday, Oct. 6. Colne; large meeting in iron school; spoke an hour.

Sunday, Oct. 7. Colne; services in the Piece Hall; fearful crowd.

Monday, Oct. 8. Salter-Hebble; opening new chapel; tea meeting. Returned home; caught cold.

Tuesday, Oct. 9. Morning in shop; many callers. Went to see old John Howarth.

Wednesday, Oct. 10. General prayer meeting at Baillie-street.

Thursday, Oct. 11. Large meeting at the Destitute. I bless the Lord for these greatly encouraging meetings.

Friday, Oct. 12. Went amongst the hills to recruit my health, find this answers much better than pills or medicine.

Saturday. Oct. 13. Much wanted at home. Left for Levenshulme; lectured. Took a cab on to Stockport.

Sunday, Oct. 14. Stockport large Sunday-school; three addresses; hundreds could not get in.

Monday, Oct. 15. Stockport. In consequence of the numbers that could not get in yesterday, I had to promise another service for this evening; upwards of three thousand at each service. The oldest teachers never saw such scenes. Came home sweating and tired.

Tuesday, Oct. 16. Bradford; lectured for the Town Mission in St. George's Hall. The most imposing scene I ever saw, except Halifax; woman fainted.

Wednesday, Oct. 17. Bradford; meeting in Salem-street chapel. Returned home late and poorly.

Thursday, Oct. 18. A shoal of letters. Feel weak and worn out. The Lord help me, and give me strength to do my work.

Friday, Oct. 19. Went to bed at noon; hope a good rest may restore me. After all, the service of my God is a glorious service. Feel calm, and thankful for many mercies.

Saturday, Oct. 20. Walked out; could not study; feel uneasy about my Sunday work.

Sunday, Oct. 21. Blank.

Monday, Oct. 22. At Grosvenor-street, Manchester, trustees gave me £5 for my poor people; was called this morning to pray with a dying child in the Gank—a bag of shavings, a bed of rags. A boy in his shirt, three drunken women, two drunken men, a child in brain fever; all in one room, with a small window; a dreadful sight.

Tuesday, Oct. 23. I do not feel at all well; fagged and weary; do hope I shall be able to get a little rest. Never had so many able-bodied poor men seeking relief. Lord give me patience; may I not say one sharp word.

Wednesday, Oct. 24. Three deputations and many letters.

Thursday. Oct. 25. Lancaster; addressed a meeting of husbands and their wives, of Miss D.'s class.

Friday, Oct. 26. Lancaster; addressed the men in the ship yard at 12-30. Lectured in the Temperance Hall in the evening.

Saturday, Oct. 27. Returned home from Lancaster. Travelled with Sir James Shuttleworth, his son, and Prof. Owen. On being introduced to Prof. Owen, Sir James said, "I hope Mr. Ashworth will present you with his books; there is nothing more remarkable in the British Museum." A very instructive conversation to Preston.

Sunday, Oct. 28. Oldham; school sermons; walked both ways.

Monday, Oct. 29. Hulme; Ragged school meeting in Town Hall; statements made respecting drunkenness.

Tuesday, Oct. 30. Southport; lectured on behalf of Lord-street chapel.

Wednesday, Oct. 31. Returned home.

Thursday, Nov. 1. Took a walk through the fields; feel better. Called at Bamford; found R. and sister both in bed. Destitute; good company.

Friday, Nov. 2. Manchester; Sunday Closing committee.

Saturday, Nov. 3. Edgeworth in the morning; Hamerbottom Band of Hope meeting in the evening.

Sunday, Nov. 4. Gave address in Baillie-street school. Destitute, evening.

Monday, Nov. 5. Ashton; lectured for debt of chapel, in the Town Hall; a perfect crush.

Tuesday, Nov. 6. Ashton; second lecture in the Town Hall. So terrible and dangerous was the crowd that six policemen were engaged in clearing the entrance. Do not know what people are so anxious to hear me for. Lord God, do help me.

Wednesday, Nov. 7. Many letters on my return home, all asking for my services; do not know what to do. Received two presents from scholars of Stockport large Sunday-school, for my services there on the 14th Oct.

Thursday, Nov. 8. Asked again to join M.'s works; Lord guide me. Destitute; C. E. took part.

Friday, Nov. 9. Four deputations. Feel better in health.

Saturday, Nov. 10. Rochdale life boat launched at Hollingworth; went to see it. Band of Hope meeting at Water-street chapel.

Sunday, Nov. 11. Baillie-street school. Destitute.

Monday, Nov. 12. Thoughts of publishing my lecture on "Young Women, Wives, and Mothers." Teachers' meeting.

Tuesday, Nov. 13. Manchester; Ormerod-street ragged school meeting. Great fall of shooting stars, foretold 33 years ago.

Wednesday, Nov. 14. Class meeting; good. Lord revive Thy work.

Thursday, Nov. 15. Destitute; good gathering. Stormy day.

Friday, Nov. 16. Making alterations at my house.

Saturday, Nov. 17. Brickfield; Annual tea meeting, about 400 present. I think Mr. C.'s work is greatly blessed in the neighbourhood.

Sunday, Nov. 18. Littleboro' in the morning, Brickfield afternoon, and Destitute at night.

Monday, Nov. 19. Leeds; lectured at three; meeting in Town Hall at seven, on behalf of a chapel for the poor.

Tuesday, Nov. 20. Leeds; lectured in Lady-lane chapel for Y. M. C. A.; not a very large meeting; either charge was too high, or people did not care to hear me.

Wednesday, Nov. 21. Returned home. Many poor creatures to-day. Class; good feeling.

Thursday, Nov. 22. Manchester; lectured at Cheetham-hill on "Three Homes."

Friday, Nov. 23. Caught cold; my head feels unusually *thick*, and I feel very restless.

Saturday, Nov. 24. Lane-head Band of Hope meeting; good company.

Sunday, Nov. 25. Morning, Blue Pits Independent Chapel. Evening, Destitute: "Backsliders."

Monday, Nov. 26. Bradford. Large meeting. Guest of Mr. D. Beautiful family scene.

Tuesday, Nov. 27. Bury. Ragged school anniversary; returned home late.

Wednesday, Nov. 28. Oldham. Ragged school anniversary in Town Hall; hundreds could not get in.

Thursday, Nov. [illegible]. Engaged with alterations in front of my house.

Friday, Nov. 30. Wrote to H.

Saturday, Dec. 1 Middleton. Annual tea meeting for debt of chapel.

Sunday, Dec. 2. Gave address at Baillie-street school. Destitute.

M[illegible]day, Dec. 3. Birmingham. Visited Reformatory at [illegible] [illegible] to 79 c[illegible]victs; gave me a regular hip, hip. [illegible] at seven; spoke to 306 young

Tuesday, Dec. 4. Birmingham. Visited the Reformatory at Stoke; spoke one hour; returned to Birmingham; addressed a meeting at eight.

Wednesday, Dec. 5. Returned home; many letters and poor people waiting me.

Thursday, Dec. 6. Halifax. Lecture, and returned home.

Friday, Dec. 7. Sorrowful letter from a friend in trouble. Many poor, mostly from the iron districts.

Saturday, Dec. 8. All day in the house; rather out of health; do not care how much work I do for my dear Lord, if He gives me health to do it.

Sunday, Dec. 9. Still unwell, but preached at the Destitute.

Monday, Dec. 10. Bolton. Lectured in Wesleyan chapel. Visited the Blind Asylum.

Tuesday, Dec. 11. Manchester. Jackson-street ragged school anniversary; came home late both evenings.

Wednesday, Dec. 12. Luton. Lectured in large Wesleyan chapel; guest of Mr. S. Terrible coal pit explosion at Barnsley, 300 killed.

Thursday, Dec. 13. Luton. Visited the bonnet factory; strange and foolish fashions; Oh woman, woman! Preached at 12-30 in the Primitive Methodist chapel, and spoke at "Friends'" adult tea meeting in the evening.

Friday, Dec. 14. Returned home. Scene at Guide Bridge.

Saturday, Dec. 15. Mr. C. gone to Barnsley. Business all confused this morning. Felt much about the sufferers at Barnsley.

Sunday, Dec. 16. Teaching, Baillie-street. Destitute at night.

Monday, Dec. 17. Attended to business. Preached at Bury New Connexion chapel; got home late.

Tuesday, Dec. 18. Huddersfield. Large gathering of poor people; guest of Mrs. B.

Wednesday, Dec. 19. Visited the Oaks colliery, scene of the explosion at Barnsley; conversed with Mrs. Winter, Barker, and Cartwright; dreadful, dreadful; pit still burning, in which 300 persons are buried. Attended Cavendish-street Ragged school meeting, Manchester; home late.

Thursday, Dec 20. Felt very sad all day from the scenes of yesterday; the burning shaft is always before me. A large meeting at the Destitute.

Friday, Dec. 21. Received a letter from Thomas Barker, Barnsley, giving particulars of his terrible search for his father and three brothers, after the explosion: all dead.

Saturday, Dec. 22. Very busy day; never so many beggars; mostly out-door workers; the long wet weather makes them very poor: preparing for Sunday work.

Sunday, Dec. 23. Lowerplace in the morning; Polly Green in the afternoon; and a service for miners at the Destitute in the evening.

Monday, Dec. 24. Began to write "Sad Story;" sorrowful undertaking; pray it may be made a blessing, especially to colliers.

Tuesday, Dec. 25. Annual tea meeting for the poor at the Destitute; 370 took tea; a very profitable meeting after.

Wednesday, Dec. 26. Crowds of beggars. Saw a sad case of distress; was glad to be able to help it. Class meeting.

Thursday, Dec. 27. Finished "Sad Story." Destitute. Thankful for God's mercies.

Friday, Dec. 28. Correcting proof; depressed.

Saturday, Dec. 29. Reading and preparing for Sunday work.

Sunday, Dec. 30. School, Baillie-street. Destitute, sermon to old people.

Monday, Dec. 31. Received Mr. D.'s account, a cause for thankfulness.

"Watch-night, Castlemere chapel; took part in the service. And now God, in His goodness and mercy, has brought me and my small family safe through another year, for which I would most humbly bless and praise His holy name. 'Bless the Lord, O my soul, and forget not all his benefits.'

"This has been a year of very heavy and extensive labour, as the Diary will show. I have travelled some thousands of miles, and spoken to tens of thousands of people. Of this I do not boast, but feel thankful that I have had health and strength to do it. The invitations to various places, from almost all denominations, for Lectures or Sermons, &c., this year, number six hundred and fifty eight, most of which I have not been able to comply with. I hope I have been guided in those I have visited. The 'Destitute' still prospers, and many souls have been saved. The 'Strange Tales,' in tracts and volumes, have had an enormous circulation. The Lord be praised! And now, my Lord and Saviour, I spend the last moments on my knees in prayer, praise, and thanksgiving. Accept, in mercy, accept my offering, pardon all my sins and shortcomings, and give me to feel that Thou dost pardon and forgive."

CHAPTER VIII.

1867.

THE ninth time I present a statement of the Chapel for the Destitute, and am thankful to say that its vitality seems in no way impaired; for all our meetings are still well attended, and in addition to our usual Sunday and Thursday Evening Public Services, our Tuesday Experience Meeting, and Wednesday's Mothers' Meeting, we have now an *Adult* School on Sunday afternoon. This School is conducted principally by members of the Society of Friends, at which middle-aged and old people are learning to read and write, and they are thankful for the privilege.

During a part of this year, two of our agents, in consequence of personal and family affliction, have not been regularly employed. This will account for our expenses being less, compared with last year. But I hope to have this part of our influence for good made stronger than ever, for I am convinced that no greater power exists for reaching the masses than the house to house visitation—for this there is no substitute. And if right agents be employed, they are an unspeakable blessing. Churches and chapels are all very right and proper, but there are more outside these places than inside, and our anxiety is to reach them.

God has been very good to me, and I hope still to serve Him all the days of my life. I pray that I may be saved from myself, and give Him, and Him only, all the glory.

JOHN ASHWORTH.

Two shillings, and several other sums, to two old men. These two old men have lived thirty years together in the same small cottage, which they keep very clean. They have a little allowance from the town, and have often thought about going into the workhouse, especially when they are hungry, and have nothing to eat; but they cannot yet give up their little cot, with its many endearing associations, for though it is indeed homely, yet it is their home.

Ten shillings for a bed. This is a case of poverty and distress, brought on by a long sickness of the husband and father. The loss of health is a loss indeed, and most valued when gone. Before sickness came they had a comfortable home; but when his strength failed, he, like thousands besides, became dependent on others.

Two shillings to a young man. I did not give this without some doubt whether I ought to give it. He was a well-educated, intelligent, professional man, and could easily have made his thousand a year. Sporting and drinking had taken his last farthing, his character was gone, and he had completely exhausted the patience of all his friends; but drink he would have, and I should not be surprised if some dreadful calamity overtake him.

Three shillings and tenpence for clogs and nourishment to a drunkard's wife and four children. Some people may object to relief being given to such cases. But we found them in a damp, dirty cellar, without food or fire, the wife sick in bed, and the naked children huddled round her, starving for want of food. Our patience is sorely tried with drunkards.

Amongst the hundreds that came in their poverty and distress to Mr. Ashworth's house during the year, were "Matthew Henry" and "William the Tutor," the subjects of two of the narratives; and we often think what a mercy it was for these, and others in like circumstances, that there was a man whose heart was large enough to look upon and lend a helping hand to such. Had Alice Blanche Oswald, the young woman who in a fit of despair committed suicide by leaping from Waterloo Bridge, been in Rochdale in place of London, who can tell but she might have been alive to-day. Are her words not the echo of thousands of despairing hearts,—"Alone in London, not a penny or a friend to advise or lend a helping hand; tired and weary with looking for something to do, failing in every way, foot-sore and heart-weary, I prefer death to the dawn of another morning. I am destitute, every day is a misery to me; no friends, no hope, no money. Oh God of heaven, have mercy upon a poor helpless sinner. Fatherless, motherless, home I have none. Oh! for the rarity of Christian hearts." Thus died the "kithless, kinless orphan." Peradventure many such deaths have been prevented by the perusal of "Strange Tales." Hundreds of poor creatures having read them, have travelled many a mile, "foot-sore and heart-weary," to see the Author, thinking if any man in this world would befriend them, it was the writer of these books. Rochdale has its thousands, and London its tens of thousands, of large, loving, liberal, sympathising hearts; but they are unknown to strangers. So it was that our two friends came to John Ashworth, and found in him that sympathy which he himself expresses in the four following verses.

Oh think it not a little thing
To lessen but one throbbing pain,
The act will surely with it bring
To you its own reward again.
To wipe a tear from sorrow's eye,
Ourselves will feel the greater joy.

How sweet the thought that we may be
A friend to some poor friendless one,
For daily round us we may see
Some suffering deeper than our own.
To wipe a tear from sorrow's eye, &c.

And should we, with a loving hand,
Take one drop from life's bitter cup,
Or help the falling one to stand,
By giving aid to bear him up.
To wipe a tear from sorrow's eye, &c.

Our Maker has for ever joined
Two blessed things in union sweet,
That doing good, we're sure to find
With getting good, will surely meet.
To wipe one tear from sorrow's eye,
Ourselves will feel the greater joy.

Broadfield, Oct. 7, 1864. JOHN ASHWORTH.

Matthew Henry Pogson (Rev.) is now a minister of the gospel, in the State of Illinois: and during a recent visit to England gave evidence, not only of his intellectual abilities, but of the great change wrought in his heart by Divine grace. On returning to his charge in America Mr. Ashworth received the following letter:—

"Huddersfield, May 28, 1874.

"Mr. John Ashworth,

"Dear and valued friend,

"After some ten months of hard and unremitting toil in the cause of temperance and the Gospel, I am making preparation for my second departure to the United States. When I contrast the two occasions—in 1867 without a friend but you and Mr. W. to say good-bye and God bless you, going to a land I knew nothing of, the victim of an appetite that had well nigh wrought my ruin, caring not whether I lived or died, without hope and without God in the world; and now, in 1874, clothed and in my right mind, with hundreds of poor drunkards thanking me for my words and experience; with many a poor wife and child now made happy who, not long ago, were miserable, blessing me for the words which, under God's Spirit, caused such a change in their domestic life; with the prayers of thousands of earnest Christian workers following me across the broad Atlantic; with the forgiveness and joyful blessing of my aged grey-haired *sire* resting upon my head; and above all with the consciousness of God's Spirit of grace to uphold me for the future. When I contrast my position thus, I cannot help but thank God for having brought me to your home. I owe all that I am, or expect to be, to your sympathy and practical Christian help, at a time when no one else would help me; and though I wandered far from your advice and the promise given to you, yet when I was brought to myself, the memory of that time spent with you nerved me to give my heart to God. Accept, then, my warmest and heartfelt thanks for all your kind interest on my behalf, and rest assured that as long as I live you will be held in my heart as my dearest earthly friend. . . . I sail on the 3rd of June. Will you before then send me a line of love that I may carry with me once more the knowledge that I have your sympathy and prayers? Remember me to your family, and Mr. and Mrs. C.

"I am, yours affectionately,

"MATTHEW HENRY POGSON."

The other, "William the Tutor," who, from the last account we heard, was in a good situation and doing well. Those who have read the narrative (No. 39) will know that the subject of it was a well educated, intelligent, intellectual man; that he was a classical scholar, and the master of several languages. Beneath some of those tattered garments there sparkles many a bright genius, as the following composition by "William" will show.

"On revient toujours à ses premiers amours."

Lonely, amid the wrecks of many a hope,
Whose radiant halo lighted Life's fair morn,
The chastened heart ceases awhile to cope
With wiser Destiny; and now forlorn
Grasps feebly at the future, till at last
It lives alone in memories of the past.

Ah! must it be that, ever as we grow
In years and knowledge, we must lose the charm
That tranced us when the pulse's quick'ning flow,
Thrill'd the young heart, and nerved the vigorous arm,
Ere trust in man's integrity and truth
Had faded with the blossoms of our youth?

Theme of perplexity! the slackening chains
Of earth, one thinks, might leave the Spirit free
To spurn the alien, adventitious pains
It feels alone through gross mortality:
The soul should warm as matter's self grows cold,
Its essence knows *no age* when *we* are old.

And yet how read we our heart's histories?
How sound the secrets of our inner life?
Sink we not baffled in her mysteries?
Come we not fallen and humbled from the strife?
While dark'ning clouds, with sombre hues invest,
Our visioned eve of calm, clear, thoughtful rest.

Time was (alas it WAS) when everything
We looked upon was fresh and fair to view,
Ah! that our "morning stars" alone should sing
For joy together! When free fancy drew
Her loveliest scenes, we knew not that she traced
Mirages only on a dreary waste.

But with our youth that Eden-time is gone,
The silver cord is now a loosening band;
Then let us sit in sackcloth, and upon
Memory's wrecked portals, with a trembling hand,
Write "Ichabod," for never more may beam
Upon our path the glory and the gleam.

The cherished idols, at whose feet we knelt,
Have proved imperfect forms of kindred clay;
Age (keenest pang of all that we have felt)
Love's "purple light has paled to dullest grey.
Meteor of life! Thy flight sped swiftly by;
No art may now recal its ecstasy."

The change has passed within us; still the spring,
With lavish beauty, decks the face of earth;

Still, as of old, the birds as sweetly sing,
Our broken chords re-echo not their mirth :
Morn comes and goes, but as the hours depart
No ray of joy revisits the sad heart.

And this perchance is wisdom : revered sage,
Thy love is dearly bought, if thou must give
For the profoundness of thy sapient age
All that made life desirable to live,
And gain thy climax only to be seen
Sitting 'mid ruins of what thou hast been.

Compare thy slow cold musings with the time
When ardent aspirations filled thy breast ;
When, as thy manhood ripened to its prime,
Even to hope was almost to be blessed,
And say if added years have kept with truth
The golden promises they made thy youth.

"Whom the gods love die young," was said of old,
(A mournful verdict for the silvered head,)
"For they depart ere feeling has grown cold,
Nor linger when the heart itself is dead,
Dragging along, in sorrow or remorse,
The living body fastened to a corse."

Sages of old ! was this the loftiest flight
Of your philosophy, when ye would solve
The problem of our life ? In what a night
Of murkiest chaos does your creed involve
The destiny of man, who with his eyes,
Ever as he treads the earth, confronts the skies !

Bethought ye not it might be thus : that, though
Each hope may fade unrealised away,
And with advancing years still darker grow
The shadows of the prison-house of clay,
Those early glimpses of pure joy were given
As pledges of our *aptitude* for heaven.

To teach man, as he contemplates the past,
Marr'd by the ruin and disorder wild
Of a fall'n world, he must become at last
Simple of heart as when a little child

His faith in all things good and lovely found
Nought to distrust, and earth seem'd hallowed ground

Whate'er of beauty in those infant years
Spake to his spirit, gently as the breeze
Of softly-breathing zephyr stirs the ears
Of the ripe corn, or whispers in the trees,
Did but reveal to him a faculty
For higher things, unseen by mortal eye.

Whate'er of purity and holy life
Affliction taught him in his fervid youth,
Whate'er of lofty sentiment could move
His sterner manhood in pursuit of truth,
All these are given him that he might believe
In what no "heart of man" can e'er conceive.

And tho' he wander on a cheerless track,
Bewildered 'mid the world's disjointed ways
And heartless dealings, he may still go back
Again in spirit to those blessèd days,
And feel how all their cloudless joys made known
What powers for happiness the soul may own.

Then thou, O weary heart, that long hast borne
The buffets of the time, the feverish fret
Of life, and art with disappointment worn,
Still cheer thee up a while, for thou mayst yet
Again behold thy childhood's visions, and
The sunny hills of Beulah's pleasant land.

And for what follies may have soiled thy name,
Even on their buried ashes thou may'st raise
Some structure of a higher, nobler fame,
Some monument of good, some work of praise:
Then let despairing thoughts for ever cease;
Think of the "Prodigal," and be at peace.

Calmly resigned, until thy course be done;
Endure, and "going softly" all thy days,
Await what time the bright millenial sun,
On a new world shall shed his orient rays,
As one who, thro' the watches of the night,
Keepeth a weary vigil for the light.

W. M.

On looking it over, Mr. Ashworth wrote to say that he thought it was still something short, when William sent the following additional verse:

Resting thy hopes in humble steadfast trust
On Christ alone, thy Saviour and thy Lord;
Low at His cross—there, prostrate in the dust,
Abide and plead the promise of His word,
That none, who feel their sinfulness and pray
To Him for help, shall e'er be cast away.

"The last verse was sent after the other as a finish."—J. A.

From a letter written to Mr. Ashworth the following is extracted:

". . . I do not know whether you received my last letter to you. It was a reply to one of yours suggesting the addition of a verse to the lines of which I had sent you some time before. I think I wrote to you by return of post enclosing a verse which I hoped would, in your estimation, be suitable. . . . I will conclude with a few words about my present condition. I am still daily striving after a fulfilment of duty to the best of my ability, and from the feeling of inward peace which I experience to a very great degree, I believe the Lord is manifesting His favour and approval. In looking back, I can see how His goodness has followed me in a very marked manner, preserving me from all harm at all times; and I do then particularly see the tokens of His watchful care, and feel my heart warming with gratitude for His wonderful mercies toward me.

"I look with abhorrence on the old temptation, and with regard to it, I may truly say 'the snare is broken, and my soul is delivered.'

"My dear friend, no words can ever tell what I owe under God to you. Had the mysterious hand of providence not directed me to your door, I know that I must have gone down—body and soul—into the depths; and yet, two hours before I saw you, I did not know there was in the world such a name as John Ashworth. True, I had heard him spoken of as a writer some where or other, but where he lived, or at what time, I never knew until the morning I first saw him, when, by a chance, which was *no* chance, the overheard conversation of two companions in misery revealed it to me.

"Mr. B. is very, very kind to me. He has employed me in the office during the winter, and I have received many proofs of his deep, quiet thoughtfulness.

"With affectionate regards,

"Your very sincere and grateful,

"W. M.

"York, 3 mo., 8th, 1869."

We also give from the same pen his experience and description of low lodging houses.

"To one who has never frequented such places—the phases of life and character which they present open up a new world. Any person who has been respectably or even decently reared, would find it very difficult to conceive any thing like the manners, customs, and habits of the human beings who make them their temporary home. The wandering tribes of a civilized community differ almost as much from the possessors of 'fixed residences' as do the nomadic races of the east, from the stay-at-home nations of Europe, and pursuing other objects, and a dissimilar scheme of life, are marked by characteristics altogether their own.

"Either from choice or necessity (chiefly the latter, I should think) a large number of persons find their livelihood 'on the road'; some of those are dealers in a small way in a vast variety of articles; others follow some rough kind of handicraft, as tinkers, umbrella menders, repairers of broken china, bellows menders, chair bottomers, and so forth; others aspire a little higher, and appear as fiddlers, pseudo Highland pipers, and general musicians. These consider themselves the *èlite* of the lodging houses which they patronise, and stand very much aloof from the 'baser sort' of itinerants. All, however, are animated by the same spirit of making out life as they can, and also enjoying their existence as much as possible. As they are not at much expense for rent, and pay no taxes, they spend most of their gains on food and drink, and seem to consider good eating and drinking the *summum bonum* of all things, the very acme of earthly felicity. Their notions of morality and religion are very lax—in fact, some ignore such ideas altogether, and in word and act plainly avow themselves to be of those who have chosen for their motto, 'Let us eat and drink, for to-morrow we die.' As might be expected from such materials, most of the grosser and more repulsive traits of humanity are certainly exhibited—gluttony, drunkenness, profanity, and indecency are so common, as not only to be disregarded, but to be looked on as signs and tokens of good sense and spirit; and he who does not take part in them is regarded with suspicion, and subjected to insult and ill-treatment. The preceding remarks apply only to the vagrant classes. In many of these lodging houses are to be found decent and deserving tradesmen, who have come from a distance, and are obliged to live in such places for want of better. Those are often men of intelligence and some education, most of them conversible. About six weeks since, I met with a very odd character in a lodging house in the town of P—. He came in one evening just at dark in a state of intoxication, and appearing much excited. He was got to bed, and next day gave an account of himself. He had been in the army in India for a many years; had risen to the rank of hospital serjeant, and been discharged with a pension of two shillings a day. On his return to this country, he quickly spent his pension before it became due in drink, and being left penniless for the time, tried his wits to make out a living.

"Having picked up some knowledge of compounding medicine while hospital serjeant, he turned it to account now, by making up pills 'to cure all diseases'; and, as he had an energetic manner and fluency of speech, with the botanical names of some plants and a few Latin quotations, he succeeded in making the vulgar believe a great deal of what he said, and found a ready and profitable sale for his nostrums. He told me he had often taken £4 or £5 in one day at a market. But the unfortunate man spent all he gained on drink, and on the evening when I first saw him, he was reduced to a sixpence. He, however, set to making more pills, and before he left the town had sold several shillings worth, most of which he duly expended on rum, going to bed drunk every night of three he stopped at P—. He was a man of very little education, but had an amazing amount of self confidence and energy. Had he been a temperate man, he might have saved a great deal of money. He left P— for Liverpool, and I have not heard anything of him since. I examined some of his pills, and believe they were made of bread, ginger, and camomile."

It may easily be conceived in looking over the Diary of the preceding year, that it would be impossible for Mr. Ashworth to continue his business with satisfaction to himself and his customers, and do such an amount of work from home in preaching and lecturing besides; one or other, he frequently said, he must give up; consequently he took what he believed to be the right course, and gave up his painting business in the early part of this year; but, to his great regret, he was induced to identify himself with a large machine business in town in the capacity of assistant, and, although relieved from the anxiety and responsibility of his own, his time was as much occupied, and his mind often much more disturbed, with the transactions of the business he had joined.

January 1. He begins the year thus,—

"I again feel glad that the first moments of the year were spent on my knees in Castlemere chapel, and that I did again consecrate myself to my God, body, soul, and spirit. O my dear Lord and Master, do give me Thy blessing again this year, let me live more and more to Thy glory. Take away pride and selfishness from my heart, and may I glory in nothing but Christ Jesus and Him crucified. May I this year again receive help from *Thine* infinite wisdom, and guidance in my writings; guide my pen, and guide my tongue in all public speaking, and greatly prosper me in all my labours in Thy cause. May I this year be greatly instrumental in blessing others and saving souls. Lord, hear my prayer, and accept this dedication."

Jan. 2. Went to the casual wards; twenty-seven men sleeping on boards; a bitter cold night.

Jan. 3. Service at the Destitute; thirty-two persons seeking relief.

Jan. 9. This day the whole of my brothers and sisters, except one, met at my house, Broadfield, with their husbands and wives. A very comfortable meeting, finished with singing and prayer.

Jan. 15. Made a member of the Manchester Exchange to-day, to represent G— machine works. Lord, Thou knowest I have not wished this, guide me in the way I ought to go.

Jan. 28. Decided this morning to give up my painting business; hope I have done right.

Jan. 31. For the first time for seven years there is a little disturbance amongst the people at the Destitute—a little jealousy about honour.

Feb. 2. One sinner destroys much good; this illustrated by a tale-bearer at the Destitute not bridling her tongue.

Feb. 9. I, this day at 12 o'clock, resigned all my right to the premises 56, Drake-street, and all the painting business to my successors. I trust I have been guided right in this matter.

Feb. 18. Batley. "Job Morley" came to see me from Sheffield—a remarkable man.

March 18. Parkinson's child come to ask for clogs; his father in prison, and his mother just come out; both drunkards; poor little thing.

March 25. H. 28 and M. J. 25 years old to-day.

April 4. A woman cut her throat to-day; she is the mother of a large family; her husband is a steady man, but she has been such a drunkard that she sold meat, coals, clothes, or anything that she could lay her hand upon for drink.

April 14. Adult school opened this day in the large vestry of the Lyceum, conducted by the "Friends."

April 25. London. Dr. Smith, of New York, and D. L. Moody, of Chicago, hearing I was in London, sought me out, and came to hear the lecture in St. John's Wood; want me to go to America.

May 22. Very poorly all night; pulse 130; retching; very sick, and not able or wishful to eat.

June 5. Girl from Middleton at my door weeping. Police after her for stealing. Sent a person with her to her master not to press the case on account of her youth; age 14.

July 18. Went to the funeral of Mary Grimshaw, of Leeds, one of "My Sick Friends," who has been on a bed of affliction 32 years; was interred amidst many tears.

Aug. 13. Dined at Mr. John Bright's, with John H. Douglass, of America, and several other "Friends."

Sept. 19. This day I saw John Stott, of Birtle, 90 years of age; been a class leader 60 years; converted when 20; remarkably happy; also an old woman next door, 83, very happy; another at Shepherd Mill, 83, very happy; all witnesses to the blessed power of saving and sustaining grace.

Sept. 27. Manchester Exchange, business, business, business. What a whirlpool this Exchange is; what anxiety, what fears, what hopes, what rapid rising and falling of men and merchandise; what a race for riches! Lord, save me from the contagion, from ever loving money for its own sake.

Sept. 28. Old scholars' tea meeting at Bamford chapel. Several present that were scholars 60 years ago. Letter from Sir J. Kay-Shuttleworth, an old teacher.

Dec. 14. My Saturdays now are very easy compared with what they were formerly, when I had wages to find, and did not know where; this has been the case hundreds of times, from which I had great mental anxiety. I feel I would rather die than live over again that struggle, struggle, struggle in money matters that I have had for nearly twenty years; I wonder how I have borne it, but God has brought me through.

Dec. 31. I here wish to record my thanks to Almighty God for His goodness and mercies during the year, and in the dust to deplore my short-comings, and want of earnestness in my labours. Oh how solemn are these moments when bowing before the Searcher of hearts. Lord God, have mercy upon my failings, and pardon all my sins, and may I feel Thee to be, more than ever, my Lord and my God. Amen.

CHAPTER IX.

CHAPEL FOR THE DESTITUTE, ROCHDALE, 1868.

"IT is now ten years since I commenced the Chapel for the Destitute with much fear and anxiety, and during those ten years I have often felt how weak I was under the heavy responsibility attached to all our operations, and I cannot sufficiently express my thankfulness that these operations are still in full vigour, and that what was at the first an experiment, has so far proved to be practicable. Perhaps the most important feature in connection with our labours, and one of the most useful in its results, has been the stirring up of others in various parts of this, and other countries, to undertake a similar work. The knowledge of this has been to us a source of gratitude to Him who alone can bless our labours either amongst rich or poor.

"Our Adult Sunday School, conducted by a few members of the Society of Friends, is still doing good service.

"Our agents labouring in town and country, almost entirely amongst the poorest of the poor, remain as last year, but have been more constantly employed; this is an important part of the undertaking, for there are thousands perishing who would never be reached by any other instrumentality than the Missionary or Bible Reader.

"Our hope and prayer is, that He who so graciously condescends to own our feeble efforts, may still more abundantly give us His blessing. With this we are strong, without it we are helpless.

"JOHN ASHWORTH."

"Five shillings for lodgings and food. This was for a servant, out of place. She had lost her last situation through getting drunk. She had learned to like drink at one of her former places, where beer was allowed for servants. She is not the only one by hundreds who have been ruined by so questionable a custom. I know a lady who allows her servants twenty shillings per annum instead of beer. She seldom changes, and they are all orderly, well-conducted servants, respectable and respected.

"Four shillings and sixpence to thirty-six wanderers that on one evening attended our service. No doubt some of these were of the Nomadic tribe; but many of them were persons seeking employment. Many thousands of such have attended our services on Sunday or Thursday evenings, and all have conducted themselves with propriety. Whatever they may be out of doors, their order and quiet respect during the services is very pleasing, and, no doubt, many received lasting good. Vast sums of money are paid to send the Gospel to such, and I think the very little given to them is money well spent, admitting the possibility of one soul being saved.

"Three shillings for lodgings. This was for a young lad, just come out of prison. This child is the son of a drunken mother, who took all his small wages for drink, and left him to starve. The neighbours often found him food, or he would have perished from want. He is truly a child left to himself, and it is to be feared that he is already ruined. He is a fit and proper subject for the Licensed Victuallers' Benevolent Society, as all drunkards' children are.

"Two shillings and fourpence, and other sums, to a cripple. This poor creature, who is nearly fifty years of age, is totally helpless, and has been so from his birth. He sits in one position by the fire from day to day, without being able to move a limb or hold up his head. He is of sound mind, and, although he cannot speak distinctly, any-one accustomed to him can understand him. His case is really pitiable; and no one, he says, came to read or pray with him till our visitors found him out, whose visits he values much, and always enquires, 'When will ye come again?'

"To M. F. and three children, a quantity of provisions. This was a case in Manchester to which my attention was requested by a person in London, where the mother had once been a respectable servant. She married, had a well furnished house and a happy home for a few years; but afterwards became a victim to strong drink, to which she sacrificed all self respect, love to husband and little ones. Her once comfortable home became a scene of desolation. Clothes, and every article of furniture for which money could be obtained, disappeared, till her husband could no longer keep a home. The mother and children came to Manchester, and had ten shillings remitted to them weekly. One of my missionaries visited the case, and, on going to the address given, found the door fastened. After knocking for sometime, he was about to leave; but, on looking at an upper window, he saw something like a human face; and, after knocking again, a little girl opened the door. 'Does Mrs. F. live here?' 'No,' was the reply. 'Is your mother in?' 'No.' After a few more questions, the visitor was convinced she was not telling the truth, and walked in. On going up stairs, such a scene presented itself as he had seldom witnessed. Not an article of furniture was there; no food, no fire, only some filthy damp straw which served for a bed, and crouching in a corner of the room was a haggard woman with emaciated face and dishevelled hair, having an old, black, ragged skirt pulled over her legs and feet to cover them. Poor thing! Once she was a bright, happy woman, picturing for herself a radiant future; and now sunk so low—the victim of an appetite which has reduced her to the deepest degradation. A few words of sympathy were spoken, and the woman wept. The visitor purchased for her some clean straw, coals, tea, sugar, and bread, and gave them in charge to Mr. Geldart, of the Manchester City Mission, who receives the ten shillings weekly from her husband, and sees that it is properly spent. How many homes, once happy, are cursed through drink."

As usual, Mr. Ashworth commences the year with self-dedication as follows:—

"In the first hour of the year 1868, I write this my dedication to Thee, my God, knowing that Thou searchest my heart and knowest all my thoughts. In Thy fear I would humbly consecrate myself to Thee, body, soul, and spirit, and pray that Thou wilt more than ever bless my labours in connection with the Chapel for the Destitute in all its operations. Guide my pen in all my writings. Give me an unbending regard for the truth in all things. Give me patience, forbearance, prudence, and judgment in dealing with the poor at my door and elsewhere. Let all I do be done to Thy glory. Keep me from trusting in myself, from the least pride of heart or self-gratulation. May I see nothing but Christ; love Him, and preach Him more than ever. Guide and be with me in all my journeys; save me from accidents; and make me an instrument of greater good in this, than in any former year. O my Lord, I am Thine; I fall into Thy hands; bless me and my house and my children, and I will love Thee with all my heart.

"JOHN ASHWORTH."

Mr. Ashworth having had for many years an intense desire to visit the Holy Land, an opportunity now presented itself, which, after consulting with his relatives, was embraced. One great inducement was, that an intimate friend and fellow-townsman was to be his companion in travel. After the necessary preparation, they left Rochdale on the morning of Tuesday, February 4th, at eleven o'clock. The excursion party, eleven in number, met in Paris on the 6th, and was conducted by Mr. Henry Gaze, of Southampton. They proceeded over the Mont Cenis pass to Susa, visiting Turin, Bologna, Ancona, Brindisi, and thence by steamer to Alexandria. After going the round of the sights there, the party proceeded to Cairo, making a pilgrimage to the pyramids of

Gizeh, the Ibis, and mummy pits of Sakkara, and to Memphis, thence traversing the desert to Suez to visit the spot where it is supposed the children of Israel crossed the Red Sea.

Returning by Cairo to Alexandria, the party started by the Austrian steamer for Jaffa, the ancient Joppa, at which point the Palestine journey really commenced. Arrangements having been previously made, a caravan, consisting of the party with thirteen servants, thirty horses, tents and all necessary equipage, started for Ramleh and Jerusalem, encamping outside the walls for the first time on Monday, March 2nd. The following extract from a letter sent by Mr. Ashworth will best describe his feelings on that occasion.

"Jerusalem, March 2nd, 1868.

"My dear ——,

"And all my dear friends, here I am at last, safe and sound, and all our company, thank God. We arrived at two this afternoon, and were so glad that we shook hands all round, with tears in our eyes. On approaching the city, I was so impatient to behold it that I rode very fast on my spirited but fine grey Arab; and when I came in sight, I dismounted, pulled off my hat, and falling on my knees, kissed the very stones. None but my God saw me, and He knew why I did it. I then rose and wrote in my note book, my horse quietly standing,—

"Jerusalem, thou city of cities!
Long have I wished to see thee.
On thee the world's eye looks
With interest deeper than on
All the capitols of many

Mighty nations; thy history
Is ever old, and ever new,
Written in songs, and sighs, and blood;
And oh, amazing truth, the blood
Of Him, who shed that blood for
Thee, for me, and for a guilty world.

"I may just say that we encamped last evening near the valley of Ajalon; see Joshua x. 13; and our ride this morning has been up the road the ark of God was drawn; See 2 Samuel vi. . . ."

On the Saturday evening previous to their arrival at Jerusalem, the party encamped at Bab-el-Wady, and after reading the doings of Joshua in the valley of Ajalon, they sang the well-known hymn,

"Come, let us join our cheerful songs."

Being only about fifteen miles distant, several of the company were anxious to push on early next morning to obtain a sight of Jerusalem, and if possible attend divine service within her walls in the evening, a proposal Mr. Ashworth strenuously opposed; for however desirous he, as well as the others, was to obtain a glimpse of the ancient city, he had a still greater regard for the Divine injunction, "Remember the Sabbath day to keep it holy," than to travel with all their equipage on the Lord's Day, and stated that if they persisted in going forward, he would not mount his horse but go on foot. It was, however, ultimately agreed that they should rest on the Sabbath, and conduct service in their tent, a practise they subsequently adopted when circumstances would permit: which was said to have a most beneficial effect not only upon themselves, but also upon their dragoman and attendants, who were deeply touched with the simplicity of their devotions, the singing of the hymns, and their resting on the Lord's Day. The party visited all the places of interest in and about Jerusalem; those that had peculiar attraction to Mr. Ashworth, he mentions in another letter, were the Mount of Olives, Garden of Gethsemane, Calvary, the sepulchres of the kings and prophets, &c. Subsequently he found his way to Jericho, where, he used to say, an old aunt had wished him hundreds of times, and there drank of the water made sweet by Elisha, which he said was really delicious; he also bathed in the Jordan and Dead Sea.

Most of the sacred spots referred to in the Scripture narrative were visited, including Bethel, Shiloh, Samaria, Shechem, Nain, Endor, Nazareth, Mount Tabor, and Tiberias, encamping on the shores of the Lake of Galilee. From Nazareth, a visit was made to Mount Carmel, and over the snow-clad Hermon to Damascus, whence the party crossed Mount Lebanon to Beyrout, and thence sailed to Cyprus, Rhodes, and Smyrna, sufficient time being allowed for visiting each. They were then conveyed by steamer to the Piræus, spending one night at Athens, five miles distant; then on to Constantinople, in which city and its vicinity nearly a week was occupied; then proceeding to Varna and Rustchuk, viewing the beauties of the Bosphorus, on by the Danube, through Hungary to Vienna and Paris; having travelled over seven thousand miles in three months. Mr. Ashworth and his friend arrived in Rochdale on Saturday, April 25th, at seven in the evening; and on reaching his home he makes the following record,—"I wish to record my gratitude to God for His mercies and providential regard to myself and fellow-travellers for the last three months; blessed be His name."

An interesting and admirable account of his travels is given by Mr. Ashworth in two volumes entitled, "Walks in Canaan" and "Back from Canaan," which no student of the Bible can peruse without interest and instruction, and being more than ever convinced that it is God's Book: as he remarks,—"Since my return from Palestine, the Bible has been to me a new, and a still more blessed book."

Although much fatigued with the journey, and greatly in need of rest, the travelling having been almost incessant from the day of their setting out, yet we find him on the following (Lord's) day conducting a service at Bury, walking to and fro, and then at his own Chapel for the Destitute in the evening. His congregation were so pleased to see his face again that he says, "My people wept on my entering the chapel."

As might be expected, when Mr. Ashworth's return became known, invitations for his services came pouring in from all quarters, especially for his lecture on "My Journey to Jerusalem and the East," which became deservedly popular; and while many were instructed and interested, it was also a source of great pecuniary benefit to many of the churches, which was to him a gratification. He writes November 24, "This journey will have yielded the Macclesfield church about fifty pounds. It may be that one reason why Providence opened up my way to go to Jerusalem, was to help poor churches."

The writer can bear testimony to the fact, that

in the course of the year Mr. Ashworth was instrumental in raising, for the various churches, many hundreds of pounds, without ever receiving one penny for himself, beyond his travelling expenses, and often, when the congregation was poor, declining even these. The smallest surplus was invariably put down towards the funds of the Chapel for the Destitute. The following morning, after returning from many of these visits, and when relating the blessed result of such services, both in a pecuniary and spiritual sense, his countenance would beam with delight as he remarked, "I am so thankful that God gives me the power to help in any way these little poor struggling churches"; and he often said the people themselves were amazed at the amount of money they could raise. On this ground the decease of our dear brother is a great pecuniary loss to the churches, and few will be able to supply his place.

It may not be generally known that Mr. Ashworth was invited, and accepted the invitation, to represent Stockport in Parliament, at the election in September, simply on the ground of closing public houses on the Lord's Day, a question he considered of vital importance to the well being of this country, and to obtain which he was prepared to make any sacrifice.

At a meeting of the Stockport electors the following resolution was unanimously passed, "That this meeting, in the event of Mr. John Ashworth coming forward as a candidate for this borough, pledges itself to support him to the utmost."

Messrs. Watkin and Smith having, however, subsequently pledged themselves to support the

Bill, the object was gained, and Mr. Ashworth withdrew from the contest, having received the following letter: "We had an official interview last evening with our members, Smith and Watkin, who came up to our standard in first class style; both are prepared to support the Sunday Closing and Permissive Bills; and we have to thank you for the importance we have attained to in this borough as an association. P.S.—I should think Mrs. A. will pass us a vote of thanks." In reference to the matter he records as follows:

"Sept. 9. Met six of the Stockport electors by appointment, to talk about my being a candidate on the ground of Sunday closing; told them I should not spend any money, or canvas an elector. Feel very anxious to be guided aright."

"Sept. 10. The Stockport matter rather perplexes me. I would not give one farthing to go into the House of Commons on mere politics; but to close public houses on the Sunday I would, and feel bound to do all I can. I dare not refuse."

"Sept. 17. Stockport; met the electors in the Mechanics' Hall; admitted by ticket; a full room. Messrs. Watkin and Smith, the present members, having both promised to vote for the Sunday Closing Bill, I refused to contest the election; all I wanted was gained. Addressed the meeting and retired, receiving a hearty vote of thanks."

Previous to the meeting he addressed the following letter to the electors:

"Broadfield, Rochdale, Sept. 12, 1868.

"Dear Sir,

"Your letter of yesterday, informing me that

your present members have promised to support the Sunday Closing and Permissive Bills, gives me much pleasure, and I am relieved from much anxiety of mind, for I am afraid of anything that would disturb my present labours, or render them less useful.

"Yours very truly,

"JOHN ASHWORTH."

Apart from the Drink question, Mr. Ashworth held, what were considered by many, both friends and foes, strong and antiquated views in reference to the imperative obligations binding upon all Christians to maintain inviolate the fourth commandment; and nothing in the world would ever induce him to ride or travel on the Sabbath, by any mode of conveyance, whereby either man or cattle were deprived of their day of rest. At home and abroad, in all kinds of weather, wet or dry, hot or cold, frost or snow, he has walked to his appointments on the Sabbath, even though the journey both ways would extend twelve miles or more. A rather unpleasant but salutary correspondence took place on the subject, between Mr. Ashworth and some of his friends, on the occasion of Mr. C.'s (the American) visit to Rochdale in 1861, and which appeared in the *Rochdale Observer*. A few extracts from one letter will best express his view of the question. "To the statement made, 'that a private Christian may use his carriage and horses on the Sabbath to go to the house of God, when distance, or the weakly condition of himself or any member of the family may in his judgment require it,' my reply is, Are not coachmen and horses working? and is not the dangerous doctrine that a man's judgment is to be the standard of right and wrong inculcated? Men's judgments vary; fifty different men may have fifty different opinions about the same thing; but the great standard of truth, the Word of God, remains. I believe such a statement is contrary to the words spoken by God Himself, and written by His own hand on a table of stone, and inexorably binding on all nations to the end of time. This same God mercifully and mysteriously clothed Himself in mortal flesh; and again speaking on the same subject said, 'Think not that I am come to destroy the law and the prophets: I am come not to destroy but to fulfil. Whosoever therefore shall break one of these least commandments and shall teach men so, he shall be called the least in the kingdom of heaven.' Now how is it that the full demands of the law are allowed except in the fourth section, and the moment we insist on its obvious intention we are called Jews? I believe Mr. C. to be a great and good man, and, in the main, as anxious for the right observance of the Sabbath as I am; and being a man of immense moral power and world-wide fame, one mistake from him whose words are of such weight and importance, on a question vital in its character, may be fatal in its effects; and those persons whose consciences are ill at ease regarding this cab, carriage, horse, and railway riding on the Lord's day will be glad to take shelter under his great name, and have the sanction of his weighty authority to their proceedings."

Mr. Ashworth's firm adherence to his Sabbath principles incurred the displeasure, not only of many at home, but sometimes those whose guest he was when away. On several occasions his host and hostess have been made very uncomfortable, as they have driven home from the place of worship in their nice easy-cushioned carriage and pair, while the preacher, after his heavy work, it may be of two or three services, has walked quietly away, thankful to use the power God had given him, and in a few instances, it was regarded as approaching to an insult on his part that he did not accept the kindness offered to him.

But more especially did it seem to Mr. Ashworth not only a great national disgrace, but a terrible desecration of the Sabbath, that 150,000 public houses should be open for the sale of intoxicating drink on the Lord's day; consequently, as shown in connection with the Stockport election, he laboured in every possible way, to his latest moments, to obtain the "Sunday Closing Bill."

In 1870, he was one of an influential deputation (said to be the largest seen at the Home Secretary's office in Downing-street since the Reform League days) from the "Central Association," that waited upon Mr. Bruce on this great question, and on that occasion said "He had laboured for thirty-five years among the masses, and had kept records in his office of the fearful facts connected with Sunday drinking. He was convinced, from that long experience, that all they could do by means of churches, chapels, Sunday schools, mechanics' institutes, lectures, and other means for promoting the religious, moral, and social improvement of the people was neutralised and counteracted by the hundreds of *public* houses which were kept open daily, and especially on Sunday. They had fought against these evils inch by inch and foot by foot, and they had now, in Rochdale at least, the working classes with them. They did not want the public houses to open on Sunday, and if the question were left to them, it would very speedily be settled. The depraving and demoralising scenes to be witnessed at these places on Sunday were something fearful. They were not places for rational and needful refreshment, but mere sotting houses, where money and time and brains were alike wasted and lost; and his experience was that their being closed would be the greatest boon ever conferred upon the working men. Every means was used to entrap them into these houses on Sunday. Even the Sunday-school hymn tunes were pressed into the service; and he earnestly urged upon the Government the imperative duty of stopping the evil at its source. He did not mean to coerce the working men or their families in any way as to the mode in which they should spend Sunday in future; but if once the public houses were entirely closed, he thought they would see a decided improvement in the attendance both at church and chapel, with a corresponding improvement in the morals and habits of the people."

The following appeal was issued, which met with a very general and liberal response:

"*To the Sunday Scholars of England, Ireland, and Wales.*

"MY DEAR YOUNG FRIENDS,

"For thirty years I have been labouring amongst you, and perhaps no man living has seen so many of your happy faces. But I have much sorrow of heart by seeing numbers of our Scholars sink into ruin, just at the time their Parents, Ministers, and Teachers joyfully hoped they would become members of the Christian Church, blessed themselves, and made a blessing to others. I know what has done this. Many snares are set for your destruction, but none so fatal as the Public House. One hundred and fifty thousand of these wicked places are open every day, undoing the good work of many thousands of Ministers and Teachers; for most of the drunkards of our land were once in our Sunday Schools.

"But the day especially given by our Heavenly Father as a great blessing, is made by these Public Houses a fearful curse, and we want our Parliament to make a law, that like other shops the drink shop shall not sell on a Sunday. To do this will require great labour and much money, for the one hundred and fifty thousand drunkard-makers will fight hard against us. But we think if all the Sunday Scholars in England, Ireland, and Wales, will give us *one penny* each, it would help to get the law made which will save millions of our youth from ruin, and be the greatest blessing to our country.

"Therefore, let all the Sunday Scholars in England, Ireland, and Wales subscribe their pennies, and send them through their Minister or Superintendent to RICHARD HAWORTH, ESQ., Treasurer of the Central Sunday Closing Association, 43, Market Street, Manchester.

"Yours very affectionately,

"JOHN ASHWORTH."

During one of Mr. Ashworth's visits to Matlock Bank, he and another gentleman were sent as a deputation to an Alliance meeting at Belper. The novel manner of their despatch, and the adventures of the journey, he describes thus:—

"Placards were posted through the country announcing a great meeting to be held at Belper on the Maine Law Question. Amongst the speakers advertised were 'two gentlemen from Matlock Bank.' Who these two gentlemen were, nobody knew, not even themselves, until a phaeton drove up to the establishment, a messenger handed a note to myself and Mr. Thomas, informing us we were the placarded speakers from Matlock Bank. We were both patients, both in low health, and great was our astonishment at the daring contract made without our knowledge or consent; but greater was the astonishment of the messenger at our daring to disobey the imperative mandate.

"'I beg of you, sir, that you will comply with *the order*. Great will be the disappointment at Belper, and Master will be made to break his word, a thing not to be thought of. Pray, do not refuse. You shall have plenty of rugs, the day is fine, and the drive is through beautiful scenery on the banks of the Derwent. Please, gentlemen, do go!'

"We were considerably amused by the earnest eloquence of the man. In his opinion, an earthquake would have been a small calamity compared with disobeying the Master. Mr. Thomas replied, 'I am not a Maine Law man. If I go I will find them something a vast deal better than the Maine Law.'

"Being rather curious to know what this 'something' was, and the day being fine, I submitted to the decree, and urged Mr. Thomas to do the same. We mounted the carriage, wrapped well up, set off, and greatly enjoyed the ten miles drive through truly magnificent scenery.

"On arriving at Belper we found the streets thronged with people of all ages, but not all sober. It was the hiring day for servants and agricultural labourers, and all seemed exuberant with excitement.

"We arranged with our coachman to be ready for the return journey at a certain given place precisely at half-past nine. We then entered a rather spacious building, crowded in every part, and received rather a flattering ovation from the audience.

"By mutual agreement Mr. Thomas was to speak first, and began thus: 'Mr. Chairman, ladies and gentlemen, my present position has been forced upon me, and it is with considerable reluctance I appear on this platform this evening, for I am not in a good state of health, nor am I a Maine Law man.'

"'Indeed, indeed; how is that?' said the chairman.

"'I see you are a little surprised at the last sentence, but I think I can find you something that will answer better, and will be a vast deal more effective and lasting than any Maine Law. Not one hundred miles from here a contractor engaged to take down an old bridge and build a new one. He built a bridge, it fell; he built it again, and it fell. Practical men were summoned together to account for this double calamity. One of them took up a brick and broke it with his fist. 'There is the cause,' said he, throwing down the pieces; 'the bricks are soft and worthless; they will not stand the compression of an arch. You cannot build a good bridge with bad bricks.' Now, Mr. Chairman, ladies and gentlemen, you want our fearful national curse of drunkenness removing. You may depend upon it, that the shortest way to accomplish your object will be to seek the salvation, the true conversion to God, of the men and women of this country; for while the heart is carnal, the carnal man will curse his fellows with either drunkenness or some other sin; the bad man will never be a good man until he is *born again.* Aim at this in all your meetings and all your agitations, and you will succeed in your desirable object, but in no other way.'

"The Chairman observed that one of the deputation from Matlock had certainly astonished them all, but he should reserve any further remarks at present, and call upon the next speaker to address the meeting.

"He, too, began, 'Mr. Chairman, ladies and gentlemen, in England yesterday about thirty thousand churches, chapels, and Sunday-schools were engaged earnestly and prayerfully in trying to be the instruments of converting the people, trying to train the young in virtue's paths, counteract the effects of sin by pointing sinners to the Lamb of God, and, by the power of the preached gospel, stem the torrent of wickedness and misery. Yesterday, the government of England, by law and license, opened one hundred thousand dens of wickedness, haunts of every description of sin, ruin, and wretchedness, to counteract all the religious efforts so anxiously put forth by ministers and teachers, thereby doing more to destroy body and soul than *all the* churches and chapels can do to save. The least-required trade, and the most fearfully productive of crime, poverty, and death, retarding all good, promulgating everything that is bad, demoralizing all classes, is the only trade government encourages and legalizes to be followed on the Sabbath day. Every one of these one hundred thousand drink-houses exists at the expense of the morals of the nation, and no man, for his own gain or profit, ought to degrade or demoralize his neighbour. We want to repeal a law that robs our schools and churches, that fills our poorhouses with paupers, our gaols with criminals, and spreads disease, lamentation, wailing, and woe throughout the land.'

"The tremendous applause that followed was partly owing to the effect produced by the preceding address. Honest opposition often improves a feeble meeting.

"Our work being done, we prepared for returning to Matlock, went to the place we arranged to meet the coachman at half-past nine, but he was not there. Ten o'clock came, but no coachman; at half-past ten he came, but as drunk as a *fiddler*, loudly protesting he was just in time, just in time to one minute.

"Seeing his helpless condition, I said to Mr. Thomas, 'My will is not made, and there are several other matters that require doing before I go into the other world. The night is very dark, and there are several dangerous places on the road, the man will kill us, so you must excuse me going to Matlock to-night. I wonder whether the coachman be a Maine Law man?'

"Mr. Thomas rather warmly replied, 'I must and will go to my own bedroom at Matlock to-night;' and, stepping into the carriage, said, 'Pray, do come in! what can you do here all night?' To please him, I consented to ride to the extent of the gas lamps, but no further.

"We had not been on the road five minutes before we were tumbling off the seats, and knocking our heads together; and, stepping quickly out, I found the blind-drunk jockey had gone against a house gable. I called out, 'Where are you going, my man?—this is no road; you are against the end of a house.' 'Am I? how is that? is there no street here?'

"Street!' replied Mr. Thomas, 'you deserve almost drowning; look how the poor horse trembles; we shall not jeopardise our lives by going another inch with you.'

"We took our rugs out of the conveyance, wrapped them round our shoulders, and turned back—to where we knew not, leaving the drunken driver to do as he liked.

"As we neared the Market Place, we found him behind us, bawling out with all his might, 'Pay me my fourteen shillings! pay me my fourteen shillings! These gentlemen are cheating me out of fourteen shillings.' Instantly crowds gathered from all sides, and we found ourselves in the midst of a dense mob of rather rough-looking Belpers. Then came the police fighting their way through the mass, and insisted on our paying the man his fourteen shillings, or they must lock us up. 'Lock who up?' we rather sharply enquired. Just then the chief constable came up, saying, 'Now, gentlemen, we cannot do with this; pay the man his fourteen shillings, or we shall have a breach of the peace.'

"We quietly informed this official how the matter stood; how we had been sent as a deputation to the Maine Law meeting, and whose the carriage is, or who the man is, we knew not. He then pushed his way through the crowd to the be-muddled coachman, and said, 'You know these gentlemen have not engaged you. This night's work will unship you; you are a ruined man, and you know it. Move off, or I will lock you up.'

"Amongst the spectators of our ludicrous dilemma was a middle-aged lady peering into our faces as we stood near a gas lamp. She asked if we were not the two gentlemen who had been speaking at the temperance meeting? 'Yes, ma'am,' was my reply. 'How is it you have not returned?' she enquired. 'Because our coachman is so drunk he cannot see his way.' 'I am very sorry,' said the lady. 'Will you please go with me? I can find you accommodation, and you are truly welcome. I am very sorry.'

"We followed the lady through a garden into a large house. Ringing the bell she ordered candles to be taken into the drawing-room, into which we were conducted by one of the servants; and, at nearly twelve o'clock, we sat down hungry and cold, wondering what next. For several minutes we were both silent, when I observed to my companion, 'I think the Maine Law is a very good thing.' At this, Mr. Thomas laughed right out: just what I wanted; for he was evidently suffering from the fatigue of the day, and I was anxious to cheer him a little, if possible, when in came the lady, saying, 'I am very sorry, gentlemen, but while I have been out, six friends have unexpectedly arrived, and they will require all my spare bed-rooms. Will you come and take a warm cup of tea, and we will think about what must be done.' We followed, as requested, into the next room, to join the six friends at tea.

"Soon there was a loud rap at the door, when a still louder voice enquired if two lost gentlemen were inside. When he entered the room, he introduced himself by saying, 'I am, gentlemen, a teetotaler of fifteen years' standing. When a drunkard I was in misery, poverty, and rags; now I am in good circumstances, having a spare bed-room, containing a first-rate teetotal bed, costing over thirty pounds. I have heard of your misfortune, and have come to beg you will accept of my hospitality.' We cheerfully complied with the request, and accompanied our friend across several streets; and, about one o'clock in the morning, lay down in the thirty pounds teetotal bed, not soon to sleep, but talk over the events of the day.

"'I suppose this is a Maine Law bed?' I remarked. 'I suppose it is,' said Mr. Thomas. 'Well, I shall not go to Matlock, but go home from here; you will please ask for my bill, and send it by post; tell them to include the rug I have with me. I wish to keep it as a memento of this deputation to Belper, and I shall call it the Belper rug.'"

On Sunday, December 27th, a casualty took place by the falling of a new Wesleyan school in which Mr. Ashworth was conducting service, resulting in injury to about forty persons; and although he escaped from any bodily harm, such was the shock to both body and mind, that he was unable to preach at his own chapel that evening, where a large congregation was awaiting him; his place being supplied by Mr. John Harley.

A fearful gale had been sweeping over this and other districts during the whole of the day, and the building, originally intended for cottages, being quite new, was exposed to the full fury of the storm. The upper portion of the gable wall collapsed, and before any intimation could be conveyed to any one, the wind seemed to gather in and heave the roof at the end, when the gable wall silently fell inwards in a compact mass. The three walls fell almost simultaneously, like a great sweeping wave; but the roof, which remained attached to one corner, came down in a slanting direction and slowly, otherwise the results might have been more serious. There was, however, no loss of life. Mr. Ashworth records the sad event thus:

"This day I was opening a new school belonging to the Wesleyans in Spotland-road, in this town, in the afternoon. While singing the last line in the last hymn about four, the storm of wind that was raging lifted the roof, and the three walls fell inside, and the roof came down, and buried all beneath the ruins without the slightest notice."

Monday, Dec. 28. "I feel very sad this morning on account of the sufferings of those injured by the falling of the school-room yesterday. How I escaped I cannot tell, but it was a fearful sight to see the walls all come down, bringing the roof with them. It is amazing none were killed on the spot. Visited some of the wounded."

Tuesday, Dec. 29. "Find that thirty-seven are hurt, some of them seriously. Many of them are poor, and will need help. Visited several of them to-day. Many letters enquiring after my welfare."

Wednesday, Dec. 30. "Saw several more of the wounded to-day. I think there will be no deaths. Miss N. bears the loss of her foot with remarkable coolness and patience."

Thursday, Dec. 31. "The last day of the year 1868. This to me has been an eventful year in many ways. My labours amongst the churches of all denominations have been great, and yet what have I done for my Lord? Spent the last moments of the year on my knees. The year is now gone, gone for ever; but still I know the Lord is my God. O how many mercies have I had by land and sea, in my Jerusalem journey especially; and how great have been my mercies in providence and grace up to the last Sabbath in the year, and on that day how mercifully I was preserved. Oh, my God, save me from ingratitude. May I always have a thankful heart, always feel my dependence on Thee."

CHAPTER X.

1869.

THE work in connection with the Chapel for the Destitute was carried on this year much the same as the preceding one. The Report states, "Our services are well attended, and the people seem more and more to hunger for the Gospel. Our encouragements are great, and I trust and pray that the smile of heaven may rest upon us, for with this we shall stand firm; and without it we can do nothing."

During the year a Sunday school was opened in town for poor children called a "Ragged school," a very significant but objectionable term, and out of regard for the children's feelings we never like to use it. The bare-footed boy, after receiving his first prize at Bamford school, went back to his seat and cried as if his heart would break, because he was such a poor poor boy, and because he thought some of the other boys sneered at his poverty. Many other poor children have similar feelings, and especially as they grow up and their circumstances improve do they dislike to be called "Ragged school" children.

The reader will easily imagine that Mr. Ashworth's early experience would naturally lead him to take a deep interest in Sunday schools and their *work generally*, but more particularly that his sympathies would be directed towards caring for and educating the poor neglected children running about the streets; such was the case. In 1848 he opened a school in Mount Pleasant for this class, and gathered together a considerable number, many of whom had been convicted before the magistrates; this may be considered his first work amongst the outcasts and destitute. He found great difficulty in getting competent teachers to assist in such work, but continued it, till eventually nearly all the scholars were drafted into other schools.

In 1865 another school of this class was opened at Brickfield, in connection with the mission work carried on in the village of Smallbridge, in addition to week-evening classes for adults. The children going to no other Sunday school were collected together, and a well organised school conducted till 1871. The Wesleyans having built one in the immediate neighbourhood, and the children greatly improved in circumstances as in many other respects, the necessity for Mr. Ashworth's no longer existed. He had the satisfaction, however, of knowing that they were all, without exception, gathered into other folds and distributed amongst the various schools in the village, the children making their own selection. Many bear testimony to the kindness shown them and the good they received.

This year, December 5th (1869), a similar school was commenced in Rochdale a second time, and conducted in the lower room of the Public Hall till it was removed to the Mission Room in School lane, where it still continues.

The other school is the one for teaching "adults"

on Sabbath afternoon at the Chapel for the Destitute, under the care and management of the "Friends." It was opened by Mr. Ashworth on Sunday, April 14, 1867, and has been the means of doing much good. Many of both sexes, who could neither read nor write, have learned to do both; and it is an unspeakable comfort and blessing to them that they can now read the Word of God for themselves.

When at home, he was in the habit of visiting both schools on the Sabbath afternoon. On one of those visits in the early part of this year, he jokingly asked the adult scholars to write a letter to him, so that he might see what progress they were making. To his great surprise, he received about twenty letters. As they speak for themselves, a few specimens are given.

(Age 60.) "January 30th, 1869.

"Mr. Ashworth,

"Dear Friend,

"It is with pleasure I write these few lines to you to show you the improvement I have made in my writing, for when I came to the adult school I began with straight strokes. So no more at present from ———."

"January 24th, 1869.

"Dear friend, a letter To you I am going to send, But what to put in I do not know, But I will study it out As far as I go. I must tell you that I love our Sunday school, our Teachers are very good and kind with us; they are not like the Teachers that I had when I was a little Girl, they used a cane and set us on to a form when we did wrong. I think the world is mending, or else the people that live in it. My desire is that you may be long spared to gather wanderers into the fold, until He the Great and Chife Shepperd call you into the fold above. And I must conclude yours truly ———."

"January 24, 1869.

"Dear Friend,

"i write a few lines to tell you that i love love Jesus; what have i ever done that he should be so mindful of me. i feel that i ham a short coming creature and unworthy. God bless our worthy friends; you do not know the kindness wich they show to us, may they never be weary in well doing for in du season they shall reap if they faint not. God bless you Mr. Ashworth, may you long be spared and may you have souls for your hire ———."

"February 30, 1869.

"Dear Sir,

"I hope these few lines will find you in good health. I was surprised when I was informed I was to write to you; we have a very pleasant class and a very good teacher, and we should be very glad to see you oftener with us. I hope you will excuse these bad spelling and bad writing, I remain ———."

"My dear Sir,

"I write these few lines to you trusting that they may meet you in good health as I am at present. As this is my first attempt to write a letter I hope you will excuse any mistakes you will expect to find, but I suppose as practise makes perfect, that by the help of God's mercy and the very kind assistance and advice both from you and all my teachers, I may be pupil of good example. I hope the Lord will bless you and all your labours to the extent of his mercy. I am yours ———."

"Dear Sir,

"I now take this opportunity of writing a few lines to you; the other Sunday when you came in the school you asked us all to write you a letter, you said that writing copies would not teach us to write, and I have begun to think so, and I am determined I will try to write letters. I am sure we are very highly previliged, and we ought to thank God for these previleges, and God will bless this cause, and I pray that the blessing of God may rest on these kind friends who come to teach us, and may God bless your labours and make you a blessing. I think that before long

I shall be able to write to my friends; please excuse my imperfections, and by and by I hope be able to write better. Yours truly ———."

"My dear friend it his a long time since I either heard or saw you, But there is one thing I have great reason to be thankful for, that his the Missionarys that gos about from house to house, it feels so cheering to a hungry soul when leaid on a sick bed to have them to come and visit us. I do feel so thankful for the many friends I have had during my sickness. And now my health is much restored again, and I hope soon to be amongst you again.

"We read in Luke, chap. 10, v. 41, That Martha was careful and troubled about many things. I think my sister is just like Martha, and its very cheering when we lie on a sick bed to know that some one cares for us. We well remember the first time that we came to the Destitute; it was a dark and gloomy time, it was in the cotton pannick, and I wish we had come sooner. The Lord never sends nothing but it is for some good, and the cotton pannick was for ours. The Lord bless you all, if I am not with you I long to be.

"Please to look over my imperfections, yours truly, ——.'

"My dear friend,

"In writing a few lines to you I think I cannot do better than let you know the state of my mind. For a long time I have been very uneasy about religion; I want to lay firm hold of it, but there is something keeps me back. We have the world to contend with, and besetting sins, and wicked temptations on every side, wile it almost makes me despair. I have said many a time to my wife after comming a way from chappel that we must live a better life, or else the Lord whould use some means to bring us to it. I said he knocks at the door of our hearts some times by sickness, some times by distress, some times by taking away a child, that as been our case. I hope that I may spend the remainder of my days in the servis of God. O that he whould make me truly one of his. Now I must finish. Yours truly, ———."

The foregoing are from persons of from forty to sixty years of age (with one exception), who have been taught in the adult school, and the letters are exact copies both in spelling and composition.

Much of its success at the commencement was due to the untiring energy and zealous labours of the late Miss White and Miss Bright, which the following letter will show:

"Llandudno, Dec. 21—71.

"Dear Mr. Ashworth,

". . . I was deeply grieved to hear of our good friend Miss White's death, and have been wondering how the school will get on without her; she was, as it were, the mainstay of the undertaking. I hear of my class through my sister, and I long to see them again; but when that will be I cannot tell.

"Hoping you are well, and with kind regards to Mrs. Ashworth and yourself,

"I remain,

"Yours very truly,

"M. H. BRIGHT."

The school is still prospering and doing much good.

DIARY, 1869.

Sunday, Jan. 3. Renewal of the Covenant in Baillie-street; a solemn time; Lord help me to keep it. Had the covenant service at the Destitute, without the sacrament; seemed to produce a serious impression on all.

Jan. 7. Feel how important it is to live to God with all my heart; to have no other God, but serve Him with singleness of heart, in order that I may have no impediment in my labours.

Jan. 27. Seventeen letters this morning, all asking for services; I am almost at my wit's end for answers. Attended class; I must keep to simple means for my own soul's sake.

Feb. 9. Went to Belle-Vue prison to see a man at the request of his wife; about seven hundred prisoners. Many visitors weeping on leaving their relatives in gaol. Officer stated that the prisoners and public houses kept about the same speed. Lectured for Wesleyans at Farnworth; returned home.

Feb. 15. Newcastle-on-Tyne; addressed one thousand five hundred mothers in the Brunswick Wesleyan chapel, from all the Mothers' Meetings in town and country; never a scene like it in this world before; feel as weak as a child.

The following is a report of his visit to Newcastle:

"For six days and nights John Ashworth, the author of 'Strange Tales,' has been lecturing or preaching to overflowing congregations. The largest chapel in town has been crowded with children to hear an address from his lips. At another time a vast assembly, chiefly of men, has listened to his lecture entitled, 'Sons, Husbands, and Fathers.' Again he has given his interesting account of his 'Recent visit to Jerusalem and the East.' Possessed of a wonderful memory for incidents, and able graphically to describe what he has seen, we do not wonder at his amazing popularity as a lecturer. Many persons wonder how he finds time and strength for such exhausting services. The truth is, having found out what he can best do to promote the glory of God and the welfare of men, he has retired from business without waiting to realise a fortune, built himself a house; and in the very neighbourhood where in his youth he wandered as a shoeless lad, he is in the habit of roaming over the hills for days together, gathering up strength for arduous services; and to use his own words, 'When I know that I am to have ten or twelve days of exciting public meetings, I go into regular training for it by a series of mountain rambles.'

"Of the meetings John Ashworth has held in the north during the past week, by far the most interesting has been that with the mothers associated with the 'Mothers' Meetings.'

"As the hour approaches, groups of women are seen collecting in the immediate neighbourhood, great numbers of them carrying in their arms living proofs that they are mothers. At a quarter-past two the doors are thrown open and the chapel begins to fill. The time of waiting is occupied by the singing of well-known hymns. We feel that it is worth going miles to see so many cleanly mothers and to hear them sing in this way. Stepping for a moment into the vestry, we see John Ashworth unostentatious as a man can be. He peeps into the crowded chapel, draws back into the vestry, walks up and down under a sense of tremendous responsibility, and whispers to us, 'There never was a gathering like that before; and only think of it, each of those mothers is the centre of a circle of influence. Who is sufficient for these things?' The service opens with singing the hymn,—

'I'm a pilgrim and a stranger,
Rough and thorny is the road.'

Prayer is offered, another hymn is sung, and then Mr. Ashworth begins to talk as he can do to mothers."

February 20. Posted thirty-two letters.

April 21. The lectures of the two last nights produced over £100. Since I returned (from Jerusalem) they have made near £2,000 for poor chapels and other objects.

May 5. Left Leicester for London; spoke in Exeter Hall for the Systematic Beneficent Society.

May 6. Lectured at St. Albans twice: at three in the afternoon and seven in the evening.

May 7. London. Many callers at my lodgings; several

D.D's. amongst them. Exeter Hall. Tract meeting, Earl Shaftesbury in the chair; spoke three quarters of an hour.

May 8. London. Preached at Lambeth out of doors, in the yard of the Wesleyan chapel.

Sunday, May 9. London. Queen's Road, Bayswater, in the morning; Victoria theatre at night. Indian officers, and many others, asked to see me.

May 10. Messrs. P. & Co., with twenty-four others, all workers and writers, met me at my lodgings to tea, to talk about various modes of doing good. Mr. S. made me a present of his works handsomely bound. Bedford Institute at eight. "Friends."

May 11. Annual breakfast of the Y. M. C. A., at six this morning; one of the speakers. Met the committee of the Tract Society at eight, also at breakfast. They presented me with a paragraph Bible. Left London at eleven; arrived home at seven, via Manchester.

May 18. Strange revelations made to me by a man at Bolton station.

June 3. At the request of Rachel Jackson, the subject of "Trials," I and my wife met several ministers and friends in her sick room, to partake with her of the Lord's Supper; a solemn time, and profitable to all.

May 5. Prevented a poor family being "sold up."

May 9. Opening of a new Independent chapel. Dined with about fifty officers, members and visitors. Toast drinking at dinner, the Queen, &c., all rising but myself. Do not approve of drinking healths, &c., by religious people.

June 24th to July 2nd Mr. Ashworth, in company with Mr. John Harley, made a missionary tour into Cornwall.

June 30. Lectured at Port Isaac at 2-30; the great and last public meeting at seven; a very powerful influence. Do hope much good will be the result of our visit to this place. The Cornish people, a fine, civil and intelligent people.

July 14. This morning my sister Peggy died, aged sixty-two. This is the first death amongst my sisters or brothers for fifty years. She died in the faith of the Gospel, and in full hope; her experience for many years has been very bright and happy; this is to us all a great comfort now.

August 27. Attended Brewster Sessions with a memorial against the granting of licenses. Crowded room.

Sept. 21. Rachel Jackson, the subject of "Trials," died this morning.

Oct. 12. This very close weather, and dense meetings night after night, make me feel very weary. O how I should like a few days at the sea side, but I have no opening in my diary; work, work, work, seems to be my lot.

Oct. 16. Left Carlisle for Edinburgh.

Oct. 21. Left Edinburgh at two; arrived home at midnight.

Oct. 26. Dined, by request, with Lord T—— at Mr. W.'s. Last Tuesday I was invited by Sir James Simpson, of Edinburgh, to dine at his house with the Marquis of T——. Must steer as clear as possible of these lords and keep to my poor people.

Nov. 6. Ragged school meeting at H.; fear I lost my temper in denouncing a foolish, vulgar piece said by a young man.

Nov. 12. Long conversation with Mr. John Bright on various matters.

Dec. 5. Opened ragged school at the Public Hall. Forty very poor children; God bless them.

Dec. 26. Ragged school; a rough lot; three caps stolen.

Dec. 31. During the year now gone I have had much labour, much anxiety about my work, many short comings, much to cause contrition of heart, many mercies, many blessings to me and mine; farewell 1869.

There is, perhaps, not a city in Europe that offers to the author and artist alike a more interesting series of subjects for pen and pencil than Edinburgh, and amongst all the places visited by Mr. Ashworth during the year, not one of them was of deeper interest or had greater attraction to him than the metropolis of Scotland, a brief sketch of his visit to which we give from his own pen.

"On my visit to Edinburgh in October, 1869, to lay the foundation stone of the first Free Methodist church there, when nearing the city, as the distant historic hills appeared in sight, and the train glided into the ancient moat of the old castle, my spirits became depressed. I knew that for the next four days I should have to address many thousands, in perhaps some of the largest halls and churches in Edinburgh; a consciousness of my ignorance and unfitness for such work in the capital of academies, colleges, schools, and hosts of men justly celebrated for their learning and labours, came over me; and when I arrived at my temporary home, the residence of two kind-hearted and hospitable sisters in Moray Place,—the noble daughters of a noble mother,—I had to seek my bed-room, and cast the burden of my oppressed soul on Him who promises to sustain us.

"On Sunday, Oct. 17, I preached at Barclay church in the morning, Brighton street in the afternoon, and Assembly Hall in the evening.

"Monday, Oct. 18. I spoke to the inmates of the Magdalene reformatory, and again in the Assembly Hall in the evening, Dr. Guthrie in the chair.

"Tuesday, Oct. 19. Laid the foundation stone of the Methodist Free Church in Park Place, addressed the children in Dr. Guthrie's ragged schools, and lectured in the Assembly Hall, Mr. Miller, M.P. for the city, in the chair.

"Wednesday, Oct. 20. Spoke to six hundred mothers in John Knox's church, visited Mr. Harrison's 'Boys' Home,' and lectured in the Assembly Hall on 'My Journey to Jerusalem,' Sir James Simpson in the chair.

"I found on this visit to Edinburgh, as in many other towns, that my safest and wisest plan was, to be just what I was; to make no pretensions to be either a learned man or polished gentleman, and then I should have nothing to sustain.

"We had several parties, but having neither swallow-tail, white waistcoat, jewelry, pomatum, nor lavender, my toilet was simple and brief; my dress plain, clean, and good, and always in fashion.

"All the three gatherings in the Assembly-hall were exciting and imposing, being crowded in every corner. Dr. Bonar, and several others who had been to Palestine, were present to hear me lecture on 'My Journey to Jerusalem,' and afterwards expressed the great pleasure they felt.

"Dr. Guthrie, in his opening speech on Monday evening, when referring to my labours and my writings, made me feel very humble and yet thankful. 'John Ashworth's books,' said the generous Doctor, 'are beyond all my praise; they are circulating by thousands, yea by millions, and not only in the cottages of the poor, but in the mansions of the rich.' But when the Doctor and his lady crossed the city expressly to take breakfast with me, and, as he said, 'have about two hours talk with one of God's honoured servants,' I felt it to be a great condescension on his part, a great honour paid to myself, and another evidence of the humility of a mighty intellect sanctified by Divine grace.

"Dr. Duff, another of Scotland's worthies, the learned labourer of the Mission field of India, being then in the city, likewise came to breakfast with me the following morning. These mornings with two such remarkable and immortal men was a privilege seldom awarded to comparative strangers, and to this day I regard with pleasure those precious hours in their company.

"Another of the Scotch divines, a mighty man, but in many respects very dissimilar to the other two, came to tell me he had read the speech of my chairman, Dr. Guthrie, in the morning's papers, giving such a glowing description of the moral improvement of Edinburgh the last twenty years; this was the colossal, iron-nerved Dr. Begg. He said, 'You must not take your impressions from the sunny-souled Dr. Guthrie. Go into the slums, wynds, and courts, especially at night, and you will witness scenes calculated to teach a different lesson. I will provide you with a couple of safe guides if you will undertake the experiment.' 'Agreed,' I replied.

"Dr. Begg sent a note to the superintendent of police, and at eleven three of us set out on our exploration through the slums, wynds, and dark courts, witnessing scenes shocking enough, scenes that told how terrible sin is, and how fearful its retribution. Our painful work finished about three in the morning. On returning to the police office to compare notes, I said to one of my guides, 'How long have you been in the Edinburgh force?'

"'About twenty years, sir.'

"'What is the criminal condition of the city now compared to what it was before the passing of the Act for closing public houses on the Sunday, called the McKenzie Act?'

"'We have not so many cases by at least one-third; the change for the better is very marked. Our average number in the city gaol before the passing of the Bill was six hundred and twenty; now it is only three hundred and thirty.'

"I then mentioned to him the observations of Dr. Begg respecting Dr. Guthrie's speech, and asked which of the two was nearest the truth. His reply was, 'I could have shown you as much drunkenness, debauchery, and open wickedness in one hour before, as I could show you in a whole night now. Since the passing of the Act, Edinburgh is greatly improved; Dr. Guthrie is right; and the old gentleman, with his ragged school and other labours, has done much towards it.'"

Mr. Ashworth loved Edinburgh for its historic associations, charitable institutions, and educational advantages, and said to a friend, "I wish I were a boy again, and living in Edinburgh." No spot, however, seemed to make a deeper impression on his mind than the martyr's grave in Old Grey Friars' church yard, a sketch of which he has given in one of his "Simple Records," entitled "A Covenanter's Grave."

Another object of interest to him in that yard was a terrier dog, called "Grey Friars' Bobby," who for eleven years slept on his master's grave. In October, 1858, a man named Grey, of whom nothing is known, except that he was poor, and lived in a quiet way in some obscure part of the town, was buried in Old Grey Friars' church yard. His grave, levelled by the hand of time, and unmarked by any stone, is scarcely discernible; but although no human interest would seem to attach to it, for eleven years the dead man's faithful dog kept constant watch and guard over the grave. James Brown, the old curator of the burial ground, remembers Grey's funeral, and the dog was, he says, one of the most conspicuous of the mourners. The grave was closed in as usual, and the following morning Bobby was found lying on the new-made mound; as no dogs were admitted, this was an innovation old James could not permit, and several times drove him out, till one wet, cold morning he saw the faithful animal, in spite of all chastisement, still lying on the grave, he took pity on him and gave him some food. From that time Bobby never spent a night away from his master's tomb. A weekly treat of steaks was long allowed him by Sergeant Scott, of the artillery corps. When the mid-day gun was fired at the castle, Bobby punctually started for the *restaurant* of Mr. John Trail, 6, Grey Friars' Place, who daily supplied him with a good dinner. Bobby, however, never went to Mr. Trail's on the Sunday, as the premises were closed on that day: but the sagacious animal saved a portion of his Friday and Saturday's dinner for the Sabbath, and had his pantry for this purpose beneath an old tombstone near his master's grave. The collector who summoned Mr. Trail for payment of the dog-tax, on the ground that he "harboured" Bobby, raised up a host of friends, who not only paid the dog-tax, but took care that his daily wants were well supplied. A photograph of the faithful creature, with a portion of his hair, was obtained by Mr. Ashworth from the keeper of the grounds, and it was his intention to have given a sketch of Bobby's sagacity. Bobby died in the house of his benefactor, Mr. Trail, on January 14th, 1872, being three years after the date of Mr. Ashworth's visit, making a total of upwards of thirteen years.

CHAPEL FOR THE DESTITUTE, ROCHDALE, 1870.

Twelve years have now passed away since I met my first congregation of *fifteen* at the Chapel for the Destitute. Since then many changes have taken place, many mercies received, and once again would we raise our Ebenezer, saying, "Hitherto hath the Lord helped us," for while our hearts have been encouraged by the kindness and contributions of friends, our hands have been upheld by the mighty God of Jacob, and we can say with gratitude, "The best of all is, God is with us."

We have added to our other operations during the year a Sunday Ragged School, referred to in the monthly accounts. I have long felt the want of this. It will add considerably to our expenses, but it is our dear Saviour's dying command, "Feed my lambs," and I have no doubt He will provide the means, which He always has done. What we want most is willing hearts to engage in teaching, hearts full of patience and full of love. "The harvest truly is great, but the labourers are few."

Our Adult Sunday School, under the care of the "Friends," is still doing much good, and greatly prized. Our Sunday School and Service at Brickfield, under the care of one of our Missionaries and four devoted teachers, is encouraging, although they have much to contend with.

Our Missionary agencies continue the same as last year. They have visited and read the word of God in many houses, comforted the distressed, preached the Gospel in the open air and cottage houses, superintended our Ragged Schools, and attended to all the various operations arising out of our work.

Our services are all well attended, and many of our poor people give evidence of having tasted the good word of God; others that gave us some hope, have gone back to sin and sorrow, but for the many that hold fast their confidence we are thankful.

It will be seen that our expenses exceed our income

by £46 15s. 6d., but we trust this will not long remain. Hitherto He, to whom all wealth belongs, has provided for us.

Oct. 1. JOHN ASHWORTH.

It was my intention to have given Mr. Ashworth's Diary in full for the year 1870, to show his abundant and incessant labours in the Lord's vineyard after having retired from business, which were continued till his last illness, but am reluctantly compelled to leave it out for want of space.

The following places were favoured with his services during the year, at many of which he spent two and three days, conducting at most of them two daily, viz.: Manchester, fifteen visits; Stockport, Liverpool, two; Denton, Leigh, Sunderland, York, two; St. Helens, Wigan, Todmorden, Barnsley, Sowerby Bridge, Saltaire, Bradford, London, three; Middleton, two; Summerseat, Ramsbottom, Bury, two; Bolton, Cottingley, Swansea, Radcliffe, Sheffield, two; Buxton, Settle, Skipton, Bolton Abbey, Runcorn, Prescot, Glasgow, Edinburgh, Rawtenstall, Poynton, Wensleydale, Blackpool, Chesterfield, Wednesbury, Dewsbury, Cromford, Matlock, Swinton, Scarborough, Oldham, Burslem, Carlisle, Whitehaven, Southport, Burnley, Louth, Brigg, Birmingham, two; Norwich, Wisbeach, Saddleworth, Cheltenham, Helmshore, Ossett, Halliwell, Leeds, Huddersfield, &c. He closes the year as follows,—"Dec. 31. The last of a wonderful year to many; a year France and Germany will never forget; a year of mercies to me and mine; a year of providential and sustaining grace. Bless the Lord, O my soul, and *forget* not all His benefits. Amen."

CHAPTER XI.

1871.

"JANUARY 1, 1871. I thank my God for His mercies to me and mine, and now, on the first day of the new year, consecrate myself to Him body, soul, and spirit. This, I trust, is done without reserve. Oh, I want to love Him and serve Him with all my powers; and I beg of Him that He will this year help me in all my labours in His cause, and give me good health for all I have to do; guide my pen, and more and more bless the writings He helps me to do, and this year help me to do more than ever. I pray for a special blessing on the Destitute, the Ragged School, the Adult Class, on our Missionaries, and the whole of our undertaking; that He will send us the funds that He sees will be required, and that this year many precious souls may be saved. Bless my wife, and all my children. Oh Lord, my God, do answer these my prayers, if it please Thee, but I submit to Thy will and guidance in all things, amen, amen, my Lord and Saviour.

"JOHN ASHWORTH."

Jan. 5. Many letters and much writing; gave many clogs, mostly to children, poor dear things; a severe cold day.

Jan. 12. Attended the funeral of Mrs. Leatham at Pontefract; she was a great friend to all the poor, but especially to the "Destitute," often lifting up my hands in my work by her timely gifts.

Jan. 20. Returned from Bolton this morning; feel quite dissatisfied with myself about the meeting; ought to have said more about the wickedness of war, but was afraid of speaking too long.

Feb. 23. Matlock; hot and cold bath this morning; walked over the high hill called Masson, a very fine view. Conducted service in the establishment this evening; an interesting company in the house at present.

Feb. 24. Matlock; walked out with Mr. and Mrs. Jarrold, of Norwich; took tea at Riber Castle by request of Mr. and Mrs. Smedley; had much conversation with both; have a better knowledge of them now, and think them true servants of God.

Feb. 25. Matlock; cold bath at seven; walked up the hills and down to Matlock Baths; a fine sweet day, greatly enjoyed the scenery, and felt much better for the change.

March 2. Feel out of health, face yellow, indicates a disordered liver; cannot tie to work, no application as I could wish.

March 7. Took Mary Jane to Mr. Smedley's establishment at Matlock; hope God will bless the means.

March 16. Do not feel that close communion with God I have often felt, an indifference to things spiritual, painful. I know I love God, and that He loves me, but want warmth and depth. Lord, revive Thy good work in my soul.

March 25. Writing to Matlock, Brisbane, and Melbourne. The Lord permits me to be greatly tried in my family. Job earnestly spoke of the days when his children were around him. Feel very sad while writing to them.

March 27. How difficult it is to do good to some persons, who are ignorant, wicked, and selfish; the more you do for them the less thankful they seem. I feel our work very hard at times; the missionaries are discouraged and sad; foolish and mortifying tattle. Lord, help us to keep close to Thee.

March 30. Feel very anxious to-day about my work at

the Destitute, and need a large increase of faith. These times of depression have their uses, but are not joyous. Lord, help me to hold fast my confidence to the end.

March 31. Received a cheque for £20, just paying all demands for school and chapel. Oh how good the Lord is; may I *never* doubt His goodness, never.

April 14. Letter from Mr. Duckworth, clergyman, tutor to Prince Leopold, informing me, "That Her Majesty the Queen accepts with pleasure the copy of the illustrated edition of Strange Tales."

May 24. Left for Plymouth at 5·50 a.m., arrived at 6 p.m. Lectured in the "Friends" large room at 8.

May 25. Rose early; walked over the How down to the sea-side; set out for Lostwithiel at 10. Spoke at the laying of a corner stone for the new Sunday school at 2. Tea in the field; walked up to Storm-hill castle; lectured at 7 to a large audience.

May 26. Left Lostwithiel early; called at St. Michael, ascended the tower, stood in the chair; dined with the governor; arrived at Penzance at 5; had two teas; lectured at 7.

May 27. Took a conveyance to the Land's End. The old Christian Thomas Thomas repeated the hymn, "Lo, on a narrow neck of land"; an impressive place. Returned to Penzance, then to Redruth, and lectured at 7.

May 29. Redruth; preached at 3 to the thousands assembled in the Gwennap pit from "Two men went up to the temple to pray." Yearly in this celebrated place open-air services are held; Wesley often preached here. Lectured in the evening.

May 30. Mullion; went down to rocks by the sea; walked in procession with the Sunday scholars; lectured in the evening; a remarkable day—the rocks, the sea, the children, the flowers, &c., &c. Bless the Lord.

May 31. Set out this morning for the Lizzard; up to the light-houses, &c., &c.; drove over the moor to Helston; lectured in the evening; a busy day.

June 1. Drove this morning from Helston to Camborne, all around was glorious—heaven, earth, and sea; lectured in the F. M. chapel; returned same evening to Redruth.

June 2. Left Redruth this morning for home, via Plymouth, Exeter, Bristol, Gloucester, and Birmingham; tired and covered with dust, but thankful for mercies. Mr. Harley was with me at all the places on this journey, and rendered me much help.

June 12. Oxford; stood on the spot where Ridley, Latimer, and Cranmer were burned.

July 8. Burton; preached in the Market-place at 8. Barrels! barrels! barrels!

July 11. Burton; went through the great brewery of Allsop and Sons; half a million of barrels going and coming—a fearful establishment to contemplate. One of those barrels, what did it do?

Aug. 31. Pic-nic with eight children to Bank-house, near Bagslate; all wild with joy.

Sept. 4—7. Ford Hall, in Derbyshire; on the moors; grand view from *Eccles Pike.* Tea with Mr. Hall, clergyman.

Sept. 22. Feel very tired with the last four days work (at Spalding, Peterborough, and Wisbeach), and am thankful that I can rest. I believe if I were to take stimulants to spur me up at these exhaustive meetings and journeys, it would be fatal to my health, and jeopardise my religious life and peace with God.

Sept 27. Opening of our grand new Town Hall; went to breakfast at the Mayor's house, Roche Mount; joined in the procession, but did not go to the twenty-one shillings dinner; felt it was no place for me.

CHAPEL FOR THE DESTITUTE, ROCHDALE, 1871.

"This year, as much as in any former, has our faith and patience been tried. In pecuniary matters I have much reason to thank God and take courage. The debt with which we began the year was not only soon cleared off, but the necessary means have been supplied for carrying on our work beyond my expectations; to God be all the praise. We believe much good has been done, but our work is so complicated, it cannot be told. In addition to our Chapel Services, and mission work amongst the poor, we have thousands of letters to answer in the course of the year;

hundreds of persons, distressed in body or mind, apply for advice as well as help; this work requires much caution and anxious thought. The narrative this year is one of these cases.

"Our Missionaries have continued their work during the year as formerly: visiting the poor, the sick, and the dying; instructing the ignorant, comforting the distressed, conducting cottage services in winter, and out of door in summer, most of which have been well attended.

"Our Adult Sunday School, under the care of the 'Friends,' has experienced a few changes. One zealous and beloved teacher has removed from town; another has been laid aside by a severe affliction, which we deeply regret; but others have taken their places.

"In consequence of trade being generally good, and perhaps to some extent owing to the operation of the 'Habitual Criminals' Bill,' we have not had so many *casuals* by several thousands, which makes the *item* of expense less than in any former year.

"We send this our Thirteenth Report to our friends, thanking them for encouragement given, and hope yet more abundantly to labour in the vineyard of our Lord.

"BROADFIELD, OCT. 1." "JOHN ASHWORTH.

Oct. 16. Liverpool; three and a half hours in the police court. Saw one hundred and ninety-eight persons brought up for drunkenness, from Saturday to Sunday night—about twenty-four hours. The governor has given me the following statement from the books:—

Bridewell, 16th Oct., 1871.

Received from Saturday,		12			
Book'd during Saturday night		174	of whom	144	were drunk.
Ditto	Sunday Do.	68	Do.	54	Ditto
Total on Books at 8 a.m.		254	Do.	198	Ditto

Oct. 29. Stockport Large Sunday School Anniversary. Afternoon, to the young. 1 Chron. xxviii. 9 and in the evening to parents, from Deut. vi. 6, 7.

Oct. 30. Stockport; Mothers' meeting at 3 o'clock, and lectured at 7 on "Young Women, Wives, and Mothers." Immense room crowded at all the services. Met the Managers of the School at Mr. J. Leigh's to tea. Much profitable conversation on various subjects. Returned home this evening. The child that prayed, mentioned in the "Dark Hour," called at my house to-day, going to be married—and well.

Nov. 13. Birmingham; lectured in the Town Hall on "Young Men, Husbands, and Fathers." Slept in my old bed.

"Persons who have travelled much and seen much of the world, have likewise seen a great variety of bedrooms, and no doubt will have experienced, along with myself, that all are not furnished alike, or all equally agreeable. I will endeavour to describe three.

"The first was a commodious, clean, well-arranged room—every thing that might be desired in the way of cleanliness and comfort. The bed, which was certainly one of the softest I had ever slept in, had been occupied by Joseph Sturge, Richard Cobden, John Bright, Harriet Beecher Stowe, and other illustrious persons, every one of whom had taken a very high position on the roll of fame. Sitting a few moments in the easy chair, a rush of thoughts in connection with the history of my noble predecessors came over me. I thought, while reviewing their characters, how every one of them was a subject for a study, and that it was indeed an historic bed.

"The second was at the residence of a gentleman who has rapidly become rich, built himself a fine Gothic hall, and furnished it at a great expense. The room that I had assigned to me as my bedroom looked on the lawn. All the furniture was blue damask—blue and silver. The sofas, the wardrobes, the bed itself were a perfect show. The mahogany carving, in connection with the bed, exceeded any thing I had before seen. The carpet was exceedingly rich, and soft as velvet. Moving about in the room for a time and surveying this very costly dormitory, I concluded that money could indeed do almost all things. My attendance was equal to the magnificence of the bedroom,—servants in livery, attention at every point, and honoured like a duke.

"The third was in the northern part of Lancashire. Arriving at a small station, the name of which I now forget, I was met by two men, one of them tall and thin, evidently dressed in his very best suit. This consisted of a coat with a very wide, thick collar, swallow-tail laps, and metal buttons. The collar was very stiff, and stuck up to his ears; the trousers were rather short, and displayed good strong brown stockings, and home-made shoes; a bell-top hat, brown with age, and I could tell by the fashion, he must have had them thirty years. He seemed a very timid man, and having gazed at me several times, he at last ventured to say, 'Are you come to open a chapel in this neighbourhood?' and I said, 'I am.' He then pointed to a phaeton, that had once been new, but had more recently been in connection with the hen-roost, the springs of which were rusty. The horse was quite in keeping, and perhaps his value might have been £3. He had four legs like table legs. The driver was a farmer's boy, with red cheeks and white teeth. The timid, pale-looking man said, pointing to the phaeton, 'Will you ride, sir'? I stepped in. He seemed afraid to get in along with myself until I urged him, and then 'our John' drove off about three miles, and with the springs going together every two or three yards, it was one of the most jolting journeys I ever experienced.

"I was driven to the middle of a long row of cottage houses, when the chariot stopped, and a stout-faced woman, with red elbows, came to the door and said, 'Well, you're welcome, I con tell yo; aw've been looking eawt for you. Come in; here is yer whoam and wheer you're goin' to stop.'

"I stepped out of the carriage into this model cottage, found that the woman was baking some nice muffins, and that she had got the floor right well washed, mopped, and sanded. Her timid, pale-faced husband sat down in the corner with nothing to say, but his ruddy-faced wife had quite sufficient.

"I went to the place where service had to be conducted in the afternoon, and found a very substantial stone building, crowded out with people from all sides of the country, and the landlady of the neighbouring public house brought a Bible and hymn-book, to present them as her share of the contribution to the new place of worship. After service, a lady came to me in great distress, saying, 'Mr. Ashworth, we are very unhappy about you.

I live in a good house, and I had every accommodation for you, and it had been arranged months ago that you should be my guest. But the woman at whose house you have been has several grown-up sons and daughters, all connected with the school and church, and all working very well. Her husband also is a very decent, but a very quiet man, and she came into the meeting last week, when we were making final arrangements, and said, 'I shall have John Ashworth as my guest; now I tell you, I shall have John Ashworth as my guest. If he doesn't come to my house, neither my husband, nor my sons, nor my daughters shall ever enter this place of worship again,—never while it is a building,' and then walked out. As she is a desperate woman, we did not know what to do, but I was requested to see you and explain it.'

"I said, 'Oh, my dear woman, don't concern yourself at all about me. If we hadn't a woman like this, we should be one character short. She seems to think it some degree of honour to have me as her guest, and if so little a matter will please her, please her,' I said, 'I will try to make myself happy and comfortable for one night, you may depend upon that.'

"When evening service was over, I returned to my little cottage home, that was crowded out with people come to see, and chat, and sing; but as time went later, they began to move off, until there was no one left in the house but the pale-faced, quiet husband, and the red-elbowed, ruddy-cheeked, strong-boned wife, and I said, 'Missus, I think I should like to retire to rest.'

"'Oh, very well, very well.' She got me a candle-stick, such as it was, showed me the way up some stone steps, at the top of which there were two or three small bedrooms, and she shouted out, 'that on the right is yours.' So I entered this bedroom on the right; there I stood looking round taking stock, with the candle-stick in my hand. There was no dressing-table, no wash-stand, no arrangement for a morning's toilet; and, speaking from the top of the steps, I said, 'Would you pray be so kind as to let me have some water in a mug, and some soap and a towel, please.'

"I heard the timid husband say to his wife, 'I told thee he's noan used to things like us. I told thee he would want something.'

"'Howd thee thy noise; I can get him something, can't I?'

"She brought me up a mug that had been in the wars, a white lead patch on one side, and a rope tied tightly round it; half a pound of soap, as hard as iron; a towel that seemed to me a washed-out dishcloth. I shut the door, and began to look at the bedroom again, and began to speak to myself as I walked about this little room, saying, 'Well, now, is that an historic bed? How many of England's celebrities have slept in that bed? Why, it is as flat as a pancake: a common, half-headed bed. A shelf at the top to set the candle-stick on, the whole painted as red as a carrot, and perhaps the market value is ten shillings. How dost thou like this (speaking to myself)? There is not much grand carving about these bed-stocks. Where is thy grand carpet, wardrobe, and blue damask, ornamented with silver, and a man to attend to thy every want? How dost thou like this? Thou hast been pampered, and spoiled, and honoured till thou hast got too highly exalted. Thou art reduced now to about a level with the prophet Elisha. He had his bed, his table, his chair, and his candle-stick, and that is just what thou hast got. Yes, but who said 'Foxes have holes, and birds of the air have nests, but the Son of man hath not where to lay his head'? I again repeated the words, 'Foxes have holes, and birds of the air have nests, but the Son of man hath not where to lay his head.' He who left His throne in glory to redeem thee.'

"'He who was rich, yet for thy sake became poor, that thou, through His poverty, might be made rich, had not where to lay His head, and thou art thinking thyself humiliated because this plain arrangement is all that is ready for thee.' Instantly that room became like a little palace,—everything appeared quite changed. I knelt down beside the plain bed, and blessed my God that, after all, I had where to lay my head.

"In the morning, on coming down to breakfast, I found the good wife had been up betimes, and had everything very nice, and what surprised me was that this carriage, this chariot, came again to the door, at which I expressed regret.

"'It is a nice morning, I can easily walk the three miles to the station, and you might have saved the expense of hiring this coach,' I said.

"The good wife stretched herself up and replied, 'We have paid for it, and you shall ride every inch; and I hope you have had a comfortable sleep, and that I have made you very happy:

and I can tell you one thing, that I shall lift up my head in this row of houses now I have had my own road, and I was determined to have it. Good morning.' I drove off in this worn-out phaeton to the station, a wiser and a better man for the last night's experience."

"Dec. 2. Gave tea to forty-five blind persons and their guides in the lecture room of the Public Hall; all seemed very happy."

The above meeting was suggested by contributions from several friends on behalf of the blind, and was the first of the kind held in Rochdale, which has now become annual. Out of it have sprung many other good thoughts: the teaching of the blind to read, the establishment of similar meetings in Bury and other places, and an excellent selection of books in embossed type, by Dr. Wm. Moon, which have been placed in the Rochdale Free Public Library expressly for the blind, including the Holy Bible in sixty-two parts, and upwards of one hundred other volumes on various interesting subjects.

Mr. Ashworth took a deep interest in the welfare of the blind. Under the title of "My Blind Friends" (No. 55, Strange Tales), he has recorded a touching narrative of John Harris, whose noble example under painful and trying experiences will, doubtless, afford comfort and encouragement to many in similar circumstances.

"Dec. 25. Had an annual tea meeting at the Destitute; never had so many of the really poor; it was indeed a good and profitable meeting. 'Happy Ned' and 'Niff,' both subjects of two narratives, were the speakers."

Amongst the places visited by Mr. Ashworth during the year were Ford Hall and Matlock, in Derbyshire; the bracing atmosphere and beautiful scenery of both were to him peculiarly attractive, hence we find him occasionally, when in a low state of health and requiring rest, visiting these places, in order to recruit his exhausted powers of body and mind. The following sketch of a visit to Matlock is from his own pen; that of Ford Hall is by a young friend who met him when on a visit there, and who drank in his words with delight as he gave himself up to the quiet enjoyment of social conversation. Such occasions were rare, but those who had the pleasure of meeting him under such auspicious circumstances will ever remember with what pure delight—almost enchantment—they have listened to his life-like and graphic description of scenes and incidents.

"Which of the forty counties of England are the most beautiful? has received forty different answers. Every division, from Cumberland to Cornwall furnishes its ardent admirers, and all conceive their own to have some special pre-eminence—some undoubtedly claim to be ranked amongst the grandest and best; nor does this feeling always arise from strongly-developed locality, retired seclusion, or a contracted knowledge of other counties or other lands. The hills of Westmoreland may not compare with the Alps or the Andes; the vales of Devon with the vine-groves of Lorraine; or the fields of Lancashire with the outstretched prairies of America. Other countries undoubtedly surpass in the vast and stupendous, but not in the ever-varying and ever-beautiful scenery, adorning almost every province of our sea-girt isle. Our countless landscapes, embellished with woods, rocks, rills, and dells; clothed with every tinge of flower and foliage, from the sombre green of the holly and pine, to the enamelled green of the oak or linden, are sweet and enchanting. And when these scenes become vocal with the choruses of our unrivalled feathered songsters, pouring forth their melodies from forest, field, and sky, the thought has often been suggested whether anything terrestrial can be more beautiful, and if there are not more Edens in this world than the one watered by Gihon and Euphrates.

"In my wanderings through the various counties, especially during summer, I have found their claims for admiration so numerous, and their unquestioned attractions so hallowed, that it seems difficult to make a selection; but it sometimes happens that these natural scenes of beauty are so mingled with other associations, that we instinctively give the preference without intending it to be invidious; and this may account for my admiration of that part of Derbyshire extending from Millers Dale to Ambergate. The whole of the valley, watered by the Wye the Amber and the Derwent, abounds with interesting scenery, and some parts with surpassing beauty. The view from the High Tor, the Masson, and the Heights of Abraham, from which parts of five counties can be seen, is most attractive and imposing.

THE MASTER OF RIBER.

"A number of years ago, a rather remarkable *young* man, residing in the direction of Cromford, found his health failing, and was ultimately reduced to great prostration of body. Many doctors, all more or less celebrated, were consulted, but to little purpose; he still remained feeble. He was one of those never-despair characters, that it was not easy even for doctors to *kill;* his mental energy seemed boundless; his convictions in either metaphysics, mechanics, politics, or religion were all positive and decided. He knew something of physiology, and believed that people ought not to die prematurely; that the machine called the human body ought to be in good working condition so long, and except wilfully and ignorantly injured, would generally work on to a good old age; but if disorder did occur, the simpler the remedy the more likely to answer the purpose. The then commenced battle of 'pathies' was raging about this time, and mankind almost distracted with the fierce medical civil war; allopathy, hydropathy, homœopathy, big-pill, little-pill, and aqua had slain each other, and all gained the victory. The result of this unseemly conduct was, that many were induced to enquire into the merits of these 'pathy' belligerents, and our young invalid, for what he thought the best of all reasons, pronounced in favour of hydropathy; he was by its application brought from the verge of the grave to health, strength, and vigour. Great was his thankfulness, and strong was his desire in some way to show his gratitude to God and man. That indomitable force of character which surmounts all difficulties and knows no defeat now began more fully to develop itself. He had no deep veneration for red-tape. He believed in doing good to the bodies and souls of men without consulting either prince or peasant, and one plan that suggested itself to him was to open an establishment for all, but especially for the indigent poor—a place of healing—a Bethesda, where the afflicted might find a home and a regenerated constitution. Matlock Bank was selected for its springs, sunny aspect, and beautiful prospect. Very humble was the beginning: a couple of cottage houses formed the nucleus; patients began .to flock in from all parts, one addition after another was made to the building, without any special regard to architectural rule, until the whole fabric became almost as singular as its controlling spirit. In a very short time the Matlock Bank Hydropathic Establishment, for many reasons, became widely celebrated: the poor, the maimed, the halt, the blind, the bloated, and the bilious, plebeian and patrician, all crowded inside or around this many shaped and many coloured hospital, until almost every house on the Bank, sloping down to the Wye, was filled with invalids, all waiting for the command of the Master, or 'moving of the waters.' It was soon found, in order to prevent rebellion and sedition amongst this heterogeneous gathering, that laws and government would be necessary. It is said that a mild, judicious despotism is the best form of government, because the most immediate and direct in its administration. Accordingly laws were framed, and the establishment regulated upon this principle, but with what success people vary in their opinion.

"Amongst the many men who have been blessed with a good wife is the Master of Riber. There are some gloomy souls, whose faces you never wish to see turn; there are others you never see too often, to meet them or think of them gives real pleasure. So it is with the genial happy soul, who shares in the management of her husband's establishments, the result of peace with God, a well balanced mind, and plenty of Christian work. She well understands, and studies the eccentricities of her noble-minded partner, shares largely in his views, and from extensive study of the human frame, and great experience amongst her sex, manages well that department. She rises early, drinks neither tea, coffee, wine, beer, nor spirits; yet she is the picture of health. She teaches in the Sunday school, and every day lives to do good; and, among the thousands that have been under her care, many will remember her anxiety for their spiritual and eternal welfare.

"There are few places in this world for invalids where there are so many scenes and sources of pleasure as at Matlock Bank. Books, music, lectures, various healthy and strengthening exercies, excursions to coves, wells, and rocks, celebrated for natural or artificial beauty, or climbing the many hills, where every step reveals wider and more expansive views, and from Riber castle the beautiful panorama stretching before you is one not often surpassed.

"There is a free and easy feeling pervading the entire place inside and out; no stiff, starched, liveried servants, no conventional chill, no miserable bonds of etiquette; all the servants seem cheerful and happy. There are not many places where you hear such down-right hearty laughing, especially in the bath houses, and oft at the expense of new comers.

"The various ablutions and transitions in the sweating, packing, washing and drying rooms; the involuntary yells, screams, sobs, and groans, often provoke the most singular speeches and greatest merriment, in which all heartily join.

"One poor fellow, with a flabby face and very suspicious nose, as he lay helpless in the packing box, said to a tall, slow-spoken bath man, 'O, sir, can you get me a glass of whisky and water; O, please do, sir, as quick as you can; I am fainting! I am fainting!' 'Whisky and water, whisky and water; you may have as much water as you like, but not one drop of whisky. We don't spoil water by putting whisky into it here; no, no, man, no whisky. I think you are not in much danger of fainting, and you will be less in a few days.'

"This packing, intended to open all the pores of the skin, is a strange, agreeable and disagreeable process, only those that have experienced it can form any conception of the negative condition to which they are at once reduced. To lie down on a double wet sheet, a double dry blanket, a double oil cloth, and then have them all brought over and wrapt tightly round, locking feet, arms, hands, and every limb, until rendered as helpless as a mummy, and told to be there half an hour, is no doubt rather trying, and certainly tormenting to the nose. One of the liberated patients took a soft dry towel, and entering the first of a long row of packing boxes, said to one of the poor helpless prisoners, 'I presume, sir, you feel much titillation of your tuberosity?' 'What do you mean?' said the man, in astonishment. 'Does your nose tickle?' 'Yes, above a bit.' 'Shall I rub it for you?' 'Yes;

but you must mind how you do it.' This good Samaritan went from box to box, rectifying their tickling noses, amidst shouts of laughter and hearty thanks."

FORD HALL.

"In a lonely secluded valley in North Derbyshire stands the old grey house of Ford Hall, with its terraced garden, its avenues of grand old limes, and its lawns sloping down to a rippling brook. Nestling in the depths of a wooded dell, furrowed among long sunny slopes of hill and moor, a pleasanter spot could scarcely be found, in which a busy worker might rest awhile from the anxieties and toil of his vocation. Those who know how intensely Mr. Ashworth admired beautiful scenery, will easily understand what refreshment of mind and body he derived from his necessarily brief visit there.

"Like most men of large heart and quick sympathies, he could derive pleasure from the simplest sources. He would go out before breakfast to watch the rooks in the sycamores, or the rabbits in the shrubbery, and interest his auditors when he returned to breakfast by some original observation upon what he had seen. One lovely summer's day, sitting under the deep shade of the old trees, he remarked, 'This scene—the trees, the stream, and the bridge—will be photographed on my memory for life!' He would enter a cottage, and win the hearts of the people by his frank friendliness, listening with interest to their tales of struggles with sickness and poverty, relating in his characteristic way, scenes in his own early life. Surrounded by friends who thoroughly appreciated him, and who sympathised with his labours for the good of the destitute and the ignorant, Mr. Ashworth would speak freely of the varied experiences of a life of persevering effort, of great sorrows bravely borne, and of such personal influence for good, as would seem incredible to those who did not know him. Well might the words be applied to him which our Lord addressed to Simon, 'Thou shalt catch men.'"

CHAPTER XII.

CHAPEL FOR THE DESTITUTE, 1872.

"WITH thankfulness, I present my yearly report, being I trust grateful for God's continued goodness in sustaining us during fourteen years of unwearied labours. The money received this year is more than on any former one, and our friends will perceive that we have a considerable balance in hand; first, because only one missionary has been engaged most of the year; second, because of a special gift; and third, because trade has been good, and we have had fewer cases of poverty to relieve.

"Our missionary, with the recent assistance of a female visitor, is still at work, as formerly, amongst the poor, carrying many a blessing into the homes of the sick, destitute, and the dying. We hope soon to add a Bible-woman to the agencies at work. This we have long desired; and our funds will now enable us to do so.

"The Adult Sunday School, under the care of the 'Friends,' has sustained another great loss in the death of Miss White, but it is still well attended, and continues to be a blessing to many persons advanced in life, who could neither read nor write, but can now do both; some of them between forty and fifty years of age.

"A Mission-room was opened in School-lane, a destitute part of the town, last November, in which a Sunday Ragged School is carried on, with very promising results, also a Mothers' Meeting, and other services.

"I again wish to express my gratitude to all our friends for their continued support and prayers on behalf of our work; thankful for what has been done, as well as for what has been received; that we should be the honoured instruments employed in wiping away the tear of sorrow, relieving the distressed, and pointing wanderers to the 'Friend for Sinners.' To God be all the glory.

"JOHN ASHWORTH.

"BROADFIELD, OCT. 1."

"Given five shillings to an old man who fell in the frost and broke his leg, his wife (who has since died) being ill at the time with dropsy, he in bed upstairs and she down stairs, a very distressing but deserving case. Our visitor at the same time took some tea, meal, and bread to a family in a cellar, where the mother was sick in bed, (since dead,) worn to a skeleton, with several little children crying for bread, and none to give them. When the husband does work he drinks his wages and takes his meals at the cook shop. The woman was pining to death for want and the children beggared and starved: all the victims of drink.

"Sent P. O. O. for £3, to relieve a widow in difficulties, her husband was a labourer in God's vineyard, and she is struggling to maintain herself and family by keeping a lodging-house. We have hundreds of letters appealing for help from different parts of the country, many of whom we find it a real pleasure to assist, but not until we have enquired into their cases from some one resident in the neighbourhood.

"Given £2 2s. 3d. to assist sick cases recommended to Southport for change of air. All of them I am happy to say got benefit more or less. Many of the sick poor pine away in their pent-up dwellings, for want of proper nursing and fresh air. We have between thirty and forty sick cases here and elsewhere on our list, some of whom have been confined to bed from ten to even forty-nine years, several of them blind, but through the kindness of one Christian friend who remembers them every year, we are the medium of conveying to them her timely gift which procures them many a comfort.

"Paid two and sixpence and several articles towards clothing a poor destitute but interesting girl, who was found by one of our visitors in a wretched home, having been severely scalded in the neck and chest while asleep on the hearth. She was lying on a little straw, on the stone flags, with nothing but her own rags of clothing, and would certainly have died had we not at once got her removed to the Infirmary, where she is doing well. She is without father, and would be better off were she without mother."

The Amount of Money received this year has been expended as follows:

	£	s.	d.
Relief given in money, nourishment, &c., to 1808 cases	73	6	1½
Salaries	93	0	0
Clogs and clogging, 163 cases	11	3	1
Clothing and Material for do.	7	8	5
Rent of Chapel, and Room-keeper	43	10	0
Rent of Mission-room, Cleaning, Coal, and Gas	8	1	5½
Furnishing do. for Sunday-school, and other purposes, including Library of 100 vols.	12	6	11
Brickfield Branch School Rent, &c.	2	2	2½
Bibles and Testaments, including the Bible for the Blind	14	3	0
Postage and Stationery	10	6	3½
Printing and Advertising	9	3	3
Christmas Tea Meeting for the Poor	9	3	10
Christmas Tea Meeting for the Blind	9	11	0
Sunday School Children's Treat	4	14	0
Schooling for Poor Children	0	17	2
Various Charities for the relief of the Poor	7	1	6
Travelling expenses, delivering Lectures, &c.	10	19	10½
Sundries	0	3	6
	£327	1	7½

Also, 108 articles of clothing to 56 cases, making a total of 1864 cases.

Balance Sheet for the year ending September, 1872.

CASH, DR.	£	s.	d.	CONTRA, CR.	£	s.	d.
To Subscriptions and Donations	361	3	7½	By last year's balance	5	2	10
„ Surplus of Expenses, Preaching, Lecturing, &c.	65	18	6	„ Cash given in relief, and paid for other purposes during the year	327	1	7½
„ Collection at Christmas Tea Meeting.........	3	11	2	„ Balance	107	19	3½
„ Poor Box at Chapel door....	9	9	5½				
„ Reports sold	0	1	0				
	£440	3	9		£440	3	9
Balance.....	£107	19	3½				

The above will give the reader an idea of the various items of expenditure in connection with the Chapel for the Destitute, which, with the exception of the amount paid for salaries, as accounted for in the preface, are much the same as they have been for several years.

The income is more than in any preceeding year, while the expenditure is less than on the three previous ones. Mr. Ashworth commenced the work with a firm conviction that God would open up his way, and send pecuniary help to any amount, or any extent that might be required, without either anniversary sermons or public collections. He believed in answers to prayer, and had good reason for so doing; and to him it was at all times, in his arduous undertakings, a great source of strength and comfort to know that hundreds throughout the land were daily remembering him and the Chapel for the Destitute in their petitions at the throne of grace. The very thought of it gave him joy; and for sixteen years, without any solicitation on his part from any human being, the necessary funds have been supplied.

From £15 6s., the first year's income, it gradually increased until it reached £440 3s. 9d.; the total amount received being upwards of £4,000, in subscriptions and donations alone; and with one or two exceptions, when the annual reports were issued, the balance was generally in Mr. Ashworth's favour. He had, notwithstanding, his times of depression in reference to pecuniary matters; hence we find the following expressions in his diary: 1865.—"Money not coming in as I did hope for the Destitute, but I wish to have faith in God." 1867.—"Feel rather depressed on account of the Destitute; everything seems low and cold. Money not coming in as formerly; my faith and love to my God requires strengthening." Such expressions were, however, rare. The principal source of income has been derived from subscriptions and donations varying from one penny to one hundred pounds, from various parts of the world. There can be no doubt the extensive circulation of "Strange Tales" increased the number of contributors, as well as his personal and valuable services. In addition to subscriptions being derived from the latter source, a considerable amount was handed over by Mr. Ashworth in the course of the year out of surplus expenses he received for lecturing, preaching, &c., as will be seen from the balance sheet, which he might justly have appropriated to his own use;

but every penny he received, beyond his railway fares or travelling expenses, was put down to the credit of the Destitute account.

The dear Rochdale friend H., who gave Mr. Ashworth the first subscription towards the Chapel for the Destitute, like many other contributors, has joined with him the church triumphant; but his family feel it an honour to continue their father's gift. A young lady in 1867 planted a Christmas tree, which yielded the first year £1 "for John Ashworth's poor people," and has gradually increased year by year, until it has produced the sum of £10 1s. The following have been selected from the Annual Reports.

"H., an egg, value 1d. The husband of this poor old woman had been confined to his bed for several weeks. I had often visited him, and thought I saw a great change in the man, spiritually. Early one morning his wife came to my door; she held in her hand an egg, and said, 'My husband died about two this morning, and I think he is gone to heaven; you have been very kind in coming so often to see him; I have brought you this egg as an expression of thanks; I have nothing else to give you, and I must give you something.'"

"From one less than Zaccheus, Luke xix. 8, £100."

"J., Bamford, 2s. There is peculiar value in this gift. It was from a young woman, long and severely afflicted. Believing her end drawing near, she requested her mother to divide the last remaining part of her savings (four shillings) betwixt myself, for my poor people, and a poor old woman residing in the neighbourhood."

"Mr. Ashworth,

"Dear Sir,—Some time ago, I read the first volume of your 'Strange Tales,' and was so much interested that I purchased several copies, so that I could lend them to others. One I sent to Peak Forest, in Derbyshire, which was eagerly *sought* after, and read by nearly all the people in the village, and was read aloud during dinner hour at one mine, bringing tears into the eyes of men (miners) unaccustomed to be impressed or moved with anything.

"I have also sent the whole of the Reports, and think much good will result from the perusal of them.

"About five weeks ago, my wife and little daughter were very ill, and I promised that if God would be pleased to restore them to good health, I would send you some money as a thank-offering. God has been so good as to give unto them their usual health, they having returned from Southport on Monday. I take this opportunity of sending you the sum of 13s., made up as follows :—

"Papa, 5s.; Mamma, 5s.; J. S., 1s. 3½d.; F., 1s. 1d.; L., 7½d.—13s.

"I should have been glad if I could have sent something more."

"Dear Brother, (in Christ,)

"It is with much pleasure, we, the following servants of God, remit you 13s. 6d., for distribution to the poor. I read one of your tracts, and I so loved you for your kindness to the suffering, that I thought I might help you a little. God, my dear Father, help and bless you! is the earnest wish and prayer of your loving and affectionate brother in Christ.

"Signed by G. A. APPLEYARD, and nine other Sailors, on board one of our war-ships, then lying at Gibraltar."

"Sir,—I read your tract, 'My Sick Friends,' last week, and it came home to me in many ways, both humbling and encouraging me. I am only just recovering, by God's great goodness, from many months' weakness and ill-health, and I find it difficult to exercise faith and patience, though my slightest wishes are gratified, and every mercy supplied. I enclose a £10 note for your sick friends who are in poverty as well as pain, and of course leave the disposal of it to yourself. I do not know your address, so send it through Morgan & Chase; and hoping you may be long spared, and much blessed in all your labours, believe me."

"Dear Sir,

"Your last report accidentally (or I should rather say providentially) fell into my hands a few days ago. The

Lord bless you in your Christ-like labour of love. Though I have never had the pleasure of seeing you in the flesh, I have repeatedly seen you in your 'Strange Tales,' and have been much affected by them. The only drawback to your admirable and simple report is a debt of £46 15s. 6d., to curtail this year's operations, and, I believe, the Lord has prompted me to send you the enclosed draft to clear it off. . . . May I ask you to pray for me, that I may be faithful to death in giving that portion of my savings that I have purposed in my heart before God? Brother, pray for me, that my faith fail not! My heavenly Father has greatly increased my power of doing good since I resolved to give systematically. May I never fall into the error of consuming it upon self. Again, I say, kindly pray for a weak brother in Christ. . . . Of course, if your debt is partially or altogether cleared off, you will appropriate the enclosed as you think best in your good work."

"Second donation from F., Prussia:

"Mr. John Ashworth,

"It is with much pleasure, my dear friend, that I enclose the promised £10 note, with the hope that it may be blessed to some poor suffering creatures. I know that the silver and gold is all the Lord's, and that He does not want any money; but I regard it as an honour and a precious privilege when He permits me to help His poor children. What a blessed thought, that we refresh Him by doing so. May you have grace and strength to continue your work. I am sorry you had the trouble of sending to the 'Revival,' as I only wished the receipt of the money to be noticed there, fearing it might never reach you from so great a distance.

"That you may be richly blessed, is the prayer of

"Your very sincere friend."

"£1, with the following letter:

"Enclosed is £1 in postage stamps, as a restitution offering to the Lord, for stealing between three and four shillings in copper from a tin contribution box, worth 3s. 6d., belonging to 'The People's Institute,' formerly held at the Public Hall, Baillie-street, about fifteen years ago.

Dear sir, if the above Institution is in existence please refund the loss with interest, with my profound sorrow and regret for the affair, and the surplus, if any, apply to your charitable Institution. If the said Institution is broken up, you can apply the whole amount to your noble charity. Dear sir, I am very thankful, that in my case judgment has been God's strange work, and mercy and love His delight, or long ago I might have been consigned to that place where hope and mercy never come. Praying that He who has kept me up till now, will do so to the day of His coming, and that His choicest blessings may rest upon your noble Institution, is the humble wish of yours,

"One plucked as a brand out of the fire."

"K., Sailor's Home, London, £1:

"Dear Sir,

"I bow my knees before my God, Maker of heaven and earth, and the Saviour of the world; I thank Him that I am able to fulfil my promise to you. You remember, perhaps, sixteen months ago you received a letter from a strange seaman; and you know I promised not to forgot you. Then I went to sea, and I have been all this time at sea; and I thank my sweet Saviour, He has been with me in storm and calm, in darkness and sunshine, and has brought me safely on shore. I have very much enjoyed reading your books, 'Strange Tales'; not only I, but many of the passengers. One gentleman told me those books were good for all classes, and had done him good. Sir, I would very much like to hear from you, and I hope that the Lord Jesus will help you in your labours. I send you £1, to be used for God's glory in your work, and for the praise of our Saviour, Jesus Christ. I pray with the whole of my heart, that God may bless you, and all what belong to you, and all your poor people."

"From the same:

"I send you, dear Master Ashworth, £2 10s., in the name of our great God and Saviour, Jesus Christ. Use this money as you think necessary in your Master's work. I have received your letter, which you wrote to me 14th June 1871, to London Sailors' Home. . . . . . .

I am now in Port Lyttleton, Canterbury province. I am going still to sea, but I get better wages here. In England I had £2 10s. per month, but I get £6 here. Thank God, I am willing to give from my heart portion of my earnings. I have much to say about God's goodness to me, sinner, but I must end this time. Please, sir, write to me. I like very much to hear from you. I have much respect for you for looking after God's poor people. May God bless you all days in your life. Amen.—Yours truly, Unworthy Seaman, J. K."

"I herewith enclose £5, to help on the good cause of proclaiming the good news to the poor, without money and without price. Though I have never had the pleasure of seeing you, yet I rejoice in being allowed the privilege of contributing a little, and what I give God always repays —how richly, even in worldly goods! That our kind heavenly Father may long spare and greatly bless you, is the earnest wish and prayer of your brother in Christ."

"In memory of a beloved sister, whom God has taken to Himself, I send you the enclosed, £1 10s. My dear sister felt a deep interest in your work, and to give your Stories to the poor whom she knew, while God gave her health and strength. She worked hard for Christ, and only a few weeks before her death, read 'My Young Ragged Friends' to us. She would have been pleased, I know, that a mite from her very small savings should be sent to you."

"Canton de Vaud, Suisse, with the following:

"A few days ago I lent the first and second series of 'Strange Tales' to a lady staying in this house. She has read them with interest, and last evening put into my hand fifty francs, requesting me to forward it to you in aid of the Chapel for the Destitute."

"I enclose a P. O. O. for 30s., part of my earnings by the sale of fancy work. Shall I be too troublesome if I ask you to spend it in four or five large type Bibles, to be given to those who would like to possess such, but cannot buy them. If this request is at all not to your mind use the money as you think right."

"I enclose a P. O. O. for 40s. towards thy feeding the

hungry and clothing the naked. I should like to know if poor Tommy Pollitt is still alive; if not, how did the poor little Christian die. Poor child! he wanted to go to Jesus. I can only wish thee God's speed in thy work of love to the ragged and distressed ones."

"£2 10s.: I hope you remember me, a poor worn-out creature, a few days over 83. I am trying to bless others, and lift up the hands that hang down, and confirm the feeble knees, in distributing tracts, &c."

"I have the pleasure to enclose you the sum of £6 for your Destitute, from our family Christmas Tree, wishing you every success in your missionary efforts among the poor."

"6s.: I enclose, dear Brother, a small token of remembrance. I will not regret it is not larger, nor give reasons why, the Lord knows and that is enough."

"4s.: Our blind friends will be expecting their Tea Party, and our young friends their poor battered clogs putting in good condition, and may eyes that are darkened and feet that are sore, have brightness and comfort and joy evermore; may Job 29 c. 11, 13 v. be your experience, and Hebrews 13 c. 20, 21 v. your daily portion."

"It is with much pleasure I elect you as steward over £10 10s. of the money our great Master has given me."

"6d.: Will you, please, accept of these six stamps for the blind; I do pity them and so does dear mother; it is a small sum, but I do hope, if God's will, it will cheer them; it is very hard to be blind, but I do hope they may have Jesus with them to comfort them."

"10s.: I have done business on the water this last thirty-three years, and this is a thank-offering to the Lord for His sparing mercies to me."

"To purchase Bibles for the blind, £30."

"Kirkby Lonsdale, on behalf of the blind, £4."

"Three stamps for a blind one, 3d."

"B. and fellow servant, £1 (two year's subscriptions)."

"I enclose £5 by cheque for your Destitute Chapel, or otherwise, as you think best, and I hope, if at any time a little money is required, and will ask me, if in my power you shall have it; I am led to this from the reading of some of your most excellent papers, some of which I have sent far away to Australia, where I hope they will be of use."

"I beg leave to enclose £10, to be employed for the benefit of the old couple mentioned in your last report, under the month of June, who have a terrible dread of the workhouse, and should like it to be administered to them in such sums as will remove that dread from their minds, and keep them comparatively comfortable."

"Enclosed I beg to hand you cheque for £50, being the amount of legacy bequeathed to you for the Destitute by the late Mr. R. H."

"I send you £20 for thy 'Sick Friends' this Christmas (1874), as I think their number has increased, and I fear some must be very poor."

Among Mr. Ashworth's many "Friends," there were none with whom he felt a deeper sympathy than his "Sick Friends," who have been for years confined to bed. To mitigate the sufferings of these poor creatures was to him a source of real joy; wherever he went he was sure to find them out. This kind donor has for several years sent a sum for distribution amongst them at Christmas. Out of the six mentioned in the narratives Nos. 1 and 2 of "My Sick Friends," only two are now alive, Naomi Taylor, Hooley Bridge, Heywood, and Elizabeth Hill, 17, Great Moor-street, Bolton. Elizabeth is sixty-seven years of age, and has been fifty-one years confined to bed. A few years ago, expecting her end was near, she asked Mr. Ashworth if he would be kind enough to conduct the service at her funeral, remarking that she had asked several ministers—the Rev. Peter McOwen, and others who had been stationed in the circuit—but that they were all dead; to which Mr. Ashworth humorously

BROADFIELD.

replied, "I had better not promise, or perhaps I shall die before you too." How strange it should be so!

Naomi has been confined to bed since 1855, has been totally blind since 1859, and is 41 years of age. She has two sisters, and a mother nearly 80, bent with rheumatism, who waits upon her with that tenderness and patience which only a mother can do. One of the sisters is also afflicted, and seldom able to work, so the support of the family is almost dependent upon the other kind sister, whose cheerful disposition and noble self-denying spirit is above all praise.

E. C., age 28—has been 14 years afflicted and 12 confined to bed. This dear child of God can only speak in a whisper, yet is very cheerful and happy; various mottoes are hung around her snow-white bed, on which her soul feeds from day to day, but she always points to one in particular, as the staff on which she leans,—"My grace is sufficient for thee."

P. R., age 65—has been 35 years afflicted, and 33 in bed.

R. S.,—54 years confined to bed.

A. B., age 20—has been 10 years afflicted and 9 in bed.

S. M., age 50—An invalid and cripple all his life.

R. T.,—12 years confined to bed.

E. E., age 40—19 years afflicted, 6 confined to bed.

E. B., age 31—12 years confined to bed.

E. McK., age 29—6 years confined to bed.

R. B., age 63—49 years afflicted, 28 years in bed, and most of that time blind.

These are a few of the cases Mr. Ashworth felt it an honour to call "My Sick Friends," and to be the medium of conveying to them from time to time a little pecuniary help gave him unspeakable pleasure; which, though comparatively small, was to them a large sum and of great value, as the following letters will show:—

"Dear Sir,—I have received your note and the money order, but if I were to try all day, I could not find words in which to express my gratitude to you for sending me part of the kind lady's Christmas gift. May God's blessing rest upon her. Many of your 'Sick Friends,' beside myself, will pray a blessing upon their unknown friend. God will hear us, I am sure. This kind gift will procure me many comforts, which, otherwise, I should have been obliged to go without; for though my dear parents do the best they can for me, they cannot do all they wish, as the constant sickness we have had in our house for the last eight years has been a sad drain upon them, yet they never seem to think me a burden, but always treat me with the same unvarying kindness. Our heavenly Father is indeed very good to me, His poor sinful child. I have proved Him in all these years of weariness and weakness to be my best friend. He never leaves me nor forsakes me. Never yet has He allowed me to want; and I believe never will. The Lord always provides for His own children; and from the bottom of my heart do I thank Him. Again I thank you for your kind gift, and praying that God's blessing may always rest upon you and your good work in Rochdale. Your's most gratefully."

"Dear Sir,—I received your kind note and the enclosed order this morning, and return you my heart-felt thanks. The severity of the weather renders it necessary that we should have fires in one's room constantly, and our kind friend's generous present will enable us to have them. I am sure my fellow-sufferers, who also enjoy the benefit of her Christian kindness, will join me in praying that God's choicest blessings may descend upon her for so tenderly caring for those who cannot help themselves. God knows I am grateful. I write lying quite flat in bed, on my left side, being unable to sit up. Yours, &c."

In a subsequent letter to myself, this dear young friend gives a touching account of Mr. Ashworth's last visit, as follows:—

"It is now two years ago this month since I saw him. The snow had been falling all morning, and I was deeply touched by his kindness in walking through it to see me; but it was just like him, was it not? He came into the room smiling, and much to my surprise refused to take the hand I held out to him. I suppose I looked puzzled at his *seeming* discourtesy, for he hastened to explain that his hand was cold, and he was afraid of giving me a chill. He then sat down by my bedside, and after telling me how long he had to stay, he began to talk to my mother and me in his own kind, sympathising manner, and after touching on very many subjects, he knelt down and prayed most sweetly. On rising he took my hand and tenderly said, 'Good bye, the Lord bless you, my child.' That is the last I saw of him, but I am looking forward to meeting him again, by and bye, in the presence of the King."

"Dear Mr. Ashworth,

"I received the P. O. O., and am very thankful to you for it, and the dear Christian lady who has sent it. I am sure many of your 'Sick Friends' will feel the benefit of it as well as myself. I hope God will still supply you with means to carry out your work and labour of love. I am very sorry to hear of your heavy affliction, and often pray for you. With regard to myself, I have been much worse this last week, and feel the cold very severely. I was 67 years last August, and I have been as you see me for 51 years; but, thank God, His grace is sufficient for me, and His strength is made perfect in my weakness, for while He afflicts with the one hand He comforts and sustains with the other. I remain your long afflicted friend, ——."

"Dear Sir,—I thankfully acknowledge the receipt of your kind letter and the P. O. O. Truly the Lord has sent it; to Him alone did I tell my need. My heart trusteth in Him, and I am helped. Bless the Lord, O my soul, and forget not all His benefits. The Lord is a good stronghold in the day of trouble, and He knoweth them that trust in

Him. I think the way in which the Lord fed His people in the wilderness is not more wonderful than the way He has provided for me during my affliction. Sir, I do feel much sympathy in your affliction. I have prayed, if it be the Lord's will, you may soon be restored to health. The Lord bless you, is the prayer of yours, &c."

"Dear and much-valued Friend,

"I received this morning your very kind note and the enclosed order, and I know not how to express my gratitude to God, and to you, and the dear lady, for such great kindness to one so unworthy. I was melted to tears at such a large sum. I can now have a warm blanket, and many other necessaries. Bless the Lord, O my soul. I shall pray to the Lord to bless that dear lady. I trust He will richly reward her and you for all your kindness to the poor and needy. With much sympathy and humble love, I remain your suffering but happy sister in the Lord Jesus. ———."

"Dear Sir,—I received your kind letter and the order. I return very many thanks for the gift you sent me. My head is almost overjoyed that you are so kind to send me such a gift. I feel I cannot express to you how thankful I am for your kindness to me. I do pray from my heart that the Lord will double it to you. I believe He will. I cried for joy when I received it; to think that I had such a dear friend as you are to me, bless the Lord. My dear father and mother return you great many thanks for the gift you sent their poor afflicted child. From yours, &c."

The other sick persons express themselves in a similar way, and they all feel that they have lost a friend, but I trust they will not be forgotten. The Lord still lives.

I would, however, add a few extracts from a letter recently received from one whose acquaintance he made while in America, and in whom he felt a deep interest.

"My dear Friend,—I well remember the visit of that man of God, John Ashworth. I have always remembered him with gratitude, and it filled me with sadness to hear of his death; for I felt I had met with a personal loss. He called in company with Mr. M—, and at once expressed much interest in me, telling me that he had visited a great many invalids in different places, and giving me some anecdotes about them. I then asked him if he could sing, and he stepped to the foot of the bed, and repeated in a way I shall never forget Deut. xxxiii. 25, 'Thy shoes shall be iron and brass; and, as thy days, so shall thy strength be.' Then he sung, in a low sweet voice, the hymn, 'Jesus lover of my soul.' It made a great impression on me. I always get people to sing when they come to see me; but I never heard that hymn sung so beautifully before. After a moment's pause, he came and knelt by my bedside, and offered a fervent prayer for me. He asked for my name. I told him that everybody in sympathy called me 'Aunt Ruth,' but my real name is R. W. B. He wished to know what to call my cottage. I told him, 'The Cottage on the Hill-side.' He said, 'I will correspond with you when I get home, and send you some books.' As I was expressing my thanks for some little articles which had just been sent me, he turned to Mr. M—, and said, 'If this poor sufferer can feel so much gratitude, how thankful ought I to be? This is a lesson for me.' We parted, feeling that though the sea might roll between us, we were one in Christ Jesus. I have never ceased to think of and pray for him, and hoped to get a line from him. The sad news of his death reached me through a newspaper before your letter came. I am glad to learn that he did remember me; and I thank you most heartily for your words of love, and for the gift you enclosed. I was born on the 12th of May, 1812; and, when seven years old, had a severe fall, which injured my spine. I recovered partially from this; but, at the age of fourteen, I had a more serious fall, which left me completely helpless. Ever since I have been an invalid. For the last twenty-eight years I have lain upon my bed, unable to move anything, except my right hand, and for the most of the time entirely blind. I have only been lifted from my bed once a year: sometimes only once in two years. Time would fail me to tell of all the different diseases from which I have suffered; but you will be more interested to know I have learned, in whatsoever state I am, therewith to be content. Jesus is my refuge; and He makes my humble cottage often seem like the gate of heaven. For many years I have had neither father nor mother, brothers nor sisters. My father's family was a large one; but, through the wonderful providence of God, I have survived them all. It was very hard for me to lose them one after another, but the Lord Jesus has filled all the gaps which His hand has made. 'When my father and mother forsook me, then the Lord took me up.' Although I have no means of support, yet God takes care of me so sweetly that I can rest the future in His hands with confidence. I am a member of the fourth Congregational church, and they come and partake of the Communion with me; and these seasons are among the brightest of my earthly pilgrimage. It fills my soul with glory to think of the land where the 'lame man shall leap as an hart.' Hoping to meet you there, and sing the praises of God with dear brother Ashworth, and many others who have gone before, I remain, yours, &c. ———."

Many of Mr. Ashworth's "Sick Friends" have been introduced by him to each other by name, and have commenced and kept up an interesting and profitable correspondence between themselves, and to some of them it is a great pleasure to do so.

CHAPEL FOR THE DESTITUTE.

FIFTEENTH REPORT.

"Our Agencies consist of one Missionary and two Bible-women, by whom the Word of God has been circulated and read, the poor and the sick visited, and our operations carried on; also a female is at present engaged in teaching the blind to read the embossed type on Moon's System, who is herself deprived of sight.

"The services at the Chapel, and the Adult Sunday Class under the superintendence of the "Friends," afford continued cause of gratitude, the attendance being good at both, and we are thankful, 'To the poor the Gospel is preached.'

"In the Mission-room, School-lane, the work prospers amidst much that is discouraging. In many of the Sunday scholars there is a marked improvement. The Mothers' Meeting is not so well attended as we wish it to be, but the other services are encouraging.

"To all our friends, who, with their contributions, have expressed, by letter, their earnest prayer to God, and deep, heartfelt sympathy on behalf of our work, I am truly grateful, and would say again, Not unto me, but to God be all the glory.

"JOHN ASHWORTH.

"BROADFIELD, OCT. 1, 1873."

"Two shillings and sevenpence for bread, butter, sugar, and tea, and an order for a cwt. of coke at the gas works, to a family in a very destitute condition, without food or fire in the house. In many cases we find it better to give relief in this way as we often discover they 'spend their money for that which is not bread.' A clean looking tidy woman, with an infant at her breast, came to me the other morning, with tears in her eyes, and such a pitiful story, that I gave her a shilling, and at night one of our visitors found her seated by her fire quite drunk, smoking her pipe."

"Threepence to a case at the door. In the course of the year, hundreds come to my door, in every possible conceivable condition of distress, either in body, mind, or circumstances. This young man was a weaver by trade, although in destitution, had evidently not long been accustomed to the life of a tramp. In a few Sabbaths following, at the close of the evening service, a well-dressed young man was waiting to see the preacher who was supplying my place, being from home. On asking what he wanted, he said he had come to thank Mr. Ashworth for what he had done for him. And on again enquiring what he had done, he said, 'I went to his door in a very distressed condition, and he gave me threepence for my lodgings, and some good advice; and I took it. I went to Bury, and got work the next day, got my clothes out of pawn; and I hope never to get into the same state again; and tell him, I am much obliged to him.'"

Such cases as the latter, that were found, like the Samaritan, returning to give thanks, were not of very frequent occurrence. Although he had the tenderest sympathy with suffering of every description, yet when he discovered that the applicant for relief was perhaps some young *scape-grace* with a good trade, who had been reduced to poverty through idleness and intemperance, he was unsparing in his rebukes, and, as some thought, rather too severe. Another similar case was the man who, as Mr. Ashworth stood on his door-step, pleaded with a pitiable look, and in a whining tone, "Please sir, will you relieve me?" With his keen discernment of character, he detected him at once, and asked the man to exchange places with him, and imitating his gestures and tone, he stood before him, whining, "Please sir, will you relieve me? Please sir, will you relieve me?" and said, "How do I look?" The man coloured up, and would have made his escape, but Mr. Ashworth then spoke kindly to him, and told him that if he had the spirit of a midge, a young man like him, with a good trade in his fingers (a cabinet-maker), would be ashamed to go about whining at people's doors in that way; he advised him to look up into God's clear blue sky, shake himself, settle down, and be respectable, gave him sixpence, and did not expect to see him again. Some months after, the same man, but very different in appearance and manners, called at Broadfield to thank Mr. Ashworth, gave him a subscription towards the Chapel for the Destitute, and hoped he would serve all such in the same way as he served him. The man said he was so vexed, that he could have thrown the sixpence in his face; but he was made so ashamed of himself that he resolved to take his advice; he went to a neighbouring town, got work, and now, he said, he had two suits of good clothes, and a few pounds in his pocket.

From no class did Mr. Ashworth receive more blessings than from the Irish, that is, those to whom he gave any relief; he used to say he would rather have their blessings than their curses. One good old woman wished that "the Lord would reward him, and that he might have a feather bed in heaven."

The year 1873 was commenced with the usual reflections, and renewed consecration to the service of God.

Feb. 3. This day a sale of property, taken by the bailiffs for a school rate, which many Nonconformists refused to pay, took place in the lecture-room of the Public Hall.

Feb. 4. An indignation meeting in the Public Hall to denounce the distraint for goods, and petition for the repeal of the 25th clause of the Education Act. The place packed full with an earnest audience; resolutions all carried with a vengeance.

Feb. 14. Mr. —, once a minister in the Methodist church, called in great trouble. Drink the cause. Gave him three shillings, and an old shirt.

March 7. Leamington; spoke in Victoria Hall to mothers at 7-30; spoke at midnight meeting from 11 to 1 to 50 girls; seven went into the "Home."

March 8. Visited the "Home"; this is truly a "House of Mercy"; left for Bristol.

March 9. Bristol; Milk-street trust sermons. *Strange attack in my throat.*

March 10. Bristol; received intelligence that my daughter is much worse. Lord, help my suffering child; I know

Thou wilt. Lectured in Broadmead rooms to two thousand.

March 11. Bristol; met the teachers and 800 mothers at 2-30; the "Friends" adult classes at 6; and lectured in Milk-street chapel at 7.

March 12. Bristol; went to the Orphan Houses; had an interview with Mr. Müller: 2,050 children in five houses; *thoughts;* lectured in the Broadmead rooms on "Young Women," &c.; place packed full.

March 13. Returned from Bristol; found Mary Jane very weak, but quite resigned; prayed with her, and greatly pleased to see her deep joy.

March 14. Writing all day; feel tired, but happy in the love of God, though in sorrow for my child.

March 15. Spent several hours with my sick child; read our Lord's last prayer, and the 21st of Revelation, and prayed. Lord, look in mercy, and help in this trying moment.

March 16. Mary still sinking; very happy; requested me to sing, "There is a happy land."

March 17. Cannot write; cannot think. Death is evidently coming to take my dear and only daughter. She now wishes to depart. Seems at times to be on the verge of heaven. She quoted many passages, and the lines, "She has found her home in heaven."

March 20. Took my place this evening beside my sick child at 9, until 9 in the morning; a night of great suffering; once heaven seemed opened; her language was truly sublime.

March 21. Again watching all night. This morning, about 3, my dear suffering child spoke to me her last words, "God is good; all is right, father; all is right! Jesus is my Jesus!" Then fell into a deep sleep, and at 8-30 breathed her last. She has found her home in heaven. Lord, help me to say, Thy will be done.

March 22. Feel this day dumb before the Lord; have no words, nor any purpose—helpless, silent, and sad. To lose an only daughter, good and affectionate, *who never gave me any trouble.* She was converted when about seven,

Had a powerful intellect, and her counsel was often valuable to me.

March 24. This is indeed a week of sore affliction. Six in paradise; no doubt of this. "The Lord gave, and the Lord taketh away: blessed be the name of the Lord."

March 25. This day interred my dear child in the Rochdale cemetery; but she will have a glorious resurrection. Oh, Thou victor over death and the grave, sustain me, help me!

March 27. Cannot bring my mind to any mental action or purpose. I hope I am not rebellious. Do wish to say, Thy will be done. Oh, my God, restore me to Thy sweet love, and help me to feel at peace.

March 28. Still prostrate, but resigned; yes, resigned.

June 4. Class-meeting. For thirty years I have only missed twice when able to go.

June 6. Whit-Friday; walked with Baillie-street school; went to our Ragged school children in the field near Hollingworth; the dear poor children very happy.

July 30. The Annual Assembly of the Free Methodist churches meet to-day in Baillie-street chapel, Rochdale; attended service; Mr. Hubbard the preacher; took my dear friend G. L. Ashworth to a seat in his old pew.

July 31. This day Matthew Henry called on me with his father. He is the subject of the tract, "Red Lamp," No. 51. He returns from America a minister of the Gospel and the Grand Worthy Chief Templar of Illinois. Father and son knelt at the *form** in my study and prayed.

Mr. Ashworth mentioned how deeply affecting this meeting was. The father rejoicing over the return of his prodigal child, and the son rejoicing that he was again received into the arms of his loving parent and of his God; that he who in July, 1867, called at that house a poor lost outcast, was now found sitting at the feet of Jesus, clothed and in his right mind.

* The form at which they knelt was the one on which the boy with the wool-sheet pinafore sat in Bagslate Sunday-school.

August 1. One of the carvers at the Annual Assembly's dinner. No beer provided by the committee. Attended morning and evening services at 7.

August 2. Man sold his grave with wife in it for *drink*.

August 6. Mr. G. L. Ashworth died this morning.

From August 8th to 12th Mr. Ashworth visited the Isle of Man for the purpose of conducting services on behalf of the Seamen's Bethel and Town Mission. He had a very cold, wet, rough passage in going, and seems to have suffered in consequence. He had a serious attack of shivering during the night, and said, he really felt he was dying, and could not tell what to do, not wishing to disturb the people in the house. He lighted the candle, and placing two chairs back to back in his bed-room, he jumped over and over these chairs till he worked himself into a perspiration from head to foot, went to bed, left the fine mould candle to burn to its socket, for he durst not get up to put it out. Next morning (Sunday) he was down at breakfast, as if nothing had happened, conducted services in the drill-room, which was packed, and lectured on the Monday evening.

August 26. Chairman of temperance meeting in Public Hall. Lecture by Matthew Henry Pogson; produced a good impression.

CHAPTER XIII.

VISIT TO AMERICA (1873).

WE now come to another very interesting period in Mr. Ashworth's life, *viz.*, his visit to America. Now that he had been to Jerusalem and the East, he felt a great desire, and was only waiting a favourable opportunity, to visit the "New World," and the land of the Pilgrim Fathers.

During the sittings of the Assembly in Baillie-street chapel, Rochdale, in connection with the United Methodist Free churches, the following resolution, recommended by the Connexional committee, was passed :—

"That the President and Mr. John Ashworth, Author of 'Strange Tales,' be kindly requested to represent the churches of our Connexion in the Conference of Evangelical Christians to be held in New York in October next.

"JOHN ADCOCK, President.
"ANTHONY HOLLIDAY, Connex. Sec.
"JOSEPH GARSIDE, Correspond. Sec.
"HENRY MAWSON, Connex. Treas."

After due consideration, Mr. Ashworth decided to avail himself of the honour thus conferred upon him by the Assembly, and made preparations for his departure. He was not, however, accompanied by the President, in consequence of family affliction.

Mr. Ashworth, having no personal acquaintance with any one in New York, asked his fellow-townsman, Mr. John Bright, for a letter of introduction to some of the "Friends" in that city, and received the following reply.

"Rochdale, Sept. 9th, 1873.

"Dear Sir,

"Unfortunately I have no acquaintance among 'Friends' in America to whom I can properly give you letters of introduction. My acquaintances there are, in the main, political, and I abstain from giving letters to them, knowing how pressing their engagements are.

"*You* will require no letters of introduction, for few men, not American, are better known than yourself among religious circles in the States.

"You will, doubtless, find many 'Friends' and others glad to welcome you, as the Author of 'Strange Tales,' and as a zealous worker in the field of Christian labour.

"I wish you a pleasant voyage, and that good to yourself and others may come from your visit to America.

"If this note can be of any service to you, pray make use of it, with any with whom my name may have any interest.

"Mr. John Ashworth, "I am,
"Broadfield, "Always sincerely yours,
"Rochdale. "JOHN BRIGHT."

About this time the Good Templar organization was spreading rapidly, and creating a great sensation all over the United Kingdom; and although Mr. Ashworth was not carried away with its novelties like many, or even favourable to its ritualism or regalia, yet at the urgent request of many of his temperance friends, who were anxious that he should join the Order before going to America, he consented to do so; hence he records, "Sept. 13th. Made a Good Templar this evening at Ebenezer Lodge. Took the three degrees by special dispensation."

Mr. Ashworth received letters from J. W. Kirton, G.W.S., Peter Spence, D.D., and others, commending him to the fraternal regard of all members of the Order in America, praying that the Divine blessing might be given to his visit to the West.

On Sunday, Sept. 14th, Mr. Ashworth visited the schools under his care, and took farewell of his people at the Destitute in the evening. The chapel was quite full, and many hearty amens went up with his prayers, that He whom the winds and seas obey would be with him, and bring him safe home again.

Having received his proper credentials from the London agent of the Evangelical Alliance, certifying his appointment as a delegate to the Conference, and secured his passage in the steam ship *Minnesota*, one of the Guion line of packets, Thomas F. Freeman, captain, he sailed for New York on Wednesday, September 17th. A young friend and myself accompanied him on board the vessel, which was lying some distance off in the river. After surveying the cabin and the little room he was to occupy the next ten or twelve days, the time came when we had to say farewell. His eyes moistened; there was no smile, but a significant warm grasp of the hand, which indicated a full heart. He was evidently thinking of those he had left behind, and weighing over in his mind the probabilities of the future.

Mr. Ashworth was preparing for publication an account of his "Rambles in the New World," but unfortunately had only completed the first chapter when his life-work was done, which contains little more than the voyage out, and is as follows.

RAMBLES IN THE NEW WORLD.

"Having seen our luggage safe on board the tender, the little steamer soon left the landing stage, and was splashing her way through the busy craft on the Mersey, until we knocked our heads against the ribs of the great leviathan that was to be our ocean home. Climbing the side ladder and receiving our precious property, we stowed it away in our state-room, and returned to the deck to witness the exciting scenes always connected with lifting the anchor of one of the line of packets or emigrant ships outward bound. On our ship there was no exception to the deafening sounds; to the bustle, shouting, laughing, and crying. Of course the doctor, the agent of the company, and the government inspector were present to perform their routine of work. The one hundred and twenty officers and crew stood bolt upright, answering to the call of their names, and their strange and comical names were not more strange or comical than their various faces. The prim saloon waiters, with their blue silk vests and lace caps, were smart as footmen; the glittering trimming on the caps and coats of the officers made them very important men, rather a contrast to Jack in his canvas trousers and slop. What a difference dress makes to-be-sure. Tailors and dress-makers are very important people; they ought to be recorded as the fifth estate.

"The click and rattle of the steam winch, slowly dragging up the huge cable, suddenly ceased; the work was done, and the deafening roar of the surplus steam was the signal for farewells and partings; but a signal from the shore told us there was another tender coming out. We all gazed on the approaching full-freighted craft, and found the cargo to consist of about one hundred additional German and Italian emigrants. Up the ladder and over the bulwarks they came pell-mell, loaded with cases, wallets, straw beds, kettles, and children,—about two dozen of the little brown-faced darlings were hoisted up and lowered down by their clothes, arms, or legs, and took the topsy-turvy tumbling very patiently; they had no doubt got used to it. A smuggled pet dog came tumbling out of a hole in one of the bags, barking with all his might to the disgust of the owner, and the merry shouts of the spectators.

"Again we were ready; the captain's voice sounding from the bridge, gave a peremptory order for friends and visitors to move off to the tender. Then came embracing and shaking of hands for the fourth or fifth time; the great screw plunged her fans into the turbid waters, and screwed us off towards the shores of America, amidst shouts, waving of hats, and blinding tears. As we glided away towers, domes, and docks of the world's greatest sea mart gradually dissolved in the distance, Waterloo and New Brighton being last in the scene. Night closed around us, hiding from our straining sight the cliffs of old England; we then turned in to a late dinner.

"There is something that calls forth restless thought and feeling at the first meal on board one of these steamships. At this sitting down we found our saloon passengers consisted of a goodly company of blushing, timid ladies, some of them with pale faces and swollen eyes; also about twenty civil but quiet gentlemen took their seats in silence. Furtive glances were the strongest marked feature of this new assembly of strangers; and as soon as propriety would allow, we one by one found our way to our allotted state-rooms, there to reflect over bags, boxes, and the homes and friends we were leaving behind, also on our coming prospects. One began to have gloomy thoughts about the lost *President*, the *Pacific*, the *Arctic*, the *City of Boston*, and the *Atlantic*, wondering if it was true that for every fifty miles ere we touched at Sandy Hook we should sail over the deep deep sepulchres of at least sixty foundered vessels. Then came the brighter thought, that these burials at sea are a very small proportion to those crossing the waves in safety; so we settled not to be drowned. It was well we had so settled, for the heavings of the ship, the noise of the heavy steps on deck, the quick commands of the captain, and loud call of the boatswain, told us there was busy work on hand.

"A slight subsiding of the storm and the lifting of the clouds the following day, revealed the coasts of Ireland,—

> The hills of Tara,
> Once the royal, regal home
> Of Ireland's ancient kings.

But as night came on heavy seas baptised our bowsprit, and here we swung round into Queenstown harbour, to give, to take, and to start again.

"We had formed some conception of the probabilities awaiting us; but we were outward bound, and bound to go outward. We therefore left behind us the sinking banks of Cape Clear, plunged into one of the world's widest and greatest seas, with the wind right in our teeth. On returning to my berth on the evening of the third day, I felt my spirits rather subsiding; rising foam looked in through the port-holes, howling winds yelled fearfully through the rigging, and all things above and below appeared either horizontal or perpendicular, amidst the banging of doors and smashing of crockery. I crept head foremost into my sleeping crib, not forgetting the packing, and began not to sleep, but to a swinging study. Here I am, thought I; and here I wish I wasn't. At that moment two leather trunks came dashing from under my sofa and banging against my berth; back they went, taking my boots with them this time, and back they came again. The packing that was to keep my body from knocking against the sides gave way, and began to race about with my trunks and boots; and to finish up with, out I came, very reluctantly, on the top of all. Being the only occupant of the state room, I had no one to speak to, but I talked to myself, and said, 'This is more than I bargained for'; and gathering myself up, began to re-dress as I sat on the restless floor. This finished, after several attempts I managed by a desperate effort to reach the saloon, which was all in darkness, with the exception of one solitary candle, near which sat the solitary night watch. On seeing me he cried out,

"'Do you want anything, sir?'

"'Yes, I want the ship to behave better,' I replied.

"'I cannot assist you in that matter, sir.'

"'Can you show me the way to Mr. Gibson, the

head engineer?' I asked; 'I must see what he can do.'

"With a curious smile he led the way, I walking after him like a drunken man, or like a man playing at blind-man's buff, through avenues of ropes, chains, and moaning, groaning steerage passengers, some of whom, like myself, had turned out, and seemed inconsolable. On, still on, until we found the engineer, who was anxiously watching his machinery. On looking twice at me, he exclaimed,

"'Is that you? whatever brings you here?'

"'Well, sir, I never object to change my quarters when I can mend myself, and I think the segment of the circle will be rather less amongst the bunkers than where I come from.'

"'But do you wish to go down amongst the firemen and stokers?'

"'I do, and work amongst them; for busy hands forget trouble.'

"'Then you shall have your desire,' he replied, with a laugh, at the same time catching hold of an iron rail to which I was clinging to prevent our being pitched on the top of one another. Down the metal steps we went; the flashing flames from the fierce furnaces revealing to the glance the half-naked, perspiring, sooty stokers. Was it Pandemonium? Was it Dante's Inferno? That it was real, was a sultry burning fact. The *boggles* greeted me with a stare, and when I took hold of a shovel to heap more fuel on the fire, knowing winks, and a new-made chalk-line told me I was a prisoner, that would require a silver key for my redemption. My labours in those lower regions, *for hot reasons*, were short. Ascending one story, we obtained lights, and explored the length of the ponderous shaft, travelling through the iron tunnel up to the great screw, then returned through endless pairs of still moaning steerage passengers back to my ungovernable state-room; tried the sofa, but was rolled off; strapped myself fast to the brass ring of the port-hole light, pulled rugs and coat over me, and in the darkness sadly wished for day.

"I believe in the Apostle's Creed, and something more. I believe in a God of infinite love and boundless goodness, whose tender mercies are over all His works; that the earth is full of His glory, and so is the great wide sea; that He gives us all things richly to enjoy. I believe in two heavens, one here and one hereafter—heaven on the way to heaven. I believe that God loves them that love Him; that He knows their hearts, sees their thoughts, accepts their praises, and hears their prayers. I believe in His omnipresence; and I presume that as the sun sheds his beams of light, and exerts a power over the stars and planets of our solar system, so the great Creator gives His presence throughout the whole universe, but more especially to those that honour and serve Him, to comfort, guide, direct, and bless. If, as Socrates said, what I believe be true, it is good to have believed it; and if it be not true, I shall have the happiness of having believed it. But the reader may say—if I have any reader—'Why bother me with your creed? who cares for your creed; go on with your storm story.' Well, I will; but you will see what my creed has to do with the storm.

"Morning came, as mornings always do (and it is a blessing that they do); the dull rays of light came creeping through the bull's eye of my cabin, revealing considerable confusion. I unstrapped myself, washed my face with one hand, making good use of the other; squared matters up a little, sat down on my sofa, strapping myself fast again; then took my companion, a companion which had travelled with me through *France*, *Switzerland*, *Italy*, *Egypt*, *Canaan*, *Greece*, *Turkey*, *Hungary*, and *Austria*, and from that companion read words that I had often read before, but never so well understood:

> 'They that go down to the sea in ships, that do business in great waters;
>
> 'These see the works of the Lord, and His wonders in the deep,' &c. Psalm cvii.

Sublime, beautiful, true, but never realised on land. No; we must be on the deep; on the depths where the stormy winds lift up the ponderous waves; be at our wits' end. Oh the grandeur, the wonders, the terrors of the great deep. How dumb it strikes the beholder; how awful. Such were my thoughts, and such my feelings, as the liquid moving hills of the heaving, rising, falling ocean, rocked and rolled our great iron ship like a feather.

"Many and rapid thoughts passed through my busy brain. One of them was precious, as it adapted itself to present circumstances. Previous to leaving home, I had gone to bid good-by to our dear, poor children in the school, who sang for me. In speaking to them, I said, 'Well now, my little folks, I am leaving you for several months, going to America, going over three thousand miles of water; will you think of me and pray for me, that

God will take me safe there and bring me safe back?' They began to nod assent on all sides. One little fellow said, 'I'll pray for you every day.'

"'What will you say when you pray, my boy?'

"'I will say, Lord, do not let John Ashworth be drowned.'

"'And so will we! and so will we!' was promised by many dozens of my young friends.

"Now, I believe in children's prayers. There is no circumlocution in their prayers; they are simple, sincere, and honest, and God hears such prayers; and I was glad to have the children's prayers. I knew, also, that many of my own people and Christian friends were making my mission and journey a subject for petition, and this, like the children, every day. These facts, to some extent, sustained and pleased me; for we like to be cared for.

"I had no destroying, agonising fears about being drowned; the probability of this had been calmly considered before leaving my home. I had no fear of death; the sting of death is sin; the sin being pardoned, the sting is gone; but there is both an instinctive and rational clinging to life, and this is a wise arrangement, that makes life precious.

"The saloon breakfast bell rung; two managed to crawl to the table, but instantly retired again, and so another day was spent in bed or in undress, in fasting and groans. But on the evening of that day the wind and waves greatly abated, the clouds disappeared; we had a promise of better days, and a night of quiet rest. What a mercy.

"The following morning found us all at the breakfast table, not one being absent; and most seemed disposed to be social, friendly, and obliging. After the repast, while walking or lounging on deck under a bright sun and clear sky, our spirits became exuberant, and we told to each other all about ourselves, and became quite one family. We were from many nations, of many persuasions, and, socially speaking, of almost all gradations; but there evidently was the greatest variety among the ladies, which was most prominently seen at the dinner table. Beginning at the eldest, she seemed disposed to superintend us all. This lady, once seen, could scarcely be forgotten: tall, fearfully thin, long neck and face, large dull glazed eyes, that never seemed to wink or close. She spoke distinct, slow, and with authority; always commencing her observations with, 'Well, I guess.' Near to her sat a little, pale, demure lady, who required great attention. She looked eagerly at the bill of fare, and tasted most of the good things. On deck she had a special easy chair and foot-stool, with large scarlet and black rugs. Her books were elegantly bound, often opened, but little read; and her looks said, 'Please keep your distance.' Opposite to her was a lady of great embellishment; part of her front hair was cut, and hung on her forehead like a short, red curtain, the rest being pulled violently back. She walked with what is called the Grecian bend, as if afflicted with a spinal curve, but it was the height of fashion. She told us 'she had given thirty dollars for the making of one of her dresses.'

"'Well, I guess,' said the old lady with the glazed eyes, 'that was a good price; did you ever sit down in it?' This observation brought a burst of laughter, in which she heartily joined. The next two ladies were mother and daughter, who were running up an extra account at our mid-ship's hotel. The next was a talkative lady about ships, ports, and distant lands. These three always disappeared during service or the reading of Scriptures. The rest of the female passengers were quiet, retiring, unobtrusive ladies. One of them had a little white woolly pet-dog, with a blue ribbon round its neck; the passage money for this pet was three guineas, but she feared 'if she had not brought it with her, the dear little thing would have fretted itself to death.'

"The gentlemen consisted of a professional singer and ventriloquist, a newspaper correspondent, a land speculator, a merchant, a cattle dealer, a missionary, three delegates to the world's Evangelical Alliance to be held in New York, one from Belgium, one from Geneva, and one from Rochdale. The rest were travellers returning home, or going to visit the 'New World.'

"The day being fine and warm, all gathered on deck; the ladies promenading, and the gentlemen smoking, chatting, or playing shuffle-board. The genial weather had also brought up hundreds of other passengers from the steerage, who squatted down on deck in groups according to their nationality: Italian, German, French, Irish, a few English and fewer Scotch. About a dozen of the Italian women were huddled together, minutely exploring each other's heads, which seemed to be a favourite occupation.

"Having provided myself with cakes, nuts, and lollipops, I took a quiet walk amongst the crowd, and soon made friends with all the children. I had also tracts, and small books, being portions of Scripture, for those that wished them.

"Two men from Derbyshire, who seemed to have suffered from sea-sickness, refused the books, but said with a queer smile they would like about four ounces of Cheshire cheese. I instantly furnished them with four ounces each, which they greedily devoured, and we became quite friendly.

"The sky was grand to-day, and as the evening drew nigh, not a cloud or speck appeared.

> "The grand red orb
> Descending, cast his fiery rays across
> The quivering dazzling deep, leaving in his wake
> A golden pathway o'er the wide expanse ;
> And, as he sunk beneath the glittering waves,
> Shot up his bright and glorious beams to the
> Vast heavens, revealing to the silent
> Wondering gaze extended glorious plain, of
> Amber, purple, blue, and burnished gold,
> That seem'd so many placed mansions
> Near the great white throne.

"Such days as this on sea suggest thoughts and emotions exalted and sublime, and open out to the mind expanded ideas seldom realised on land. After all, the peradventures of an ocean journey are well worth the risk.

"A calm night, and a night of quiet rest, was again followed by a bright, lovely, sweet morning. That morning was the Sabbath, and Captain Freeman came to remind me of our contract the previous night, that I would preach in the saloon at half-past ten. At a quarter-past ten the poop-bell began to call the worshippers from all parts of the ship; fifty-six seamen, including half the officers, steerage and saloon passengers, had all gathered before the bell ceased, and constituted a large congregation. The chief engineer conducted the singing, the captain read the prayers, and, by request, I preached.

"Three of the saloon and many of the steerage passengers kept aloof from the service, being taught by their priests never to attend Protestant worship, under pains and penalties; but they could dance, play at cards and other games on the Lord's Day, which they did to a painful extent, rendering the blessed Sabbath a day of sensual indulgence and dissipation.

"On the evening of the same day I passed through three companies of Romish card players and dancers, seeking the steward of the steerage. On finding him, I expressed my astonishment at this open defiance of God's laws. He beckoned me into his little box on the forecastle, requesting me to be seated, and said,—

"'Have you talked with the captain about it?'

"'Yes, I have.'

"'And what does he say?' Informing him what the captain said, he replied, 'I can confirm all he says and much more, for I come in contact with thousands of Catholic emigrants, and I have found it positively dangerous to either offer them a tract, or speak to them about the Bible. I will relate to you an illustration, which I am not likely to forget.

"'The office I now hold on the *Minnesota*, I held on board the unfortunate steamship *Atlantic*, which was wrecked on the shores of Nova Scotia on the morning of April 1st this year. We had a crew of one hundred and twenty officers and men, thirty-five saloon and seven hundred and eighty steerage passengers: amongst the latter were many emigrants from Devon, Cornwall, and other English counties, but more from Ireland. Judging from their hymn books I thought many of the Cornish men dissenters; they frequently gathered in groups to read the Scriptures, and sometimes for singing and prayer; but they had to encounter storms of abuse from their Catholic neighbours, who would crow like cocks, scream like cats, roar like bulls, or bark like dogs, and sometimes throw their mess-cans or other missiles at them. To screen them from these insults as much as possible, I divided their berths, placing the mockers on the larboard, and the mocked on the starboard side of the ship. The night of the wreck was a bitter cold frosty night; the officers and firemen, thinking they would be short of coal, determined to run for Halifax instead of New York; but they got out of their reckoning. All the women had retired to rest, except the ladies who were in the captain's state room. Crash, crash, and again crash went the ship, grinding her keel on the sharp jagged rocks; down in deep water went the stern, and instantly drowned the three hundred women and children. The larboard side also went down into a deep creek betwixt the rocks, sinking all on that side beneath the surging waves. The mockers were drowned to a man; but the praying, singing, Bible-reading men, being on the other side, were saved.'

"'You seem to think it was a judgment on these Bible scorners and mockers?'

"'I have thought so,' he replied.

"No doubt it is very sad, but it is not wise to judge. Our Saviour, when speaking to the Jews *about* these things said, 'Think ye that those eighteen on whom the tower of Siloam fell and slew them, were sinners above all men that dwelt in Jerusalem? I tell you nay.' We may fill up the measure of our iniquities, and have no room left for repentance, for God's Spirit will not always strive with man; yet it is well not to judge.

"'How many were saved in all?' I asked.

"'The females all perished; two ladies, and the only two I saw, one died of cold while clinging to the ropes, and the other fell from the deck and was washed on shore. I saw them both on the beach stiff and dead. Out of nine hundred and thirty-five souls on board, six hundred and forty perished.'

"In the evening, my co-delegates to the Conference from Geneva and Brussels, conducted service in the forecastle to all their countrymen and women that would attend, to the evident mortification of the dancers and card players.

"There was also another scene on board this day that could not be witnessed without mingled feelings. The French children, boys and girls, gathered in a circle on the quarter-deck, and began to sing, not only their popular national airs, but songs descriptive of their late terrible war with Germany, and their sufferings during the siege, in the chorus of which the children's parents joined. The following is the English of one of the songs:

"'The bravest soldiers of France have fallen,
The earth has closed o'er the glorious dead;
O'er their graves the herb puts forth its flowers;
Heroes, martyrs, we will watch over them;
Sleep in peace, till the day of hope,
When the clarions shall sound triumphant,
And France shall then avenge her children.'

It was pitiable to see these dear innocent children trained in the miserable spirit of war, who may one day (like their fathers) reap a harvest of tears and blood.

"Those who have crossed the seas will know that various inventions are devised for mutual entertainment and amusement in songs, riddles, recitations, tale telling, &c. I here give the tales of one evening; the captain's first.

"'An English man of war was anchored in Port Royal, Jamaica; several of the crew, according to rotation, were allowed to go on shore. An old planter, hearing the screaming of his fowls, ran out to see what was the matter, and found one of the tars wringing their necks. The thief seeing the planter, took to his heels, but not before he was seen to have only one eye. The enraged owner of the fowls went down to the commander to complain of the theft, vowing vengeance on the one-eyed Jack, and insisted going on board to detect the villain. All hands were piped on deck for inspection, and all had heard of the scrape which their one-eyed ship-mate had got into. As they came on deck and stood before the planter, to his utter astonishment every man had one eye shut; he gave up the search and bolted from the ship, declaring he never saw a crew like that in all his life, for they had only one eye apiece.'

"The next story was from the reporter, about the old clerk of a country church, who was passionately fond of his little fiddle. He one day said to *the minister*, 'I think, sir, that the two lines,

'O may my heart in tune be found,
Like David's harp of solemn sound,'

might be much more suitable if rendered,

'O may my heart be tuned within,
Like David's sacred violin.'

To which the minister gravely replied, might it not be still better rendered, and say,

'O may my heart go diddle, diddle,
Like David's little fiddle, fiddle.'

The old clerk was content to let the hymn alone; and is an example to others who would try to mend many of our noble hymns."

CHAPTER XIV.

RAMBLES IN THE NEW WORLD (CONTINUED).

"DURING one of the fine days, our captain entertained us by sending out a current indicator. This consisted of two boards about six feet long, fixed together in the form of a cross; in the centre was a strong glass bottle, containing a document signed by the captain, myself, and several others, with the date, name of the ship, latitude and longitude; with a letter requesting the finder to forward the bottle to the office at Liverpool. On the indicator was also placed a small red flag, and about two pounds of pork for the birds. To witness the launching of this, and to watch the red flag with our glasses, till it was lost in the distance, was interesting. Some of those indicators have floated for years, and been found on the coasts of Lapland, Cornwall, New South Wales, &c.

"Our captain was a man of about sixty-two years of age, and looked like a captain. For forty-nine years he had been battling with the waves, and during a great part of that time a commander—a post for which he seemed well qualified; kind, courteous, affable, yet firm; and, in danger, cool and courageous. When quite a boy his good old grandmother used to take him on her knee, and on *one* occasion he remembered her saying, 'Thomas, your grandmother is getting old, and will not live long, and I am very anxious you should be a good boy and live for both worlds; will you learn one of my favourite hymns, and say it to yourself every Sunday morning as long as you live? Now promise me that, Thomas.'

"'What is the hymn, grandmother?'

"'It is—

'Be it my only wisdom here,
To serve the Lord with filial fear,
With loving gratitude;
Superior sense may I display,
By shunning every evil way,
And walking in the good.

'O may I still from sin depart,
A wise and understanding heart,
Jesus, to me be given:
And let me through Thy Spirit know,
To glorify my God below,
And find my way to heaven.'

"Thomas promised; and those two verses have had something to do with regulating an adventurous life. Speaking of his early days, he said,—

'"I went to sea at fourteen; one day when on the yards the mate cursed me, and called me disgusting names. I cried bitterly. I thought it was so different from home, where the Bible was daily read. The captain, who was a coarse, wicked man, hearing of my crying, and being informed I would not swear, mocked and laughed at me, and asked me to open my box and show him my books. He took them out, and looked at the titles only. They were a Bible, Simpson's *Plea for Religion*, Doddridge's *Rise and Fall*, Booth's *Reign of Grace*, and several hymn books. He then ordered a table to be placed near the bulk-head, with a chair on the top, tied my foot on the chair, and insisted on me reading a passage in the life of Joseph, when he was in the house of Potiphar, amidst the shouts and laughter of all the crew, who had gathered to see the fun. That was a day of great agony to my young heart, and I wished myself at home. Day after day it was little better; they were all wicked, but the captain was the worst.'

"'Where is the captain now?' I asked.

"'Where is he? why in a short time after he was dismissed, and became so degraded he could not get any other ship. His friends got him a situation in a government store; he was again discharged, became a hanger-on and a tramp, and died in a common lodging-house. I am always thankful for my early training. My grandmother's hymn has been a constant warning and help to me. I have been in many dangers. I have been three times wrecked; and not long ago this very ship was on fire. We were from New York laden with cotton, and when about mid-ocean, a smell of burning told there was something wrong. Search was made, and we soon found—what sent a thrill of dismay through the entire crew, our cargo of cotton was on fire. All hands were instantly in readiness to obey orders; only one voice was heard; bale after bale of the blazing cotton were cast overboard, but still the smoke increased. I ordered one of the hatches to be cut open, a questionable act some might think, as the increased air might fan the flames. The ship was rolling at the time. Burning bales were again and again thrown into the sea; still the fire gained on us, and all seemed hopeless. O how I prayed God would have mercy and save us; though I know I showed no fear, bu kept all hands hard at work; when we shipped a sea, and a large volume of water rushed down the hatchway, extinguished the burning mass, and we were saved. Not a man flinched so long as there was danger; but the moment the fire was overcome, many fell down sick and insensible, and lay helpless for several hours. I have always believed, and still believe, and will believe, that God sent that big wave just in time to save the ship.'

"The captain's early training had evidently influenced his conduct and principles all through life. He recognised the hand of God, believing He held the winds in His fists, and the waves in the hollow of His hands. He was also blessed with a good wife, who daily followed him over the seas with her prayers, and strengthened his confidence in the providence of God by her strong faith in His promises; she was one of those who carried the one hundred and third Psalm in her countenance.

"On going into my room one day, I found a large yellow envelope, addressed,—

'Anglo-American-Ocean-Accommodation Mail
(runs once a-week only), Limited.

'Mr. John Ashworth,
'Room No. 25, Minnesota House,
'Atlantic Avenue,
Neptune's Villa,
Pre-paid. North Atlantic Ocean.'

"This contained the following letter and poem:

'S. S. *Minnesota* at Sea.
'Noon, Sept. 22, 1873.
'Lat. 48·50 N.; Long. 31·20 W.

'Mr. John Ashworth,

'Esteemed Sir,—Here, then, you will see I have fulfilled my promise, and have written you an exact copy of that inimitable piece of poetry you were reading in my scrap book. I hope you will derive as much pleasure from the oft perusal of those beautiful lines as I have myself. Whoever the author was, he appears to have entered into the spirit of the beloved disciple, judging from what we read of him in his Epistles. I have been thinking what a beautiful piece it would be for some of your Sunday-school children to recite, at one of their Sunday-school anniversaries at Rochdale. I will give one sovereign, to be divided amongst any who recite it to your satisfaction at the next anniversary. I remain, dear sir,

'Yours very truly,
'THOMAS FORTUNATUS FREEMAN,
'Commander S. S. *Minnesota*.'

ST. JOHN THE AGED.

'I'M growing very old. This weary head
That has so often leaned on Jesus' breast,
In days long past that seem almost a dream,
Is bent and heavy with its weight of years.
These limbs that followed Him—my Master—oft
From Galilee to Judah; yea, that stood
Beneath the Cross and trembled with His groans,
Refuse to bear me even through the streets
To preach unto my children. E'en my lips
Refuse to form the words my heart sends forth.

My ears are dull : they scarcely hear the sobs
Of my dear children gathered round my couch.
My eyes so dim, they cannot see their tears.
God lays His hand upon me ; yea, His HAND,
And not His ROD—the gentle hand that I
Felt, those three years, so often pressed in mine,
In friendship such as passeth woman's love.
I'm old, so old ! I cannot recollect
The faces of my friends, and I forget
The words and deeds that make up daily life ;
But that dear face, and every word He spoke,
Grow more distinct as others fade away,
So that I live with Him and holy dead
More than with living.

Some seventy years ago
I was a fisher by the sacred sea.
It was at sunset. How the tranquil tide
Bathed dreamily the pebbles ! How the light
Crept up the distant hills, and in its wake
Soft purple shadows wrapped the dewy fields !
And then HE came and called me. Then I gazed
For the first time, on that sweet face. Those eyes,
From out of which, as from a window, shone
Divinity, looked on my inmost soul,
And lighted it for ever. Then His words
Broke on the silence of my heart and made
The whole world musical. Incarnate Love
Took hold of me and claimed me for its own.
I followed in the twilight, holding fast
His mantle.

Oh ! what holy walks we had,
Through harvest fields and desolate dreary wastes ;
And oftentimes He leaned upon my arm,
Wearied and wayworn. I was young and strong,
And so upbore Him. Lord ! now I am weak,
And old, and feeble. Let me rest on Thee !
So put Thine arm around me. Closer still !
How strong Thou art ! The twilight draws apace.
Come let us leave those noisy streets and take
The path to Bethany, for Mary's smile

Awaits us at the gates, and Martha's hands
Have long prepared the cheerful evening meal.
Come, James; the Master waits, and Peter, see,
Has gone some steps before.

What say you, friends?
That this is Ephesus, and Christ has gone
Back to His kingdom? Ay, 'tis so, 'tis so,
I know it all; and yet, just now, I seemed
To stand once more upon my native hills
And touch my Master. Oh! how oft I've seen
The touching of His garments bring back strength
To palsied limbs! I feel it has to mine.
Up! bear me once more to my church,—once more
There let me tell them of a Saviour's love:
For, by the sweetness of my Master's voice
Just now, I think He must be very near,—
Coming, I trust, to break the vail, which time
Has worn so thin that I can see beyond,
And watch His footsteps.

So, raise up my head.
How dark it is! I cannot seem to see
The faces of my flock. Is that the sea
That murmurs so, or is it weeping? Hush!
My little children! God so loved the world,
He gave His Son: so love ye one another;
Love God and man. Amen. Now bear me back.
My legacy unto an angry world is this.
I feel my work is finished. Are the streets so full?
What, call the folk my name? The holy John?
Nay, write me rather, Jesus Christ's beloved
And lover of my children.

Lay me down
Once more upon my couch, and open wide
The eastern window. See! there comes a light
Like that which broke upon my soul at eve,
When in the dreary Isle of Patmos, Gabriel came
And touched me on the shoulder. See! it grows
As when we mounted towards the pearly gates.
I know the way! I trod it once before.
And hark! it is the song the ransomed sang

Of glory to the Lamb! How loud it sounds!
And that unwritten one! Methinks my soul
Can join it now. But who are these who crowd
The shining way? Say!—joy! 'tis like the eleven!
With Peter first: how eagerly he looks!
How bright the smiles are beaming on James' face!
I am the last. Once more we are complete
To gather round the Paschal Feast. My place
Is next my Master. Oh, my Lord! my Lord!
How bright Thou art, and yet the very same
I loved in Galilee! 'Tis worth the hundred years
To feel this bliss! So lift me up, dear Lord,
Unto Thy bosom. There shall I abide.'

[The reader will excuse a little digression here when I relate the sad sequel which follows. We might well pause, and think how strange and mysterious are the vicissitudes of life. This was Captain Freeman's last voyage, as captain; he returned home as a passenger, and was intending to settle down and enjoy the evening of his days in rest and quietness, having been at sea since December, 1824. Alas! alas! Captain Freeman, his dear wife, and John Ashworth are, within this short time, numbered with the dead; but without doubt have joined the great multitude which no man can number. The following extracts from letters reveal the sad facts.

"Bootle, Liverpool, Nov. 13th, 1873.

"Mr. A. L. Calman,

"Dear Sir,—Your kind favour was forwarded to me at Buxton this morning, where I have been for the benefit of my health. At the same time I received notice my dear wife was quite ill, so I left Buxton and arrived here at noon. Enclosed I send you P. O. O. for one pound, and shall be glad to hear you have those among the children who will be able to learn the poetry easily. It will strengthen their memories to learn to recite. I can recite hymns my mother gave me to learn when I was only *four* years old, and many a time at sea, as I have paced the deck thinking of home, and father, and mother, have I repeated some of these hymns. . . I hope some day I shall have the pleasure of again meeting good John Ashworth; and if ever I felt a reverence for any man it is for noble John Bright, and I hope I may have the pleasure of seeing and speaking to him. Yours truly,

"THOMAS F. FREEMAN."

"Bootle, Liverpool, Nov. 27th, 1873.

"Mr. A. L. Calman,

"Dear Sir,—I must apologise for not answering your kind favour earlier; but, just at that juncture, I was in great distress of mind, for my dear wife was taken violently ill. . . The last Sunday the doctor told us what was the matter—cancer in the breasts. Four years ago she apprehended this. . . I leave you to conceive how sad it makes me feel, but we trust to have patience imparted to us under our grief and affliction. I am obliged to you for the invitation, but I cannot leave my wife twenty-four hours; for though I cannot do any thing to arrest the terrible disease, yet I can do much to console and comfort her. . . We do both feel so thankful that Providence has been so kind to us that I am enabled to quit the sea, and you can imagine what a comfort it is to her. . . I am thankful I am somewhat better myself. Yours, &c.

"T. F. F."

Mrs. Freeman died on January 14th, 1874. In the month of August, 1874, Mr. Ashworth received, indirectly through a friend, the sad intelligence that Captain Freeman was dead. I wrote on behalf of Mr. A. to his son's wife, and received the following reply:

"Bootle, August 31st, 1874.

"Mr. Ashworth,

"Dear Sir,—I received your note from your friend, and am sorry to hear of your illness, but hope your useful life may be spared yet a while. It is quite true father has gone home. When you were here, he was suffering from cancer in the liver, and he gradually got worse, and wasted to a skeleton, until dropsy set in. . . It was a long tedious illness, but he was very patient and happy, and could look forward to his death without fear or doubt. . . His mind was very clear and bright, and he could enjoy to hear some of us read out of the old Book, a sermon, or a hymn. He was very fond of the pilgrim song, 'A few more years shall roll,' and he would ask friends to sing for him when unable to do so himself. . . Hoping you may be restored, I remain, yours respectfully,

"A. W. F."]

"We were now approaching the virgin rocks that stretch out seventy miles from the coast of Newfoundland, and over which we should sail at a depth of about forty yards. In the distance was an immense bank of mist, out of which came dashing the No. 8 pilot boat, one of the eight constantly cruising about to meet the ships approaching the American shores. Our engine stood still for the first time since leaving, to take up the pilot, who had brought with him the American papers; and at the same time to take soundings. The bank of mist gathered thick around us, and we soon found ourselves enveloped in a dense fog; and then began the dreadful roaring of the fog-horn, and continued every two minutes night and day, which had a depressing effect, until we got clear of the gloom, and glad we were to hear the last doleful depressing sound, and once more see the expanded open clear sky.

"The brilliancy of the night kept us long walking on deck, and made the captain eloquent in his description of former scenes, especially on the night of Nov. 7th, 1870, when one entire side of the skies was lit up with the aurora borealis, or northern lights, with their shooting flickering hues; and the masts, yards, ropes, and chains of the ship illuminated with will-o-the-wisp, leaping from stay to stay, or hanging in separate luminous balls, and the whole sea radiant with phosphorescent waves, making everything look unreal by the strange lurid glare.

"Our night on that calm quiet evening was perhaps less memorable, but not less glorious than the one described by the captain. The clear immeasurable expanse above seemed literally crowded with countless worlds, that sent down their soft resplendent beams, making the outstretched ocean look like a sea of glass, and as I sat alone near the bowsprit singing Addison's .

'Spacious firmament on high
With all the blue ethereal sky,'

and looking on the 'spangled heavens,' I seemed surrounded with invisible beings that joined in the stanza, and echoed back the words—

'The hand that made us is divine.'

"And who could gaze on such scenes, and think of the vast western continent we were now approaching, and not remember the brave Italian youth that first pioneered our passage over those seas.

"This young Genoese, from the study and copying of maps, had a strong conviction that there must be a great land over the great sea, and for seven years besieged several kings and courts: John the Second of Portugal, Henry the Seventh of England, Ferdinand and Isabella of Spain, entreating them to render him help in his great undertaking. The latter yielded to his entreaties, and furnished him with three small ships, the *Mina*, the *Pinta*, and the *Mary*. He sailed from Palos August 3rd, 1492, and for nine weeks battled not only with the waves, but with the fears, superstitions, and frequent mutiny of his crew. Day after day he entreated them to go on one day more, promising the man that should first see land a blue silk waistcoat. Then floated past the ship a twig of hawthorn with red berries; the sight of this ominous branch made the heart of Columbus leap for joy. Then followed a handful of moss and a carved stick, which brought tears to his eyes, saying land must be near. And land was near; he himself saw it first, and got the blue vest. The ships reached the shore, the sailors leaped on land, rolled in the grass like dogs, and shouted again and again, hurrah! hurrah! hurrah! and now almost worshipped their commander as a god.

"Columbus, with a heart full of gratitude, went on shore, fell on his knees and thanked God for His mercies; and on October 12th, 1492, christened the land San Salvador.

"But also over those seas followed another ship, whose name history will never let die.

'A solitary bark,
A lonely speck on the wide seas,
Battling with winds, and waves, and storms,
To seek a home where high priests were
Unknown. Prayers from that lonely bark
Daily went up to heaven, for heaven's
Preserving care; those prayers were heard,
And He, who stills the boisterous storms,
In peace and safety, brought them to
The longed-for, long-sought land.'

"This ship, the *May Flower*, sailed from Delft Haven, in Holland, July, 1620, with one hundred emigrants, who twelve years before had, with their minister, John Robinson, been driven from England by James the First and his prelacy, because they wished tc worship God according to their conscience. Their beloved pastor suggested to his flock the crossing of the great sea, and forming a colony in the far west, to be called *New England*, and there enjoy that freedom of worship their own country denied them. The proposition was gladly accepted, and it must have been an affecting sight to see the congregation gathered on the shore, and listening to what proved to be their minister's last sermon, from Ezekiel viii. 21, after which they all knelt down, while the good pastor, with bare head, grey locks, and tremulous voice, commended them to the care and guidance of Him who made the sea and the dry land; then embarked the Pilgrim Fathers, all English. At first they had two vessels, the *Speedwell*, sixty tons, and the *May Flower*, one hundred and twenty tons; but the *Speedwell* speeded badly. Both ships put into Plymouth, and all went on board the *May Flower*, that now historic ship; and that frail bark, like the little ships of Columbus, for nearly nine weeks ploughed the stormy Atlantic, during which time John Carver, William Bradford, John Holden, and thirty-seven others, drew up that immortal constitution that afterwards became the foundation of American freedom and greatness, and John Carver was elected the first president or governor.

"The late hour reminded me I must draw my reflections and soliloquies to a close; and as I descended from the stem of the great vessel to my snug little state room, I felt truly thankful to God for such a glorious day on the mighty deep. Again the Sabbath morning came, and again the poop-bell rang out its notes of invitation to come and worship. A clergyman read prayers, and I preached. That evening we sent up two blue lights to signal our arrival, to be instantly telegraphed to the world, and to many that would rejoice; then quietly glided through the straits into the bay betwixt Staten and Long Island; and after having, at the request of the saloon passengers, presented an address to the captain and officers of the *Minnesota*, we disembarked, and for the first time stood on the shores of the New World."

The two following letters, one addressed to his congregation at the Destitute, and the other to the teachers and scholars of the Sunday-school in connection with it, were written by Mr. Ashworth on the voyage and posted at New York on his arrival.

"Middle of the Atlantic Ocean.
"Fifteen hundred miles from land.
"September 25th, 1873.

"My dear Flock,

"On board our great ship, now leaping and rolling amidst surging billows and a wide, wide sea, I think of you, and feel thankful to think you do not forget me. I have already seen, as I never saw before, the wonders of the Lord in the great deep, and on that deep have I read the 107th Psalm with a full heart, and an interest never before experienced. Truly God is great, and it is sweet to feel that He is affectionate, kind, and good. Through many scenes it has been my lot to pass, one consideration never yet left me, that God would guide me by His counsel, and surround me with His providence; and now, while rocking in the stormy sea, this conviction is more and more precious.

"You are often in my mind, and have been the subject of many prayers. I believe that some, who once mingled in our assemblies, have passed away to their heavenly mansion, and that some of you are on the way to that prepared place, for a prepared people; but I fear all of you are not now ready to enter the pearly gates of the realms of glory. This often gives me much concern, for it is a sad thought to me—and I know it is to Mr. Calman, and our Bible women—that any of you should be lost. It would rejoice me greatly to hear, on my return, that you had found peace with God, through faith in our Lord and Saviour, Jesus Christ. Let me plead with you, and beseech you, no longer to defer this all-important question. Jesus will receive you; Jesus will pardon and bless you. No true penitent was ever rejected, or sent away by Him, and His blood can save to the uttermost; yes, to the uttermost: and, I pray God, that His holy, converting, saving, consoling blessed Spirit may descend on you every one; yea, every one.

"I trust you will diligently attend the various means of grace, and by living in peace and joining in prayer, uphold the hands of my fellow labourers.

"And may I request you not to forget me in the various services, or when bowed before your Lord. I think much of your prayers for me. Pray that God will guide my steps; bless me while labouring in the New World; preserve me on the sea; give me health, and bring me home again in peace, a better and holier man. Again the Lord bless you, and greatly bless you.

"From your affectionate Minister and Pastor,

"JOHN ASHWORTH."

"On the wide, wide Ocean.

"More than a thousand miles from land.

"September 25th, 1873.

"Dear Teachers, and

"My dear Young Friends,

"Though our big ship is now plunging through waves and under waves almost as high as my house in

Broadfield, yet I do not forget you. The captain wanting to talk with me about our schools, I mentioned you to him. About five hours after, on going into my berth, or box, or little bed-room, I was astonished to find a large letter addressed to me, containing a very beautiful piece of poetry, also the offer of a reward to the boy or girl that will learn and repeat this poetry before the whole school.

"We have a great many passengers in our big ship, coming from many countries, also a number of children, and little folks, boys and girls, in what we call the steerage or fore-part of the ship. I go amongst them every day; give them nuts, laugh, and talk with them.

"When I give them nuts the Italian children say for thank you, 'Grazio'; the French children, 'Merci'; and the German children, 'Danke.'[1] When it is not stormy, they sometimes sit in groups on the deck, and sing the hymns of their own country.

"I hope you will be obedient to all your teachers, also kind to one another, and not keep company with bad boys or girls, who will not go to any Sunday school. That little beautiful first Psalm tells you what to do about keeping company with the ungodly. I wish all of you that can read would learn that Psalm, and say it to me when I return. If you do what that Psalm tells you, God will bless you all through life.

"TEACHERS,

I would also say a word to you. And, in the first place, express my sincere thanks for your untiring patience in trying to do good to those little cared for at home. God sees you, and knows your labours, and He *will* bless you, and make you a blessing to the dear children. The promise to us all is, 'If we sow in tears we shall reap in joy; and in due season we shall reap if we faint not.' The Lord keep you from fainting, from being weary in well doing.

"Do not forget me when you pray together or in private God bless you all.

"Yours affectionately,

"JOHN ASHWORTH."

CHAPTER XV.

RAMBLES IN THE NEW WORLD (CONTINUED).

"THE point of land on which we first set foot in the New World has had several names. The Indians sold it to a Dutchman for four pounds sixteen shillings worth of rum, or what they called *fire-water*, and got drunk. To commemorate this event the Indians called the island Manhattan, or the place where they got drunk; this was in the year 1626. The Dutch christened it New Amsterdam, then New Orange; and when it came into possession of the English they named it New York. The first view of the city from sea or land, when remembering its recent birth, reveals a wonderful evidence of energy and enterprise that has no parallel in this world's history; the rapidity of development, moral and natural, of all the cities of the States, has astonished all nations; but that of New York is the most marvellous. Its three hundred churches; its charitable and benevolent institutions, embracing and mitigating almost every human woe; its colleges, public libraries, museums, parks, and palaces, all tell of surprising intelligence and industry. But there was one building in Third Avenue, the first in which we entered, that in my opinion explained the why and wherefore of all this prosperity and greatness; this is an immense pile, occupying an entire block of land, six stories *high,* lighted with upwards of four hundred windows, and adorned with the grandest inscription that ever designated any institution, and that is, "*The Bible House,*" the temple of God's Word, the depôt of the Book from heaven; and heaven's decree relative to that Book is, that whosoever meditates in it, delights in it, whatsoever he doeth shall prosper. There is not a nation on the face of the earth can boast of such a palace, for such a purpose; and it is no wonder, so long as the hand of God is recognised in the history of the rise and fall of nations, that He should honour the nation that honours Him.

"And then the question comes, Is not this splendid Bible House the fruit of the *May Flower?* Did not the germ of mighty empire move within that fragile bark that braved the waves of the Atlantic, carrying to these shores a band of consecrated men and women whose hearts God had touched; dauntless in freedom's holy cause, and liberty to worship God according to their conscience, are the seeds of this noblest of all the noble institutions of the greatest city in the United States.

"To this Bible House, in the first place, came the delegates and representatives of many cities and many climes—from Asia, Europe, Africa,—to present their credentials to the world's Evangelical Alliance; a place truly in harmony with the object and purpose of the great gathering; and it was curious to see the constant arrivals of men of all ages, all customs, and all colours, the chosen of many Christian communities, whose fame had long preceeded them, handing in their testimonials to the Executive, and receiving the first billet for their temporary home.

"The Gramercy Park Hotel was my first appointed residence; trunks and other property followed by express. In this hotel were two hundred and fifty beds, and one hundred and fifty-seven servants of all colours. My room was two hundred and nine, the key of which was handed to me, and of which I was the sole proprietor. Descending to breakfast the following morning, I found a large troop of liveried waiters, and a good dining room, containing fifteen circular tables, and six chairs to each; the ceiling was hung and entirely covered with graceful festoons of pink gauze or muslin; the floor polished oak. A German waiter led me to my seat, and then immediately placed before me two peaches and a glass of iced water, as a prelude to what was to follow; he then handed me a bill of fare, containing thirty-seven articles; and had I been disposed and possessed of sufficient capacity, I might have begun at the top and eaten down to the bottom. On the list of good things was the word 'mush'; speaking to my German servant and pointing to the word, I said, 'What is this?'

"'Mush, sir, mush.'

"'I know that; but what does it mean?'

"'Meal milk, sir, meal milk.'

"'Do you mean porridge?'

"'Yes, sir, porridge; yes, porridge.'

"'Then bring porridge instead of peaches, please.'

"'Yes, sir; and will you say five or six other things, and then you can go on.'

"Seeing that he wished to economise both time and labour, I complied with his request.

After breakfast I took a walk round a miniature

park, the property of the owners of the surrounding buildings, and was glad to seek the shelter of the overhanging trees from the hot beams of the morning sun. While pursuing my leisurely stroll, I was surprised to see a large number of boxes fastened to either the stem or branches of the trees. Speaking to a gentleman who sat on one of the park seats reading the morning's paper, I asked,

"'What mean those boxes suspended in the trees?'

"Rising, and rolling up his paper, he replied,—

"'Well, sir, had you been walking in this park twelve years ago, you would not have seen a single leaf on any of these trees, now so covered with beautiful foliage. At that time there was a small grub, called the inch-worm, that bred in the bark, climbed up the boughs, and utterly stripped them, leaving them as destitute of foliage as in the depth of winter; so with all our orchards, gardens, and parks in many States of the Union. An intellectual man, a student in animated nature, suggested a remedy, and it was this: to import several thousand English sparrows, provide them with little wooden houses, and feed them daily until they become settled and contented with their new home. The sparrows were got, thousands of beautiful little boxes were volunteered, and fixed in the trees ready for their reception. A State law was passed inflicting a penalty of one dollar or a week's imprisonment on any person killing one of them. And now, sir, you see the pleasing results: the inch-worm is destroyed, the trees are healthy and green, and the little spirited English birds are found hopping and chirping in every garden and park in the Union.'

"'Are you an American?' I asked my civil informant.

"'Yes, sir, I am,' he replied.

"'Well, sir, I am an Englishman; and as our English sparrows have done you such invaluable service, ought not this to have been reckoned in the Alabama claims?'

"A louder laugh I have not heard for some time than came from the lungs of my new friend; it made many of the sparrows over head look out at their front doors and give an extra chirp.

"'Well, sir, I have one more question to ask; some of the sparrows' houses have small white steeples, making them look like little churches, while others are plain and without spires; what does that mean?'

"The American evidently determined to have the upper hand of me; with a second laugh, but not quite so loud, he replied,—

"'If I were in England I should say the sparrows in the steeple houses belong to the state church, and the others are dissenters.'"

Here the chapter left by Mr. Ashworth in manuscript of his "Rambles in the New World" closes; and the writer can well remember that, when recommended by his medical adviser to relinquish all mental effort for a time, with what reluctance he laid down his pen. At first there was a great inward struggle, wondering what was going to be the result, and he said, 'Well, if I must give it up, I must give it up; God's will be done, and not mine.'

What follows of his visit to America and the *voyage* home, is taken from his diaries.

"Oct. 1. Met Mr. H. Tarrant, of Leeds, and Miss Kipling, of Darlington, England, in Broadway this morning. Attended the daily prayer meeting from 12 to 1 in the old North Dutch church, Fulton-street. Many present, from many nations. This hour of prayer is truly a precious hour. Letters were sent to the conductor with fourteen requests for prayer. The meeting closed precisely at 1. The daily prayer meeting in Fulton-street, New York, was first commenced in the former lecture-room of the old North Dutch church on Sept. 23rd, 1857, by Mr. Lanphier, a city missionary, who day after day, and many times a day, continued in earnest prayer for a revival of God's work; and on going his rounds one day, as he was walking along the streets, the idea was suggested to his mind, that an hour for prayer from 12 to 1 would be beneficial to business men. He opened the above room. The first half-hour he sat alone, and at half-past twelve a solitary individual was heard upon the stairs. On the 8th Oct. the meetings were removed to the middle lecture-room, being more commodious. This meeting, we learn, was one of uncommon fervency in prayer; deep humiliation and self-abasement, and great desire that God would glorify Himself in the out-pouring of His Spirit, which was followed by the great American revival.

"Attended the daily prayer meeting of the Young Men's Christian Association from 4 to 5. This is a truly noble building—the library, lecture-hall, reading-rooms, and valuable paintings, all constitute a great attraction. To this prayer meeting three requests were sent.

"Thursday, Oct. 2. Went with my English friends to the Central park. Worthy of any city in the world; laid out at great expense and taste. Had luncheon at the 'Friends' *Dinery*, Broadway; a sensible eating-house, and reasonable.

"At 7 this evening the reception service for the Delegates and friends of the Alliance was held at Steinway Hall; great crowd. Met some of my Co-English Delegates for the first time—Mr. Reed, M.P., Dr. Parker, Dr. Rigg, &c. Many fine men from almost every land, of all costumes, nations, and colour of skin. Ladies of average beauty: some of them wretchedly spoiled with the Grecian bend.

"In the hall were mottoes, inscriptions, and flags of all nations. The service was opened with the hymn—

'From all that dwell below the skies,
Let the Creator's praise arise;
Let the Redeemer's name be sung
Through every land, by every tongue,'

which was sung with great power. Prayer followed; address of welcome by Dr. Adams, masterly and impressive; Christian speeches of other Delegates from many lands, all of a fine Christian character. The meeting was indeed a great success; all must return happier and holier men and women.

"REFLECTIONS.

"Before retiring to rest read Acts ii., and felt that I had that evening witnessed a scene much like that mentioned from the 4th to 11th verse.

"O for a pentecostal shower on this wonderful gathering in America. God and Father, in mercy, send down the blessing on us."

Mr. Ashworth often spoke of the wonderful effect which that meeting had upon him, especially when the great gathering rose and sung, as he had never heard it sung before, the 'Coronation' hymn—

"All hail the power of Jesus' name."

He said he never saw or felt anything so like heaven.

He was introduced to many foreign delegates, and amongst them Narayan Sheshadri, a distinguished high caste Brahmin from India, who had come fourteen thousand miles to attend the Alliance Conference. He is forty-six years of age, has been a Christian about thirty, and has laboured with great success among his countrymen all that time, as a missionary. He has a pleasant voice, speaks a number of languages, and his English education is good. His Christian experience is clear, and he is a constant and careful reader of the Bible. It was when about fifteen years of age he was led to give some attention to the teachings of a missionary, and his mind became awakened to the foolish, degrading, and ruinous fables of the heathen priests. Having read the twenty-second Psalm in connection with the recorded scene of Christ's crucifixion in the New Testament, he was so powerfully led to apprehend the truth as it is in Jesus, that he exclaimed, "If there is a book given of God to man it is the Bible"; and when he came to contrast the miserable legends of his heathen education with the God of the Bible, and the history of the creation and redemption of man, his heart was filled with wonder and delight.

He gave an appalling account of the terrible condition of the vast multitudes in India. Of the children alone there are thirty millions taught to worship idols. Each one of the inhabitants may have as many gods to worship as he pleases; as there are over five hundred and thirty millions of these imaginary deities, any man may worship a thousand gods or more all at once if he choose.

The devotional services of the Conference were conducted in the Madison Square church daily, at nine o'clock, a.m., and the business meetings in Association Hall, in all of which, suffice it to say, Mr. Ashworth took a deep and lively interest from first to last. Among the numerous subjects brought before the Conference those specially noted in the programme by him are under the head of "Christianity and Social Reforms," embracing—

I. Christianity as a Reforming Power.

II. The Working Power of the Church—how best to Utilise it.

III. Temperance, and its Suppression.

IV. Crime, Criminals, and Prison Discipline.

V. Christian Aspect of the Labour Question.

VI. Christian Philanthropy—Hospitals—Deaconesses—Refuges—Ragged Schools.

"Oct. 3. Removed my lodgings from Gramercy Park Hotel to the private residence of Mr. E. C. Wilder, 122, West 45th Street, merchant, and the President of the N. Y. Sunday School Union Association, at his request."

As soon as it became known that Mr. Ashworth was one of the delegates to the Conference, he had many enquiries after him, many visitors, and many requests for his services, with which he complied as far as possible. Advertisements such as the following, "Can any one inform me where a letter will reach Mr. John Ashworth, of Rochdale, England, delegate to the Evangelical Alliance," were frequent; and he says, "Three deputations waited upon me this evening." He often spoke with gratitude of the obligation under which he was laid to his kind host, Mr. Wilder, for undertaking the responsibility of replying to his numerous letters.

"Oct. 4. Prayer meeting at 9 this morning; largely attended. The converted Brahmin, from Bombay, in his white turban and blue tunic, the six swarthy African bishops, and pastors, French, Italian, English, and Russian, all joining in prayer with one heart and mind; a glorious sight. Rose to give my seat to a black woman in the rail car, which astonished the whole company. Ice vans, in various streets, sold at halfpenny per pound. Two ladies admiring a lap-dog without tail; one observed it was now *fashionable* to have lap-dogs without tails.

"Oct. 5. Sunday. Came last night to Brooklyn to be ready for my engagements, for I was determined not to ride on the Sunday here, as I do not at home; rose early; mingled with the Catholics; visited three Sunday schools —Primitives, Baptists, St. Peter's; the last a fine school, and all the rooms richly carpeted, and seats cushioned. Here, as in all the American and Canadian schools, rich and poor, old and young, sit down together; the best talent and wealth of the church devoted to the schools. Teaching strictly scriptural; one lesson for all throughout the States, and in the Dominion, on the same day. Singing an important part; all have notes. Great order and quietness. This I observed in all my travels in all places. Preached in Prospect Park at 2; a great gathering. Walked to Association Hall six miles, and preached to a large audience at 7-30. Walked home; weary. Pained to see street cars running, and all crowded.

"Oct. 6. Prayer meeting at 9; large company. Like this feature of the Alliance; precious means. Introduced to Philip Philips, Drs. Angus and Stoughton, Bishop Simpson, and the Honourable E. Dodge, a good Christian worker. . .

"Oct. 7. Prayer meeting. Attended morning sittings; a good feeling. Many invitations to occupy the pulpits of the New York churches.

"Oct. 8. Met Miss Weston, formerly a missionary in Constantinople; met her last in Edinburgh. The committee provided Foreign Delegates with twenty-four carriages, containing four each, with two horses to take us to Greenwood Cemetery, Central Park, &c. Sat with Mr. Newman Hall, of London; interesting conversation on the way he was led to write his 'Come to Jesus'"

One day, after dining with a large company who began to drink toasts, he and another slipped out, and resolved to hold a service in a neighbouring street. A few people soon gathered round, and the Methodist ditty, "Come to Jesus just now," was sung. Mr. Hall thought he could not do better than base his remarks on it. So he began, "Come to Jesus! Yes; but who is He? He is God. He is man. But where is He? In heaven; here. How can we come to Him? By faith; by prayer," &c., &c. The next Sunday evening he enlarged on it to his own people. Soon after he was seized with rheumatic fever. When convalescent he amused himself during his recovery by writing one section of this tract; and as he resolved every section should occupy just two pages, it was a pleasant puzzle so to work down what he wrote into the required size. This led to the use of the shortest words and simplest sentences, for condensation, and this has caused it to be so extensively translated and circulated, the style being so easy.

"The Park very fine; the Cemetery truly beautiful, not surpassed in the world; drove six miles in it. Visited the Academy of Music at Brooklyn; dined there.

"The meeting in the evening in Broadway Tabernacle on Sunday Schools. Dr. E. F. Cook, of Paris, stated that they durst not sing in Protestant schools, lest they might be shut up.

"Oct. 9th. By invitation of the Mayor and Corporation of the city of New York, we visited the institutions under the charge of the Commissioners of Public Charities and Correction, the city authorities providing us with carriages and steamers for the purpose of conveying us; the institutions being situated on four islands, viz., Blackwell, Randell, Wards, and Harts. Our visit to the various places painful, yet to some extent pleasing. The welcome shouting and speeches of the boys and girls in Randell's Island deeply affected us all. They marched out to meet us, on landing, and a little boy stepped out from the ranks, and pulling off his cap, said,—

"'Gentlemen of the Evangelical Alliance, we bid you welcome, and we are glad you have come to see our noble refuge and home. You come, gentlemen, from many lands, and have crossed the wide seas to teach all nations love and unity. May God bless your efforts, and crown your Christian labours with great success.'

"Another bright little fellow then came forward out of the second company and said,—

"'Gentlemen of the Evangelical Alliance, we do not think that the senior boys ought to have the exclusive honour and privilege of bidding you welcome. We are happy to see you; and, if any of you come from lands that have no shelter for poor children, may what you see to-day induce you to promote such an unspeakable blessing; and may God bless your meetings, and His providence guide you safe home.'

"Then from the third company, all girls, one of their number, Emma Gardener, came forward blushing, and said,

"'Gentlemen of the Evangelical Alliance, you have come to the Free States of America on a glorious errand, to teach all sects and parties how beautiful union with Christ and each other is. May all nations be blessed by your Christ-like work. But we, though only girls, do not think that either the senior or junior boys ought to have the exclusive joy of bidding you welcome. We, too, would say, gentlemen, that we hail your visit to our country and this noble institution. May God send down his blessing on you and your children.' At the close of these speeches, the Mayor stepped forward and kissed the ruddy-faced darling. It was a scene."

Mr. Ashworth is said to have been deeply affected, but it would not be the first time he was moved by the eloquence of little folks. Amongst the two hundred and seventy-two boys in the training ship *Mercury*, anchored near Hart's Island, he discovered an English lad, and found that he was a runaway. Mr. Ashworth, on his arrival in England, wrote to the boy's mother, and received the following reply:

"B——, Dec. 2, 1873.

"Mr. Ashworth,

"Sir,—Many thanks to you for your very kind letter, giving me an account of my poor boy, who I've known nothing of since February last. . . So, kind sir, I must leave you to fancy the distressed state of my mind—thanks to a kind Providence for raising me a friend. Will it be troubling you, if I ask you to give me a little information how I can get him home, and if you think he is kindly treated there? Can you tell me how long, and how he came to get on the training ship? . . I hope, sir, you will excuse an anxious mother's freedom by asking you to give me another letter. . . With many thanks, yours, &c.

"C. J."

"P.S.—Kind sir, I have not expressed my thanks and gratitude, half as much as I should like to do, if I could see you. From an anxious mother."

In the published list of the delegates meeting in the Institution, Mr. Ashworth is designated "Rev. Dr. Ashworth, Rochelle." *(New York Times.)*

"The other institutions we visited are melancholy evidences of fallen nature and depravity. Dined with the Mayor, W. F. Havemeyer, and the city council, in the large hall of the Inebriate Asylum, Ward's Island. Much talking and considerable excitement to-day; many tales told. One about a 'Universalist' who kept a little lonely wayside inn, that asked his customers, who put up their horses, what their creed was—

"If a Methodist, he gave them corn; but no rubbing.
"If a Churchman, rubbing; but no corn.
"If a Baptist, plenty of water; but no corn.
"If a Universalist, corn, water, and rubbing.

A minister, when questioned, told him he was a Methodist, but his horse was a Universalist.

"I preached this evening to a large congregation of coloured people, all black; they sang lustily, and seemed very happy. The Gospel has done much for this race; heard many terrible accounts of their sufferings during the civil war. Learned to-day that all the Methodist local preachers in America are styled 'Reverend.'

"Oct. 10. Attended a reception given this evening by the Honourable Mr. and Mrs. W. E. Dodge, at their residence, 225, Madison Avenue, to the Delegates of the Conference. About five hundred ladies and gentlemen present. Had a fair specimen of American ladies; looks, dresses, &c. Pleased to find no intoxicating drink—good feature; cakes, lemonade, tea, and coffee.

"Oct. 11. Attended the last morning prayer meeting (in connection with the Conference) in Madison-street church; quite full. Last meeting of the Alliance, impressive and effecting. Attended the gold market at 2; admitted, and conducted through by one of the members; a fearful scene, all seemed absolutely crazed. The market given on tape by telegram; got one day's market to bring home.

"Oct. 12. Sunday. This day will not soon be forgotten in New York. Many of the large halls and churches were thronged to hear the farewell sermon and addresses of the most popular Delegates, and a powerful influence rested on all the vast crowds.

"I was engaged for smaller places: Allen-street (Methodists) in the morning; Baptist Sunday school, Fifty-fifth-street, an address at 3; Baptist Sunday school, Fifty-third street, at 4; and spoke at St. John's Methodist church at 8. Returned home weary but happy.

"October 13. Two hundred and fifty of the delegates set out this morning at 9 by special train, in grand saloon carriages, to Philadelphia and Washington, on a visit to President Grant and his cabinet. Called at Princetown college; were met by three hundred students; cheered vociferously, always finishing with, 'Tigar—ysh—bum—yah.' Arrived at Philadelphia at 4; were driven direct to Independence Hall; examined the relics of the revolution. Banquet given by the Philadelphia branch of the Alliance; truly gorgeous; new to me; four hundred present; Bishop Simpson and principal clergymen, Judges Peirce and Allison, Ex-Governor Pollock, &c.; orations at Agricultural Hall after. The stage was beautifully decorated, as was, indeed, the whole room. Stretched across the stage were three high arches of evergreens studded with various coloured natural flowers. In the centre arch were the words, formed in flowers, 'All One in Christ.' On the other two arches similarly formed letters read, the words being on either side, 'Let Brotherly Love Continue.' The decorations around the wall were handsome and appropriate. Near the ceiling were festoons of American colours. At intervals around the walls were fixed the names of Calvin, Knox, Wesley, Luther, Zwingle, and Huss, the letters being in white roses in evergreen frames, the designs being beautiful. Across the front of the balcony was a handsome silk banner bearing the inscription, 'The Church of Philadelphia Saluteth You.' Under this was the name 'Wickliffe' in floral letters. Under each gas jet was a hanging basket filled with creeping plants and the American flag affixed to one of some foreign nation waving over it. Beneath the floral designs were placed shields bearing the colours and coats of arms of France, Spain, Russia, Germany, Turkey, Italy, and Persia.

CHAPTER XVI.

RAMBLES IN THE NEW WORLD (CONTINUED).

"EX-GOVERNOR James Pollock, on behalf of the citizens of Philadelphia, extended to us a hearty welcome. He said :—

"Your mission to us is one of peace, unity, and love. The work of the great Alliance has filled our hearts with joy, and we are glad it was so great a success. And is it too much to say that the city to which you have come is a mark of the great work you have performed. Love prompted your meeting and consecrated your labours. You are with us now, but you do not come to recognise the governments of men, but the hearts and sentiments of a Christian brotherhood, in which there is no geographical boundary. You have come to us at an hour when the world's great heart is beating. Mind is moving, as does the world, and progress is the word.

"The centuries of the past have made their impress on the present. You are here to witness the operations of a free government by a free people. You will ascertain our failures and our successes. Our mountains are high and our valleys deep, yet over all we have free thought, free speech, a free church, and a free people to worship God as we please.

"In the providence of God the people of other lands are epitomised in ours. In the names of the people of this city we welcome you as being of the same household, as brothers. Welcome then, thrice welcome then to our hearts and homes.

"Bishop Simpson, on behalf of the ministry of Philadelphia, also extended the delegates a warm welcome :—

"The motto of our hearts has been prepared on the gallery beyond, 'The Churches of Philadelphia salute you.' We welcome you to this city, not because you are men of prominence at home, nor because you are ministers of Christ, but because you come among us to represent Christian oneness, which the peoples of the earth begin to yearn for. I rejoice that a brighter day is coming. Men can differ and yet love one another. I rejoice to welcome men far in advance of popular sentiment which they may possibly suffer on account of. May God sustain them! I rejoice to see your colours beside those stars and stripes, which we would love to talk about, if it were not for our proverbial modesty. We do not welcome you as Baptists, Presbyterians, Lutherans, or anything else except as Christians beloved.

"The hymn beginning—

> "All hail the power of Jesu's name,
> Let angels prostrate fall,

was then sung, nearly every person in the hall joining. Mr. Stuart then introduced the Very Rev. the Dean of Canterbury, of London, who was received with great applause.

"He said it gave him great pleasure to come here, and it was no more than right to come here after the Alliance had closed their business, because it was the City of Brotherly Love.

"We have lived, said the speaker, to see America and England settling their disputes by arbitration. If the decision has gone against us I feel that we did wrong, for I cannot but believe that we were guilty. A strong feeling of love in England is growing for you, and I believe that the two countries should and will be united in love and amity. I trust all feelings of difference have passed away. But after all this earthly love, what is it to compare to the love in the hearts of Christian men for Christ and for each other? The true thing that binds men and nations together is God's love. Men who feel that they are monuments of *God's love* in Christ, what feelings should we have for our brethren but love? Every one is yearning for peace, and we are looking forward to a better time, when, instead of these disputes we shall have a proper feeling of the love of Christianity.

"The time has come when in all our hearts there is springing up a yearning for a closer union, and we have been brought nearer by railroads, steamships, and other rapid methods of travel. We feel very differently of men we have seen in the flesh to those we have but read of. We have come to see you in your great country, and have felt your kindness and hospitality. You have done everything for our comfort, and we cannot but feel for you because we love you. Beside this friendly feeling I trust there will be that higher feeling, the sense that we are brethren in Christ. I do earnestly trust, and I believe the meetings of the Evangelical Alliance will bring about a better idea of our duties to each other. We do form the one army of Christ, and should love our various regiments, and not turn upon each other to destroy. We should turn against the sin of the world, and, feeling ourselves of the same army, our feelings of love and attachment should be pledged in the warfare of Christ and the destruction of all his enemies.

"The next speaker introduced was Rev. N. Sheshadri, of Bombay.

"He said he was formerly a Brahmin, and had claimed divine honours from the poor people who had fallen down at his feet to worship him. He thought he was a great man, and who would not have felt so. The speaker related a native story about a monkey god who had lost his wife, which was returned by a giant who had stolen it. He took revenge on the giant by setting Ceylon on fire, and, the speaker said, his countrymen believed the island was still on fire. This was too much even for his credulity, and he could not believe it. Through the influence of a good missionary he had been led from the errors of Hindooism to the love of Christ. I made up my mind that I should love the Lord, and on the thirteenth of September, 1843, I was baptised. It was a very severe ordeal to leave my kindred, but I did it, and I considered my sufferings were of no comparison to those of Jesus. Thirty years ago these things made a deep impression on me, and it is still as deep, if not deeper, than it was then. The Lord Jesus was proved to be the Saviour of the world, and there is no other way to be saved. This Alliance has one of the grandest objects before it, and that is the establishment of a unity between the members of the Church of God.

"It matters little where we live, for we are all members of the great brotherhood of God. He is our head, and we are its members. He wishes to gather all His children together, and then we shall go forth to the world as members of the host of our Lord Jesus Christ. My presence here has given the lie to the statement that the missionaries are not doing a good work. I am but one, but there are hundreds of others, and Brahmins, too, who love the Lord. Among us we have two hundred and fifty thousand Christians, and some of these are martyrs who have suffered for Christ. We have only five hundred missionaries in our large country—not as many, perhaps, as you have here in Philadelphia and New York. May God so stir up your hearts that you may be the first nation to evangelise the world. You have done nobly, but I trust you will send forth a larger number of workmen unto my beloved countrymen.

"We were billeted at the Continental hotel; my room No. 289.

"October 14. Left Philadelphia after breakfast for Washington. Presented with an address at Baltimore. Arrived at Washington at 2-40. We were conveyed in coaches to Willard hall, and were presented to Governor Shepherd, who gave us a cordial welcome. When assembled in the Blue room the Rev. Dr. O. H. Tiffany, pastor of the Metropolitan Memorial church of this city, addressed the President as follows:

"Mr. President: The Evangelical Alliance which has been in session in New York, was a gathering of Christian men representing the Protestant faith. They came from many lands and uttered the maturest thought of the churches. They deliberated on topics of common interest to all Christians, and it is confidently believed that thus great stimulus has been given to Christian scholarship, enthusiasm awakened in Christian work, and that the ties of Christian fellowship have been greatly strengthened.

"The churches and citizens of Washington have extended, through the local metropolitan branch of the Alliance, an invitation to foreign delegations to visit the national capital. They have come in response to that invitation, attended by many of their American friends. I now have the honor of presenting to the President of the United States and his Cabinet the officers and members of the Evangelical Alliance.

"The President, in reply, said:

"It affords me a great pleasure to welcome to the capital of this nation this Evangelical Alliance. I feel that this country is the freest one to work out the problem of your association.

"Mr. Stuart, of Philadelphia, then introduced to the President the entire delegation.

"In response to a call, Mr. Sheshadri said that he had been very much impressed with what he had seen in this country, especially its independence. He was glad to be in free America, and to feel all its kind influences. He hoped its future would be as glorious as its past, and that its religion would ever be that of the Lord Jesus Christ, and that the rulers of this land would ever show an attachment for it, and remember that it is righteousness that exalteth a nation.

"Mr. Henry Ward Beecher was requested to address the audience, but declined to do so, only remarking that he entertained the highest respect for the President of the United States, because he is one of the very few great men who can hold his peace. The President, in recognition of the compliment, took occasion to respond that Mr. Beecher is one of the very few men who, speaking frequently, yet always says something worth hearing when he does speak.

"Services in various churches in the evening, and addresses by delegates.

"October 15. Our visits in the city of Washington. The Treasury, Senate House, Capitol, &c.

"The Capitol was staked out the year after Franklin's death, thirty years before the death of George III., in Goethe's fifty-second year and Schiller's thirty-second, sixteen years before the first steamboat, two years before Louis XVI. was guillotined, when Louis Phillipe was in his nineteenth year, while Count Rochambeau was commander of the French army, two years after Robespierre became head deputy, five years after the death of Frederick the Great, while George Stephenson was a boy of ten, the year subsequent to the death of Adam Smith, the year John Wesley and Mirabeau died, two years before Brissot was guillotined, in Napoleon's twenty-second year, the year before Lord North died, in the third year of the London *Times*, just after Lafayette had been the most powerful man in France, three years before the death of Edward Gibbon, while Warren Hastings was on trial, in Burke's sixty-first and Fox's forty-second and Pitt's thirty-second, three years after the death of Chatham, in the Popedom of Pius VI., while Simon Bolivar was a child eight years of age, the year Cowper translated Homer, and in Burns' prime.

"The old Capitol, including the works of art which belonged there, cost two million seven hundred thousand dollars. It covered considerably more than an acre and a half of ground. It was three hundred and fifty-two feet four inches long, seventy feet high to the top of the balustrade, one hundred and forty-five feet high to the top of the old dome, and the wings were one hundred and twenty-one feet six inches deep. These dimensions show a sufficient edifice for the period to have been truly a national Capitol. The part which the British burned had cost about seven hundred and ninety thousand dollars; to restore those parts cost about six hundred and ninety thousand dollars; the freestone centre cost about six hundred and ninety thousand dollars. The park enclosing this old Capitol contained twenty-two and a half acres.

"On assembling, we joined in singing,—

'All hail the power of Jesus' name,'

in such a way that made the great dome ring. Reaching the eastern front, a photographic view of the assemblage was taken, after which we sang, 'Jesus shall reign,' and 'Blest be the sacred tie that binds.' At the Treasury were three thousand five hundred clerks, five hundred ladies. I went into the safe, containing four hundred millions of dollars. Visited the room where President Lincoln was shot, and the little room in which he died. Visited the patent office and museum, &c. Were entertained to lunch by Governor Shepherd, of Columbia, at Willard's hotel.

"At the close of the entertainment, Governor Shepherd arose and said :—'I am honored, gentlemen, by your presence as my guests to-day. Although from want of time the entertainment offered you may not be commensurate with the occasion, your welcome is none the less hearty and sincere. Your visit to the seat of government, gentlemen, will long be remembered by our people, and, if you will take with you as agreeable recollections of Washington as you leave among us of yourselves, we will be gratified indeed.

"We have welcomed you as leaders in a great movement for the regeneration of our race. We will part with you with wishes of God-speed in the noble work which claims the best energies of your great minds and noble hearts. Our regret is that your stay with us is so brief; our joy is that though brief, during your sojourn you have inspired our people with new zeal in the interest of the Christian Church. Allow me to conclude with this :—'The Evangelical Alliance—May its results be equal to the grandeur of its conception and the nobleness of its ends.' This speech was applauded by the guests.

"We then returned to Philadelphia, to the same hotel, where the delegates dined together for the last time. A prayer meeting was held in the large room, and all seemed full of gratitude to God for His goodness and mercies, and prayed for His protection during our return over the wide sea to our distant homes.

"Oct. 16. Visited many institutions in Philadelphia. The Normal Training school for young ladies. Five hundred and forty pupils, averaging eighteen years of age; for twenty-five years not one has fallen. The coloured Normal Training school, male and female; the head teacher, Miss Fanny Jackson, was a slave nine years ago. Many of the pupils very beautiful; most of the females in Bloomer costume and high heeled boots. Visited the common schools; Penn's hospital; the Mint. Ten million sovereigns in bars. Spoke to old William Long, who has been making gold dollars forty-two years, about the danger. Pointed upwards to heaven, saying, 'My home is there.' Machine stamped fifteen thousand dollars in ten minutes. Saw many coins of many countries. 'The widow's mite.' The similar coin that Judas sold his Master for. Nine hundred English sovereigns worth nine hundred and sixteen American. Masonic Hall, just opened, cost £400,000; sixty-seven different lodges meet in this room; an imposing building; had a view of Philadelphia from the tower, two hundred and seventeen feet high. The Gerard school for orphan boys. By the will of the Founder, no priest of any sort allowed to cross the threshold of this school. Stood in the pulpit of Albert Barnes. Saw many 'Friends.' Servants' wages fourteen dollars per month; washerwomen one and a half dollars per day and food. Servant told me she gave twenty-two dollars for a dress, not silk; ten dollars for making: ladies often pay twenty dollars.

"Oct. 17. Attended the Women's Congress in Union League Hall, Twenty-Sixth Street, New York. Mrs. Livermore, Chicago, in the chair; opened with prayer by Mrs. Lozee; two hundred present, amongst them Mrs. Peabody, Mrs. Harriet Beecher Stowe, and her sister; speeches from gloves and dresses. One of the speakers said if they intended to have healthy children they must not marry men whose blood was corrupted with drink. Mentioned the case of a son that shot himself in the *delirium tremens*, and his last words to his father were, 'Would rather sink into a dishonoured grave than transmit a taste for drink to my children.' The speaker said the array of fifteen thousand idiotic, fourteen thousand deaf and dumb, eleven thousand blind, and twenty-four thousand insane is sufficiently strong to appeal to the sympathies of men and women. This day amongst the ladies was one of singular experience.

"Oct. 18. Saw Mr. Tarrant and Miss Kipling sail for England. Met two beggars, one asked ten cents for his lodgings, the other confessed his wife was earning ten shillings per day in washing. Paid ten cents for my shoes blacking; asked thirty-five cents for my hair cutting."

Mr. Ashworth considered the last item so exorbitant, that he went to several hair dressers to ask their charge, but found they were all alike, and offered the last one he visited twelve cents (6d.), asking him to take off as much as he could for the money, as he thought it was quite enough to pay for hair cutting.

"Went over to Brooklyn; guest of Mr. Ladd, 294, Lafayette-street.

"Oct. 19. Preached for the 'Friends.' Visited many Sunday schools. Heard Mr. Talmage in the evening.

"Oct. 20. Went to the court; heard 'Stokes' tried the third time for shooting 'Fisk.' His grey-headed aged father and mother sat near him; a scene. Spoke at a large gathering of Sunday school teachers in Dr. Crossley's Presbyterian Church, Fourth Avenue, Twenty-Second Street.

"Oct. 21. Left New York at 9 this morning for the Falls of Niagara; passed through New Jersey, and arrived at the 'Falls' the following morning at 1-30, having travelled four hundred and fifty-six miles through almost every variety of scenery, upwards of one hundred miles on the banks of the Delaware, and a long distance on the

Susquehanna; the whole deeply interesting. The autumnal tints of the dense forest of trees, beautiful, all colours—red, crimson, yellow, brown, green, &c.; many white churches on the way.

"Oct. 22. After breakfast went out to see the world-wide famed Falls of Niagara; undressed and redressed to go under in a suit of flannel, and over this a suit of oilcloth, with hood oil cap. We descended the spiral steps down to the rocks over which the mighty mass of waters rolled, thundered, boiled, and foamed; the noise beyond all my former experience. Saw what cannot be described. Viewed the 'Falls' also from the tower of suspension bridge, one hundred feet in height, the bridge itself being nearly two hundred feet above the level of the lake."

Mr. Ashworth left the "Falls" on the 22nd for Toronto, where he remained until the 28th, when he left for the Indian settlements, spending a night at Hamilton on the way. At Toronto he was the guest of Daniel McLean, and had eight public engagements during his stay there. He notes, "Public houses closed from seven o'clock on Saturday evening till eight on Monday morning. No cabs on the stand; no bus or car in the streets. Collections in the churches twice every Sabbath." The following extract from letter sent home details his experiences until his return to New York.

"New York, Nov. 1st.

"I have been exploring the dominion, calling and speaking at several towns (the last being Hamilton), where I received a hearty welcome, many Englishmen and women crowding around me. I have indeed witnessed strange scenes during this journey; standing on the banks of Lake Ontario, beholding cities entirely made of wood; pushing on through narrow openings of dense forests, covering thousands of square miles, portions of which had been on fire, leaving openings of immense trees, remnants of ancient days, standing like tall bare piles without a branch; here and there a farm clearing of a few acres, the rest stumps and a wooden shanty, sheltering the hardy spirited owner and his family; then merging from the deep dark forests to find a more open country with improved dwellings, but still all wood; the farmers here are all dwelling on their own estates. At last I arrived at the nearest rail point to the principal object of my journey. Here I engaged a buggy, or light carriage of mere frame work, with four spindle wheels, drawn by two spirited cobs. On we went through the woods and clearings, bump and splash, over seven miles of such a road as I have never before travelled. Every moment I expected to be thrown out behind or over the horses' heads. At last the huts of the Indian settlements came in view on both sides the banks of a great river. These Indians are the Minicoys, the Oneidas, and the Ojibbeways. Driving up to the Wesleyan mission station, I enquired for Dr. Evans, and dismounted. My buggy driver, fearing he would be overtaken by the night, whisked round and left me standing at the door. Soon the doctor appeared, a tall, thin, grey-headed man about seventy; then a brawny Indian with raven locks, a Christian, who speaks English well, and to my astonishment informed me he had read and explained my books to the Indians in the woods. This was a passport to me, and soon all combined to make me welcome. The same evening about thirty Indians, mostly strong, brawny young men, and women with jet black hair, but shy and timid, came to sing for me. The whole was pleasing, strange, and romantic. I spoke to them about half-an-hour, prayed, and then shook hands with them. After a long conversation with Dr. Evans, I retired to bed amidst the tribes made immortal by Catlin and Cooper. My work the following day was to visit their chapel, school, and mission station. When I told them I must leave, Dr. Evans insisted on himself driving me those terrible seven miles through the woods. Two light grey ponies were yoked to a covered buggy, and on we went, the Indians watching our departure. During the journey, the doctor said it was a long time since he spent such a happy day. I arrived at the 'Falls' about eleven o'clock, started next morning at four, crossing the immense chasm of the 'Niagara' in total darkness. I reached my home at New York in the evening at ten, after travelling yesterday about five hundred miles, through wooden towns and villages, down the banks and winding gorges of the Delaware, by forests, clearings, stumps, shanties, and cities of timber, with here and there a white painted wooden church, which always did my heart good to behold, for these little scattered white temples erected in the clearings of mighty forests to the worship of God are the hope, the ornament, and the joyful gathering places on the holy Sabbath, where the hymns learned in the Sunday schools of Fatherland will be sung with a depth of emotion that only the emigrant knows. I have been a little surprised and much pleased with one fact. Out of the hundreds I have spoken with, *every* man and woman is dead against being annexed to the United States, and at one gathering at Toronto of two thousand Sunday school teachers and members of various churches, our national anthem was sung with an effect I never heard exceeded, the chairman remarking, 'Let Mr. Ashworth tell what he has now seen in England, and that Canada is intensely loyal to the beloved old country'

"Yours, &c.,

"JOHN ASHWORTH."

From the 2nd to the 10th November Mr. Ashworth made another tour to Newhaven, Plymouth, Boston, and Albany, visiting the schools and benevolent institutions in each place, and conducting several services. At Plymouth he says, "Standing on the rock on which the Pilgrim Fathers first landed in 1620, I sang with deep emotion,—

'The breaking waves dash'd high,
  On a stern and rock-bound coast,
And the woods against a stormy sky,
  Their giant branches tossed;
And the heavy night hung dark
  The hills and waters o'er;
When a band of exiles moor'd their bark
  On the wild New England shore.'

He then visited the burial place of the Pilgrims, and speaks of the kind hospitality he received from the Rev. George Morse, Wesleyan minister, and his family, whose guest he was at Plymouth. On his return journey to New York he sailed down the Hudson river, and describes the scenery as grand. Stood in the pulpit of the late Rev. John Todd.

From 10th to 19th November Mr. Ashworth's time was occupied about New York and the neighbourhood, conducting religious services and visiting the various institutions. He visited Staten Island, where he lectured, and had many Lancashire and Yorkshire people to hear him; sailed round the island; visited "Snug Harbour," or home for invalid sailors; conversed with old tars; heard the following tale: "An aged minister was refused communion with a certain Baptist church, and observed, 'Oh, I thought it was the Lord's supper, but I see it is a private affair of your own.'"

"Sunday, Nov. 16. The last Sabbath spent in New York. Preached in St. Luke's Methodist chapel in the morning, and at West Presbyterian church in the evening.

"Monday, Nov. 17. A farewell service was held at Dr. Crosby's church; singing by Phillip Phillips.

"Tuesday, Nov. 18. Visited and spoke at Mr. and Mrs. Palmer's meeting for promoting higher Christian holiness. Met forty 'Friends' at Mr. Tatham's; much conversation.

"Wednesday, Nov. 19. Mr. Wilder, my kind and patient host at New York, invited a number of friends to breakfast, after which we had singing and prayer. The singing by Phillip Phillips, 'Loved ones gone before,' and prayers, deeply affected me; it was a scene. Telegraphed by cable to my wife, 'John Ashworth, Rochdale, England, sailed *Minnesota;*' cost one dollar each word; would get it in one hour. Went on board; many friends from various parts came to say farewell. Went into my bedroom, fell upon my knees, imploring the continued protection of my God."

Captain Freeman having retired from the sea, the *Minnesota* was now in command of his late chief officer, Captain Beddoes. The vessel left New York at 2-30 p.m., amidst the cheering of friends and the waving of handkerchiefs. They had on board about twenty saloon and one hundred and thirty steerage passengers. Among the former were two Catholic priests, who addressed each other as Father P— and Father D—, and made themselves very conspicuous during the voyage in a variety of ways. "In carving a fowl or cracking a lobster they were A1, and took more delight in drinking porter or listening to comic songs by a fellow passenger from Ireland, than the reading of Scriptures or prayers. The moment service began they bolted."

For several days they had moderately fine weather. On the 22nd, however, they had indications of a coming storm: in the setting of the sun, the frisking of the cats, in washing their faces and not putting their paws behind their ears, which the sailors regard as ominous signs. On the following day the captain was heard giving orders to make all fast, and see the boats secure. As night came on there was no setting sun visible. The skylights were boarded over, and all retired with rather gloomy forebodings.

"Nov. 24. Noon. Hail and snow; wind still rising, roaring in the sails and yards; ventured on deck, holding fast by the ropes. What a sight! The rolling, foaming waves as far as the eye can reach. The stormy wind being in our favour the ship was driving at a fearful speed, and dragging her screw, which made the vessel tremble from stem to stern. Passed a three masted vessel with all her sails torn, and though within two hundred yards we afterwards lost sight of her behind the huge waves; around us these majestic billows often seemed higher than our topmast. As night came on, a booming sound was heard: one of our sails was blown to pieces. We all sat in the saloon as quiet and silent as possible; several were sick and depressed. The two priests requested the funny Irishman to sing them a comic song; he looked, and appealed to me whether, under the circumstances, such a request was proper; for Solomon said there was a time for all things. 'I am no admirer of comic songs at any time;' I replied, 'but now, when so many on board are in fear and distress, it would seem strange. I will join in singing—

'God moves in a mysterious way
His wonders to perform,'

if you please.' At this, the priests again bolted into their bed-room, and soon a porter bottle went *plop*.

"Nov. 25. Did not undress last night; a heavy sea broke over our vessel, keeping her on her beam-ends for some time. Deep seemed calling unto deep, and the roar of the sea was fearful. Could take no food, only a little rice milk; could not stand, sit, or lie down: strapped myself fast to the ring of the port-hole.

"Nov. 26. Feel very restless; no sleep for twenty-four hours. Went amongst the poor steerage passengers, found I had much to be thankful for. Passed a large mast, and other floating wreck; fearful signs these."

They were not far from the spot where that terrible collision of the French steamer *Ville du Havre* and *Loch Earn* occurred, on the morning of the 22nd, when two hundred and twenty-six lives were lost. Probably it was some of the wreck of that ill-fated vessel.

"Nov. 27. A turkey for dinner to-day for all that could eat; a universal dish in America, being thanksgiving day in commemoration of the relief of the 'Pilgrim Fathers.' The funny Irishman, and the 'illigant' lady had something beside turkey, and sang foolish songs.

"Nov. 28. Had a fearful restless night; no sleep. The vessel rolling and plunging, deep in on starboard side; still strapped fast to the port-hole ring. Read and tried to study a portion of the Gospel by John. How truly precious are my dear Saviour's words, as given by His beloved *disciple*; I do love Thy word. Rose thankful for great mercies, but feel my health suffering by being not able to rest night or day. At the request of the saloon passengers, I presented the captain and officers with an address expressive of our thanks for their care and kindness.

"Nov. 29. Very restless and distressed night; I felt really poorly, my head like fire, and my appetite gone; could neither stand, sit, or lie. Shipped a great sea about 2, which dashed open my port-hole window, and deluged every thing in my berth—sofa, bed, books, and myself; twenty gallons of water at least came rushing in. Went on deck; beheld what I can never forget. It seemed as if the ship would be swallowed up every moment. Had more conversation with the captain on prayer; said he was so thankful I had told him of the prayer meeting held at New York previous to our sailing, and remarked how applicable the 107th Psalm was to our condition. The 'illigant' lady was asking what sort of theatres there were in Liverpool, and expected to see 'illigant' playing. The 'Farsnet' Lighthouse was sighted about 8 this evening, amidst the shouts of the passengers, and a greeting to the captain. 'Ye are the lights of the world.' Got into smoother water; retired to bed; slept soundly; heard nothing of our call at Queenstown.

"Nov. 30. Sunday. Sun rose clear and bright; all seemed like heavenly peace compared with what we had just experienced. Oh, what happy hearts will hail this morning on shore, sweet Sabbath, sweet Sabbath. Preached to the steerage passengers, at their request, in the steerage; seemed to enjoy the service. A fine moonlight evening; walked the deck praising God; many lighthouses, 'Skerries' and 'Holyhead.'

"Dec. 1. Monday. As daylight dawned we saw New Brighton, and the glimmering lamps on the shores at Liverpool; and about 7 we bid adieu to the captain and officers of the *Minnesota*, amidst the shouts of fellow passengers, and went on board the tender. On reaching the station, found a train ready for starting; arrived home at 11 to my own great joy and thankfulness to my God for His great mercies. Bless the Lord, O my soul."

As might be expected, Mr. Ashworth looked

fagged and weary. On the following day he says, "Slept almost all the afternoon, and sat by my comfortable hearth in the evening"; probably it never felt or seemed so comfortable to him as then.

He complained of sore bones for several days, but by quiet rest and good nursing soon recovered his usual vigour, and was again engaged in active service for the Master. He says, "Had many friends to see and welcome me back again. I am thankful for this." On the Saturday he presided at the annual tea meeting of the blind, and on Sunday preached at the Chapel for the Destitute to a crowded congregation, and was heartily welcomed both by his blind friends and poor people. Invitations came pouring in from all quarters, which, with the accumulation of letters awaiting him, the correspondence for some time was excessive. He closes the year with the following reflections: "The year is now gone, and we are one less in our family. God took my dear Mary Jane on the 21st of March last, took her to her home in heaven, after great pain, and through much tribulation; she loved her Saviour, and now reigns with Him."

CHAPTER XVII.

JOHN ASHWORTH, AS AN AUTHOR.

AS has already been intimated, that which gave Mr. Ashworth such a world-wide reputation was his writings, more particularly those entitled "Strange Tales from Humble Life." Previous to the publication of these he was comparatively little known, and laboured for years without much public recognition or public sympathy; although his first literary productions, years before the issue of "Strange Tales," were of considerable merit, and attracted the attention of a few, who discovered in these early essays the germ of a successful future in the pathway of literary fame.

In 1853, when attending a meeting of the Peace Society in Edinburgh, he met with John W. Barber and his daughter Elizabeth, two celebrated American writers of historic and other works, who were at that time making a tour through Europe; and as if there was a kind of spiritual magnetism between kindred souls which recognise one another, so in a few days an intimacy was formed, such as might only be witnessed in those who had known each other for years.

This young authoress, as with prophetic eye, in writing to Mr. Ashworth from London a few weeks after they met, said, "You have no ordinary talent in writing. This is sufficiently proved by that fine article on American slavery, which you so kindly sent us. Who knows what time may yet bring for you, with a cultivation of the *heaven-born* talent with which God has endowed you? Perhaps I shall yet see your name enrolled amongst English authors, and your productions always, I know, on the side of truth, justice, and liberty. At Glasgow we found a kind little token of remembrance from you, in the form of some lines addressed to my father and myself, which I have copied agreeably to your request, and enclose with this."

The lines are as follows:—

TO MR. AND MISS BARBER.

IMPROMPTU.

"We met on Scotia's classic ground,
 Where Burns and Scott have sung;
We met on Calton's Grecian mound,
 Where city's hum unceasing rung.

"We saw the gory Pentland hills,
 Where struggling virtue fell,
Beneath the ruthless tyrant's hand,
 Fierce vagabonds of hell.

"We saw the place where martyrs sleep—
 The bold, the great, the good;
We saw the stone on which they sealed
 The covenant in blood.

"Three happy kindred spirits met:
 When shall we meet again?
Columbia is your distant home,
 And mine Britannia's plain.

"JOHN ASHWORTH.

"GLASGOW, OCT. 15TH, 1853."

Miss Barber, who afterwards became the wife of Captain Barrett, died of cholera in the Chinese seas, when accompanying her husband, the following notice of which is from an American journal:—

"We are surprised and pained to hear of the death of Mrs. E. G. Barrett, better known by her maiden name of Miss E. G. Barber, which occurred at sea on the 19th of July last (1868). Miss Barber was widely known as a writer of rare merit. Her poetry and prose, each showed a purity of heart, a depth of feeling, and a refinement of intellect that entitled her to a position among the best authors in the country. Her death will be deplored by those who knew her through her writings, but more deeply by those acquainted with the nobleness of her personal character."—*Newhaven Journal.*

It may be mentioned as an exemplification of the importance of what may appear to be little things and small services, that the career of the subject of this memoir as a public writer was to no small extent determined by an incident of that description.

Many Rochdale people will remember with what éclat a person who called himself Mr. Henry Box Brown, and represented himself as an escaped slave from one of the Southern States of America, for a goodly number of successive nights lectured to overflowing audiences upon the then flourishing, but now happily exploded social institution, slavery; the lectures being rendered doubly attractive by a dioramic exhibition of scenes touched upon. This lecturer added to his popularity by what appeared to be profuse liberality. He offered a prize for the best essay on slavery which should be composed by a Rochdale workman.

On the day appointed for the reception of the competitive essays, Mr. Ashworth's nephew and namesake, passing the shop of his uncle, observed him standing pensive at the door, and jocularly enquired if he was a competitor for the coveted prize. It transpired that he had entertained an intention, but was reluctant to present his production for two reasons: one, that the term workman might not be construed to extend to him; the other, that the time was too brief to permit him to finish before the precise hour. Encouraging him to risk the question of advisability, the nephew promised, and the promise was accepted, to re-write at the uncle's dictation, &c. The result was, that the paper was *just in time*, and was adjudged *the prize, viz.*, a handsome family Bible.

It is the same article referred to by Miss Barber, and is as follows:—

THE HORRORS AND CURSE OF SLAVERY.

BY JOHN ASHWORTH.

Being the Successful Essay for the First Prize, given by Mr. Henry Box Brown, an American fugitive slave.

> Has Beelzebub a rival?
> Is there a wretch in all his vast domains
> That seeks to be his peer? That wretch
> Would surely be the owner of a slave!

"Slavery! the very word is odious; the bitterest part of the curse is summed up in the sickening sound. Its history was never written. Wilberforce, Clarkson, Buxton, Thompson, Burritt and others have hurled their denunciations against it: but who has not felt that even these men have failed to delineate its hideous form?

"There are subjects that defy the highest powers of the loftiest intellects. Slavery is one. Its crimes are stupendous; it is sublime in its very atrocity.

"AFRICA! AMERICA! who does not associate with the

very utterance of these words the most painful recollections? Africa has drunk deep the bitter cup: its plague-smitten cities, the Simooms of its deserts, the ferocious beasts and deadly reptiles of its forests are but as the gentle breeze to the tornado, compared to the appalling horrors inflicted on it by the accursed Slave Trade. Could the bones of its victims be collected, there might be reared on the banks of the Nile another Pyramid—of skulls! Could the waters of the Western Hemisphere be dried up, the grim monument of death would shew the track of the Slave Ship from the banks of the Gambia to the shores of the Atlantic.

"The African mother, while watering her rice-ground hangs her basket-cradle on the low branches of the Mango tree, and sings in plaintive accents:—

When bad men shall come to steal thee
Hush baby, Ho!—
May he be good massa to thee
Hush baby, Ho!—
If he will not take me with thee
Hush baby, Ho!—
Then I'll pray him not to flog thee
Hush baby, Ho!

"How often has this song been interrupted by the loud yells of the captors, rushing upon a peaceful village! and the morning sun has risen over the dun smoke of its smouldering embers; its youth dragged away in chains to the suffocating hold of the Slaver, while the aged and infirm are left to perish broken-hearted.

"The horrors of the middle passage do not admit of description. Gnawing hunger, burning thirst, madness, suffocation and death; bodies cast overboard to be devoured by the shark, who ever fattens on the wake of the Slaver.

"Whither are these cargoes of murder bound? Let the features and contour of the Slaves of Columbia tell! Let Georgia, Maryland and the other Slave States of America tell!

"AMERICA! *thou paradox of Nations!* the whole earth ought to put on sackcloth and mourn for thee. The names of thy thirteen Slave States ought to be graven in letters deep on a blood-red ground, and publicly exhibited in every hamlet in Christendom. America! perfidious and guilty America! Slave-buying, Slave-selling, Slave-breeding, and Slave-destroying America!

"In North Carolina the punishment for teaching a Slave to write, giving or selling him a Bible, or any other book, is a fine of two-hundred dollars. In Georgia, seven Slaves found together without the presence of a white man shall be punished by flogging: if a master offer an insult to a Female Slave and she resents it, he may order her to be flogged; and if she still rebels, he may order her to be shot; if a company of Slaves be discovered holding a prayer meeting, any magistrate can, without a trial, inflict, on each, twenty lashes.

"There is no cruelty, no pain, no torture however refined, but what has been improved upon by the American Slave-holder. The poor, weeping, suffering, helpless, and unpitied Slaves have their quivering flesh lacerated in a thousand varied forms by the scourging lash of their inhuman owners or reckless drivers, and often when their bodies present one mass of clotted blood, turpentine, pepper, salt, or mustard is rubbed into their bleeding wounds, to aggravate and prolong their suffering. They are stamped upon; their limbs are often broken, joints dislocated, faces bruised, eyes and teeth knocked out, ears cropped, slit, or shaved entirely off, red-hot branding irons stamped on their flesh, maimed by guns, pistol-shots, and knives; they are forced to flog one another,—sons to flog mothers, fathers their daughters; if they attempt to escape, they are hunted and worried by blood-hounds;—and this in proud, pompous, boasting America! Thirty-three thousand additional Slaves are annually required to supply the places of those destroyed by these dreadful tortures: for American Slave-holders, in public assembly have decided that it is more *profitable* to work them to death, by forced labour, than to prolong their lives by humane treatment. And this in the land of freedom! the land that every fourth of July hoists its countless flags of Liberty and Independence. Liberty and Independence, forsooth! The American flag instead of being bespangled with stars ought to be broad and black, distinguished from others by its death's-head and cross bones.

"Tell us not of the mental inferiority of the coloured

race! who that has read the appeals of the fugitive slaves to British philanthropists, can for a moment doubt their intellectual powers? Who that has heard the searching eloquence of Frederick Douglas or Henry Box Brown can accuse them of natural incapacity? In the likeness of himself the Great Spirit made them all, and has pronounced a curse on every man that makes and holds his brother a slave. Measure the black man by the wisdom that formed him, the benevolence that watches over him, and the destiny that awaits him: measure him by his hopes, his fears, his joys, his sorrows and by his crimes, and then appears *the man*; and Newton was no more.

"But the knell of Slavery is sounded; the vampire that that has sucked the blood of earth's continents has received its death-wound; the light of truth and of freedom has shot its beams athwart the dark caverns of the craven Republican: and if vengeance overtakes not the oppressor, it is because the oppressed have learned to shew him mercy.

"O Slavery! what tongue can thee describe? to call
Thee fiend were mild—to compare thee
With the fearful aggregate of
Ills that crush earth's hapless sons, would
Be to honour thee. Earthquakes, storms,
Tempests, and thunderbolts, with all
Their train of horrors—compared with thee—
Are mercies.—To draw thy portrait
The pen must be dipp'd deep in
Stygian dye, and shaded by a
STUDENT OF THE SCHOOL OF HELL.

"JOHN ASHWORTH,

PAINTER.

"*Rochdale, October 3rd*, 1851."

Although born in a rough school, John Ashworth was a man who was sure to rise in the world, notwithstanding every drawback of birth or circumstances. His sturdy independence and self-reliance preserved him from the fatal tendency to lean on others for success. The help that weaker natures seek from their fellow-creatures, he sought only from God; as when told by a friend of sums of money given to a man who was failing in business, he shrugged his shoulders, and with a most impressive gesture, said, "I would never have received them." In youth, he grew up in the constant presence of the misery that results, even here, from sin; and of the consoling and elevating power of godliness. What guilt can do, and what grace can do, were among the first lessons he learned; and let boys and young people remember that it was owing to his energy and determined perseverance that he rose step by step, as they will learn from his own account of the way in which he obtained his first book.

"I am not an old man, but the youth of the present day have many privileges which I had not when I was a lad. I remember how I got my first book. I shall never forget it—I don't want to forget it. I was in the habit of going to a place in Rochdale called Providence Chapel. From childhood I have never been an absentee from the means of grace, and I need not speak of the great boon that it has been to me. There was a little pew in that chapel, so small that it would not hold more than one. Whether they collected any rent for the pew I do not know. I never paid anything for it. I had nothing to pay with. Well, I used to get into this triangular-shaped pew. One Sunday, the minister, Mr. Eli, who subsequently went to Leeds, made use in his sermon of the word 'prerogative.' Why that word should have so impressed itself upon me I do not know, but it did. It bothered me the day after, and I sought the assistance of an old man in our neighbourhood, named Adam. I said to him, 'What is the meaning of the word prerogative?' He said, 'I do not know, and there is nobody in this country knows.' He said, 'Where didst thou hear that?' It was a poser for him. I told him where I had heard it, and he said, 'Thou may go and ask *Eli,* then. 'Now,' said I, 'is there a book that tells the meaning of words?' 'There is,' he said, 'there is what they call a Johnson's Dictionary: but there isn't one in this neighbourhood.' He said, 'Possibly the number man,' the travelling bookseller, 'may have one when he comes.' 'My father takes in 'Buchan's Domestic Medicine,' in parts, and the man calls every month.' The 'number man' came in due time; and after he had put down the part of Buchan on the table and had gone out, I followed him. I followed him about two hundred yards before I durst speak to him, and then I called to him from behind 'I say.' He turned round with, 'What do you say?' and nearly drove all my say out of me. I said, 'Have you a book that tells the meaning of words?' He said, 'Do you mean Johnson's Dictionary?' and I replied 'Yes.' He said, 'Yes, I have it; how much will you give a month if I bring you one? The price is two shillings and sixpence: how much can you give a month?' That was a very serious question, and, after hesitating, I replied—stretching to the very utmost I durst—'twopence.' Well, his good nature prevailed; he burst out laughing and said, 'You shall have it.' I am thankful to this day that the man's good nature did prevail. You know twopence is twopence if you haven't got it. Some of you may laugh at the idea of being fast for twopence. Well, twopence is twopence, and it was so with me. I knew my mother's circumstances. I knew that she had not a farthing to spare, and that she had never what she ought to have. I was determined I would not ask my mother for it: I would get it somewhere without asking her for it. I saw a load of coals thrown down belonging to an old bachelor called 'old James,' and I thought I would get these coals in. I did so, and then opening his door I said, 'I have got your coals in.' 'Very well,' he said. I thought, was that all? I swept up the coals and went again and said, 'James, I have got your coals in.' 'Very well.' I was astonished; I had expected a penny. I went and swept again, and then ventured down the third time. Just as I opened the door out sprang 'James' with an 'Off; I will coals thee if thou comes here again.' I ran up and ran away. I was mortified to an extent I cannot tell. I felt as if I would have scattered his coals all over Lancashire if I could. There was a woman in our neighbourhood called Lucy, and sometimes she had to pick up a lad to take her husband his dinner. I went to her and said, 'I will take Jack's dinner three times for a halfpenny.' 'Very well.' Three times there and three times back, six miles, for a halfpenny. Four times six are twenty-four miles for my first twopence to pay the first instalment for my first book. Now I want to know if there is a lad here who labours under greater difficulties than I did. I made a bargain with myself I would never pass a word I did not understand without consulting this book, and it was in that way I soon acquired a knowledge of the meaning of words."

John Ashworth's first appearance as an author is said to have been in 1845, when he contributed some articles to "The Sabbath School Friend," published by Jesse Hall, of this town (Rochdale), vol. I of which was presented to him by the Rochdale Sunday School Union; but we know that he was the author of several anonymous productions of an earlier date, one of which was a dialogue, published in 1843, entitled "Women's Lodges; a bit o taulk obewt um, between Mary and Nancy," in the Lancashire Dialect, a style of language he became much averse to in after life, either in speaking, writing, or reciting, and frequently brought himself into collision with the conductors of Sabbath schools by denouncing it. He thought young people ought to be trained to speak properly. The moral of the dialogue, however, is good, and intended to teach mothers some wholesome lessons; for example,—

"*Mary*—Wel, realy, Nancy, dusn't te think ut it's o gret shome for us ut ur mothurs to goo on so? Con we expekt ur childer to be whot the' shud'n be, wol we setten um sich paturns? Nobut last Tuesday neet aw went into Cathrun's for th' stokin' needle ut ho'od borrow'd, un little Cathrun sed ur mam wur go'on t' th' Lodge, un ud nevur us'd it;

for ho'od sin ur poo ur stokin' dewn so us oles cudn't be sin.

"*Nancy*—Wel, wot dos that mathur wen one's in o hurre?

"*Mary*—But ther wur sich o hewse, fur pots wur o durt, un cindurs wur up t' th' bars, un little Ned wur o sleep o' th' floor wi' o fase us blac' us soot, un us rag'd us o file-fole; little Cathrun ud dun o ho cud t' keep chilt quite, un aw seed ut ho'od bin cryin' ursel, un a took un gin th' chilt o pap; but sob'd so wol i' made moy hart wartch, un it isn't lung sin Bil un ur wur feghtin obewt ur bein' ut ur Lodge so lat.

"*Nancy*—Un ar foke nevur t' goo ewt o th' dur? Chilt ud sleep no wur fur havin' o good skrike, un ho'od soon wesh pots un gethur up sindurs wen ho geet back.

"Ut th' Lodge they're drinkin,' un dancin,' un yellin',
Wol ther hewses ur durty, un ther childur ur bellin'."

Many of the narratives comprised in "Strange Tales" were written years before they were published, such as "My Mother," "Sanderson, and Little Alice," and others. The former, the author informs us, was written eleven years before it saw daylight; he had an impression no one would care to read such tales, far less did he ever think they would be so acceptable to the public, or that they would be in the least remunerative; and when, in 1860, he went with his manuscript of "The Dark Hour" in his pocket to the publisher, Mr. Bremner, he would have been thankful to be assured against any loss in its publication, as the following circumstance will show. On that memorable day, he was passing through St. Ann's Square, in Manchester, when he met a friend from Rochdale, Mr. John Petrie, Jun., who noticed that he was looking exceedingly dejected, and addressing him, said, "John, whatever is to do with you? you look down and gloomy." He replied, "I never was so fast in my life, or so cast down. I've been to Bremner about publishing the first narrative of 'Strange Tales,' and he says it will cost £100 to bring it out, and I don't know what to do. I was just thinking of going home, and giving it up altogether, as I have not a hundred pounds to spare, and I think it would be wrong in me in my present position, with my family, to risk the loss of so much money." Seeing him so much dejected, and knowing from previous conversations that he had long set his heart upon the publication of these "Strange Tales," Mr. Petrie said, "Well, if you will agree to give me half the profit, should there be any, I will give you the £100, if it is wanted." The expression of his countenance changed in a moment, and his face beamed with delight as he replied, "I will give you one-third." "Agreed," said his friend; and they shook hands to ratify the contract. Addressing Mr. Petrie he then said, "You have taken a load off my mind; I'll go back to Bremner, and tell him to go on with it, as I have found a friend who will find the money." When the publisher saw he had a friend at his back, he willingly undertook the work, and said he had no need to have troubled him.

About eighteen months after, Mr. Petrie was one day surprised by Mr. Ashworth calling upon him, and saying, "I have to-day received the first thirty pounds for 'Strange Tales.' I don't know whether you expect some of it or not; but if you do, it is yours." His friend, wishing to try him, replied, "Of course, I am entitled to one-third;" but generously added, "I do not want it; I am glad you have succeeded, and you are quite welcome to the whole of it."

Sixty-one of these narratives of "Strange Tales, from Humble Life" have been published singly, and also in five Series, the first of which was issued in 1863; the second in 1865; the third in 1867; the fourth in 1870; and the fifth in 1874. There is also what is called the Illustrated, or Queen's Edition, containing the first and second Series, a copy of which was presented by the author, and graciously accepted by Her Majesty Queen Victoria, and duly acknowledged as follows:—

"77, Hamilton-terrace, N.W.,
"April 14th, 1871.

"My dear Sir,

"I am commanded by Her Majesty the Queen to assure you that Her Majesty accepts with pleasure the copy of the beautiful edition of 'Strange Tales,' which I have had the honour of presenting on your behalf.

"Believe me,
"My dear Sir,
"Very faithfully yours,
"R. DUCKWORTH."

"Mr. John Ashworth,
"Rochdale.

Upwards of three millions of these Tales have been circulated, and are now translated into several languages, *viz.*, Welsh, French, Dutch, Russian, Spanish, and Swiss; and there is scarcely any part of the civilized world where they have not been read, and the name of the author become familiar. When visiting one of the Indian settlements, during his American tour, "Strange Tales" were his passport, and he was at once recognised and welcomed as a brother.

The narratives display great descriptive power, pathos,- and beauty. They are substantially true; not mere creatures of the author's imagination, but portraitures of real men and women. They are written with a masterly hand, in simple but expressive language; show great insight into character, and intimate acquaintance with many phases of human life. Objects the author came in contact with, which many would have passed unnoticed, served as material for thought, and were made available by his pen, and wielded with such graphic power as to stir the deepest emotions of the heart. Who could read "The Dark Hour," "Mary, a Tale of Sorrow," "Niff and his Dogs," or the deeply touching sketch of "My Mother," for the first time, and not weep?

Some, in depreciation, have said many of the Tales are highly coloured and overwrought.

While it is admitted that the author had a warm imagination, and his feelings were of the intense kind, so that he could sketch the incidents with such power as to make them seem incredulous, the writer can testify to their truthfulness; having been associated with him in his work for upwards of ten years, known and conversed with more than twenty-five of the subjects of the narratives, and visited many of them in their sickness and on their death-beds.

The author, in his preface to the first and second series of Strange Tales, writes, "The reader may rest assured that these Tales are true, as hundreds in Rochdale and the neighbourhood can testify; and perhaps nowhere are they so popular as in this locality, *because* they are known to be narratives of facts."

Mr. Ashworth was at considerable trouble to collect vouchers to the truth of most, if not all, of the narratives which he intended to publish. The following are selected.

"THE DARK HOUR."

"I have read your narrative called 'The Dark Hour,' and know it to be true. I sold you and helped to carry the second-hand furniture into the cellar the night you mention, and my wife attended Mrs. Johnson in her sickness.

"George Crowther.
"Mary Crowther (her × mark)."

"Wardleworth Workhouse,
"Rochdale, March 24th, 1868.

"I have read Mr. John Ashworth's tract, entitled 'The Dark Hour,' and so far as regards the condition of the family, when residing in Cheetham-street, have no hesitation in declaring the same to be true.

"Robert Whitworth,
"Relieving Officer."

"THE TWO OLD MEN."

"I have read your narrative of 'The Two Old Men,' and as far as regards my father, old Lawrence Hoyle, your description of him, and also of my mother, I know to be true. I am the son William that you mention as playing the flute at the Destitute.

"William Hoyle."

"Pleasant View,
"Hopwood, February, 9th, 1864.

"I wish to add my testimony to the truth of your narrative of my father, Lawrence Hoyle, in conjunction with my brother William. Much more might have been said.

"Peggy Clegg,
"5, Robert-street, Rochdale.
"Maiden name, Peggy Hoyle."

"Pinder, or Joseph Taylor, mentioned in your narrative of 'The Wonder; or, The Two Old Men,' was my grandfather. What you have written about him I know to be true.

"SARAH LEES (her × mark).

"Witness, A. Barraclough,
"January, 1868."

"SANDERSON AND LITTLE ALICE."

"I have seen an attempt by the Secularists to prove your narrative of Sanderson not true; and I feel I ought to say that I knew Sanderson well, I was much in his company, and am surprised how very correctly you have described every thing about him.

"JOHN MILLS, Regent-street,
"Rochdale, Wool Sorter."

"Having read your reply to the attack made upon your tract, 'Sanderson and Little Alice,' by the Secularists, I beg to say, that the statement you have given respecting our interview with them is perfectly correct; and, I have no hesitation in saying, that if they had published the whole of the notes then read by them, on that occasion, any reply on your part would have been entirely unnecessary.

"THOS. SCHOFIELD.

"Castlemere, Jan. 28th, 1864."

"Mr. Ashworth's story of 'Sanderson and Little Alice' I have read. I knew Sanderson well; he was always reckoned an Infidel. It was always said he believed neither in God nor Devil, Heaven nor Hell. What Jane Moorhouse said to Mr. Ashworth about Sanderson's principles was true.

"23rd Feb., 1864. "HARRIET JOHNSON."

"WILKINS."

"We have read your narrative of 'Wilkins,' and know it to be true. We are the persons mentioned in the narrative.

"MICHAEL TODD.
"MARY RICKSON (her × mark),
"Housekeeper to Michael Todd."

"Livesey-street,
"Feb. 5th, 1866.

"I have read your narrative of 'Old Richard; or, The Dark Night,' and know it to be true. Richard lived with me a long time, and died at my house, at a place called Springs, near Bagslate and Bamford. I frequently called for the money, at your house, you allowed him weekly.

"WILLIAM FOULDS,
"Feb. 6th, 1864. "Union-street, Lower-place."

"I have read your narrative of 'Old Richard; or, The Dark Night,' and know it to be true. I well remember the Sunday he was bidding us farewell before going to the Workhouse, and heard him telling how that the Lord had provided a friend. Richard was a good old man; known to many, and all loved him.

"JOHN BROADBENT,
"March 26th, 1864. "Chapel Keeper."

"JOSEPH; OR, THE SILENT CORNER."

"We have read your tract called 'Joseph; or, The Silent Corner,' and know it to be true. Joseph was a long time sick in our house, and at last died in a small back place called the hen-cote. You (John Ashworth) visited him a long time, and helped to carry him to his grave.

"JOHN SMITH (his × mark).
"Feb. 5th, 1864. "SARAH SMITH (her × mark).
"E. Ashworth, married daughter, Witness."

"NIFF AND HIS DOGS."

"I have read the narrative by John Ashworth called 'Niff and his Dogs,' and know it to be true. I am the person called 'Niff,' though my proper name is Nathaniel Kershaw, but am seldom called anything but 'Niff.' I am sorry to say that the description of my former life of wickedness is too true; but am happy to say that I am now, by the grace of God, a new creature in Christ Jesus.

"NATHANIEL KERSHAW."

"MY MOTHER."

"We have read our mother's narrative, entitled 'My

Mother,' and hereby declare that we know all the statements therein made to be true.

"SARAH MILLS.
"LUCY ASHWORTH.
"ABEL ASHWORTH.
"MARGARET SHEPHERD (her + mark).
"ABRAHAM ASHWORTH.

"Witness to the Signatures,
"A. Barraclough."

"MY NEW FRIENDS."

"We keep the Lodging-house you mention in the Tale called 'My New Friends,' and well remember your first congregation going with you from our house:—old Solomon, Boswell with the wood leg, Bill Guest, Solomon's wife, and others.

"JOHN SMITH (his × mark).
"SARAH SMITH (her × mark).

"Signed in the presence of—
"E. Ashworth, } Married daughters
"Mary Richards, } of the above.
"February 5th, 1864."

"We have read your narrative of 'My New Friends,' and remember most of it, and know it to be true; for we are two of the persons mentioned, and have attended your chapel almost from the beginning.

"MATTHEW SHEPHERD (his + mark).
"JAMES CLOUGH (his + mark).

"Alice Leach, Scripture Reader, Witness."

"JULIA."

"John Ashworth has read over to me the narrative of my life, and it is all true. He is at liberty to call it 'Julia.'

JULIA B——.

"John Hey, Witness."

"Having called in to hand to my friend John Ashworth a small donation which I had received to encourage him in *his labours* of Christian love and benevolence. . . He was *engaged* in conversation with Julia B——, whose character and destitute position I heard narrated, and read the touching letter from her parents, who had been greatly distressed at the loss of their child, not knowing what might have befallen her; having now found her way to John Ashworth, who wrote to her parents, and has now undertaken to return her safely to the bosom of her family.

"JOHN YEARDLEY.

"1864, 6 mo., 18."

We have similar vouchers for "Sarah; or, I will have him"; "No Cotton"; "George"; "Old Adam"; "Old Ab'"; "Little Susan"; "William the Tutor"; "Job Morley"; "Emmott"; "The Widow"; and others, which we cannot possibly find space for. We trust sufficient have been given to satisfy any unprejudiced mind of their truthfulness. I would however again refer to one living witness, and that is Nathaniel Kershaw, or "Niff," whose reality has been frequently called in question. Had the thrilling narrative of "Niff and his Dogs" been written twenty years after his decease, it would have been no more wonderful if sceptics had doubted the truth of it, than that they should "Sanderson and Little Alice"; but that they should do so while the subject is still alive is something marvellous. Not long ago Nathaniel heard of an infidel in a neighbouring town denying his existence, and his informant having given him the the man's address, Niff took the trouble to pay him a visit. After wishing him good morning, he offered him his hand; and as the man exchanged these friendly greetings, he said to Niff, "But I don't know you." To which Nathan replied, "But you shall know me; I am the man they call 'Niff and his Dogs,' and I heard tell of you saying there never was such a man, and I thought I would just come and let you look at him." This is not the only occasion on which Nathan has had to vindicate his reality. He is now in his eighty-second year, and thinks God has spared him on purpose for people to look at, and show them what grace can do.

Mr. Ashworth received hundreds of letters testifying as to the good, in various ways, resulting from the reading of "Strange Tales." Many conversions, many prodigals returned, and many of God's people led to seek after the outcast and wanderers, and open chapels for the destitute, to which we think it unnecessary further to refer.

Other works by the same author followed the publication of "Strange Tales." Two volumes,—"Walks in Canaan," and "Back from Canaan"; the first published in 1869, and the second in 1873. "Simple Records," published in 1871-2. The former is the description of a tour in Palestine and the East; and the latter a number of short sketches delineating, with that pathos natural to the author, the various phases of human nature, as affected by the gospel and grace of God, which makes them almost as interesting as "Strange Tales." Amongst the many testimonials as to the merits of "Simple Records," the following criticism from a disinterested writer is selected:—

"I cannot allow myself to say less than this, *viz.*, that both for the true touch of nature which makes the world akin; for the humane element which pervades the stories; for the chaste and touching pathos so delicately and yet tellingly brought out in many of the 'Records'; and for other points, but chiefly for the testimony most of them yield to the value of living, loving, practical Christianity, *and the* lessons suggested both to the saved and the unre*pentant* sinners, I exceedingly like the book.

"Even as a literary production, although I don't profess competence as a literary critic, I consider the book to rank respectably.

"I have the more pleasure in speaking with unqualified admiration of the 'Records' because you know that I am combative enough to express an adverse opinion when I cherish it; and also because on some points upon which you have written we do hold opposite opinions.

"Believe me, very sincerely yours,

"GEORGE JACKSON."

Mr. Ashworth also published several tracts on "War," which did not meet with the same reception as his other works; and while some commended him for his fearless attack upon a system he regarded as odious and degrading, many more of his professed friends and admirers wrote and said bitter things of him; and one of them (a Major in the 33rd L. R. V.) offered to provide him apartments at Cheadle (asylum), as the most suitable place for a mind so distorted. He, however, notwithstanding all the opposition he met with, maintained his peace principles with unflinching firmness, believing that war was an unmitigated evil, and opposed to reason, morality, civilization, and the spirit of Christianity.

In early life, Mr. Ashworth identified himself with one or more debating societies, which no doubt tended to develop those faculties that made him so popular and successful as a public speaker; and when a comparatively young man he was found on the platform taking part in any matters that concerned the welfare of his fellow men, whether social, political, or religious. He could always command the attention and respect of an audience, whether acting in the capacity of president or speaker, as the following incident will show.

In the year 1843, during the period of what was then called the Chartist agitation, Mr. Joseph Sturge visited Rochdale, with the view of originating a complete suffrage union. Meetings were held for this purpose, and many who disapproved of the extreme opinions of the Fergus O'Connor chartists joined this organization, regarding its programme as a solution of the vexed question of the suffrage. After considerable discussion in the committee, a public meeting was resolved upon, for the purpose of placing the views of Mr. Sturge before the people, and it was held in the Assembly Room, behind the old theatre, then existing in Toad lane. Opposition was expected from the physical-force chartists, who did in fact muster in overwhelming force. Mr. John Ashworth, then considered as a representative working man, was proposed as chairman, and accepted by the meeting. Mr. Jacob Bright was to have been the first speaker, but the meeting was uproarious and refused to hear him. A socialist lecturer was then put up by the chartists, who harangued the meeting at great length, in a violent speech, and proposed a resolution in favour of the charter, condemning the proceedings of the Sturge party in strong language. This resolution was carried amidst great excitement, and it was owing to Mr. Ashworth's excellent tact and good sense that a collision between the contending parties, which might have resulted in blood-shed, was avoided; and the meeting passed off without violence.

CHAPTER XVIII.

LECTURER AND PREACHER.

AS a Lecturer, Mr. Ashworth was not what may be termed eloquent, but he had the power of gaining the attention and working upon the feelings of his auditors in a manner few could equal or surpass. At one moment the faces of his audience would beam with pleasurable emotion; while the next, their smiles would be turned into sadness, and the tender tear be trickling down their cheeks. His expressions were always plain and simple, yet forcible, so that his hearers could understand what he had to say. He addressed himself to the heart, and by pointing his morals with some striking incident of which he had a fund at command, he never failed to gain the attention of his audience. Another secret of his success as a lecturer was his thorough earnestness and sincerity. Mr. Ashworth had about twelve different subjects upon which he lectured at various periods, *viz.*,—"The Scotch Covenanters." "The Puritans of England." "The Jesuits." "War." "The Origin and Progress of Baillie-street Sunday School." "The Division of 1835." "The Three Homes." "Young Women, Wives, and Mothers." "Young Men, Husbands, and Fathers." "Journey to Jerusalem and the East." "Rambles in the New World," &c.

Of late years they have been confined to the last

five; the most popular of which, and perhaps the most useful, were those to "Young Men," &c., and "Young Women," &c., from which we give the following extracts.

"YOUNG WOMEN, WIVES, AND MOTHERS."

"There is a great deal more misery and suffering in this world than God Almighty ever intended there should be; and I believe a great portion of that misery and wretchedness and suffering is of their own making. They were miserable because they would be miserable, or else they did not know how to be happy. God had His watchful eye over all, and if they followed out the plans which He had laid down in His Blessed Word they might be immeasurably more happy than they were. Some people—good Christian people, too—were not happy, but they said they were going to be. They sang of 'the realms of the blessed—that country so bright and so fair,' and they seemed to have an impression that they should have no joys until they got there. I think it quite possible for a good man to be happy on earth, and believe in the powerful influences of circumstances. The Bible recognised the doctrine of circumstances: 'Train up a child in the way he should go, and when he is old he will not depart from it.' That was the doctrine of the Bible.

"Man could be influenced by his fellow-men. Man was a moral agent, made in God's own image; and, being a moral agent, he was conscious of moral obligation. Man did understand the ten commandments and his moral obligation. The influences thus brought to bear have a tendency to mould the character of man with a will which is supernatural, and it may act upon him either for good or for evil. Man was a creature of circumstances, and, with a supernatural will, he has a tremendous power; and if any age of the world has ever developed that power, it is the age in which we live.

"Suppose that two girls were born on the same day—one of rich parents and the other of poor parents—both saw the light at the same time. (For convenience I will call *females* 'Mary,' and all males 'John.') When the child of the rich parent attained the age of eighteen or twenty she has become an accomplished lady through education, all through the power of circumstances. Some gentleman John might then see her, and he told her that he had seen her; and he told both his parents and her parents that he had seen her; and, if it was agreeable, they were engaged. The other little Mary came into the world in a poor cottage, perhaps well filled before she came, and was very likely one too many. No nurse was got for her, except some old woman who had perhaps half-a-dozen on her hands, and who knew the use of Godfrey's cordial, and who can keep the little baby quiet until the mother comes home from the mill, to which she had to return, perhaps, before the yearnings of nature had been attended to, and before she could caress her babe to her satisfaction. I hope the time will soon come when there will not be a single mother in all our mills. It was not a mother's place. A mother's place is at her own fireside, and if fathers would bring all their pence home I am persuaded that mothers could stop at home. This poor little Mary was not sent to the boarding-school, but at the age of eighteen or twenty years, if anyone said to her, 'Well, Mary, you are a fine lass; how have you been brought up?' she and hundreds could reply, 'I have been thumped up or kicked up, but I am up.' At that age, I know what young women are thinking of. They are wondering what sort of a one *he* would be; whether he will be long or short, and what trade he will have. They could not help thinking thus, nor their mother nor grandmother could not. Some of them could not wait, but must go to some old hag and give her a shilling, and they would see a man with a hat on, and that would be *him*. She was a very silly Mary who would do that, and if I were a young man, and knew that she had been to a fortune-teller, that would settle the matter at once. If their training had been what it ought to have been, at this most critical period of their lives—a period in which thousands have been wrecked,—they would have proper guides at home.

"There were, perhaps, some who had a desire to do right, and wished to be guided aright, but their training at home had been so wretched that they dare not speak a word to their parents upon the subject of their love. What a terrible position for a young woman, at that awfully critical period! Where such was the case there has been a want of mutual confidence between parents and children; and if you have no guide at home, I urge you to seek the guidance of your Heavenly Father on the matter. There was One who had said, 'In all thy ways acknowledge Him, and He will direct thy path.'

"There are some parents who believe their children would not think about love if they were not told about it; but they would, and if Mary could not go out of the door she would go out at the window. I would advise that their training should be such as Mary would go honourably out at the door, and consult her father and mother about John, by telling them of her affection for him. I can very well picture Mary on some night when her father and mother were sat quietly reading and sewing, although it cost her many an effort, but with great courage saying, 'Father, do you know John?' 'Yes, Mary.' 'Mother, do you know John?' 'Yes, Mary.' The father would say, 'Have you committed yourself in any way, Mary?' and she would say, 'No, I have not.' I can easily picture such a scene; and there should always be such affection between parents and children that they could tell them about such matters before it was too late to receive good advice. If Mary could not consult her parents about this, there was something radically wrong, and if she could not have this parental advice, an injustice had been done to Mary.

"Suppose some John proposed to Mary when she was about eighteen or twenty years of age, I would advise Mary to be extremely cautious. When a young man proposed to her, whatever their parents' conduct had been, they should not be deceived. They had a duty to perform, and they should perform it at all risks. They might have to suffer from it, but they were suffering in a right cause.

"I would advise them before making an engagement to ask John if he attended any place of worship. If he did not, where was he on the Sabbath? Young men did not stop in bed all day, and if they would go to the corner of the street, they would find them talking about dogs or pigeon flying, and Mary was hard up if she would have one of that class. She would be a foolish Mary if she expected happiness with a man who did not attend any place of worship, or a Sabbath school. They should ask another question—Is he good to his mother and father? for if he were he would be good to Mary, and if he were not he would not be good to anybody. I would urge Mary to stand on her self-respect, and go only where modesty could be maintained. No modest young woman would go with a man into a public-house, where she was sure to hear some obscene sentence. If Mary stood upon her self-respect she had a tremendous power. If young women stood upon their self-respect men would follow them through fire, but if they lost that self-respect they would have to follow men through tears. If man admired anything it was retiring modesty in young women, and that he did fervently admire.

"I would also advise Mary not to go with a young man with sly ways or dark ways. I could tell them of four sisters, one of whom had been in a bye-way with a young villain, and the three remaining sisters dared not be asleep all at one time, for their poor sister had attempted to hang herself. There was terrible ruin in those bye-ways, and any John worth a straw will never think the better of Mary for going with him there. There were hours besides courting hours, when John would think over every slight particular, and he would then weigh his Mary in a most critical scale, and John would think of her imprudence and bring in the verdict against her. If Mary stood upon her self-respect she would rise in John's estimation every time he saw her. I would advise Mary never to be whistled out, for it engendered deceit to their parents. I will suppose Mary and John were going to be married. He wanted Mary to go in her own clothes—clothes which were paid for. A good John would like her a thousand times more with a worsted dress paid for than with a satin dress unpaid for.

"They must not begin housekeeping on too large a scale, but have all according to their means, and all paid for, and not have a lot of fine things to be paid for at so much a month, but have all paid for upon entering the house. Mary must not go a gossiping, and when any gossip came into the house she should shut her mouth, and the gossip would never come again. They should be determined that their little cottage should be like a little palace, and also resolve to save a little, which could be done if things were managed aright. When a ready-money customer went into a shop she was treated with the greatest respect and courtesy, but when a customer who was behind with her payments came, how different was her treatment. The poor Mary had to stand with her thumb in her mouth whilst the other was served, almost afraid to speak. What John would like his dear Mary to stand in the shop with her thumb in her mouth? I would advise you to abhor those shop books and to regulate your expenditure according to your income.

"Some women when married thought 'Ah, now I have him,' and did not care what they did. But they were greatly mistaken. When the husband came home all was confusion, dirt, and disorder, and thousands of husbands had been driven into the Red Lion with such conduct. If they thought it did not matter what they did after marriage, they had fallen into a terrible mistake. If Mary kept her house neat and clean, and herself tidy, John would love her the more, for no matter what a man's exterior might be, he had an eye to the beautiful, and could see a clean cottage and a tidy wife, and set a proper value upon them.

"A woman who lived very uncomfortably with her husband, was one day advised to cure him by having everything nice and clean, and herself nicely washed, and have his tea ready when he came home, and to see what effect it would have upon him. After a vast amount of persuasion she promised to do it, and after leaving the place where she charred earlier than usual, she went home and said, 'Well, I guess I mun begin.' So she got everything nice and clean, and all about the fireplace as bright as a bell. Nothing escaped her ready fingers until all was as neat and clean as could be. She then said to little Mary, 'Well, I guess I mun now begin o thee.' So she washed her, combed her hair, and made her nice and clean. She then began and made herself clean and tidy, and said, 'Well, I suppose I mun get th' gentleman's tea ready now.' She did get his tea ready, and put everything nice and clean on the table ready for him and awaited his arrival. Now John had threatened to kick Mary out of the house, upon his arrival home at tea time, but upon his nearing the door, fully intending to carry out his threat, he saw a clean door step. He went and leaned his shoulder against the door-post and looked in. His little girl met him and said, 'Eh, father.' He took a very long stride into the house, over the step, on the mat, and saw all nice and clean and his wife tidy, but with her back turned to him. He kissed little Mary and said to his wife, 'Now, Mary, let's look at thi face,' but she would not turn round, so he walked round her and looked into her face, at the same time saying, 'Ah, God bless thee, Mary, I have not given thee a kiss these three months, but I'll give thee one now.' He was so highly pleased with this state of things that he said to his wife, 'Ah, Mary, I wish thou'd always do like this.' Mary said, 'Well, I will, if thou'll keep out of th' Red Lion.' He said, 'Come, that's a bargain,' and he had kept it, and they afterwards lived happily together.

"Many a man went from his work and found his wife dirty, her face unwashed, her dress unhooked—'slip slop.' He looked at this picture with sorrow, and said to himself, 'Is that her whom I fancied to be an angel—that dossy?' He walked out of that wretched house into the Red Lion, and many thousands of noble-hearted men had thus been ruined. If women would only stroke men down the right way, there was no man in the world who would not be hen-pecked. I urge Mary to make John as comfortable as she can, and not go to the pawn-shop, for that is the cousin to the gin-shop. Those were the best mothers who would sit in a house, and make their daughters do the work. Mary did not think so now, but when she grew older she would thank her mother for thus instilling into her mind all the little things which could only be learned by practical experience; and as a means of educating wives in common house duties, the mothers' classes were grand instruments, and I hope they will prosper. When John came home if the house was nice and tidy, with the tea nice and hot, he would be comfortable, and if Mary would bring him his slippers he would not stir far out of his comfortable corner. Mary should shake the cushion up on his chair before he came in, and welcome him with a bright smile, and all would go on happily. These were little things, but John would set a very high price on them. When John saw his wife clean and nice, he would say to himself, 'God bless that little body; I made a good day's work when I wed her.' If John came home surly, Mary should smile at him, and if he would not smile back she should smile again and again, for he would count every one of them. Mary might say, 'I will smile if John will smile.' That was very fair, but it did no good, and it was Mary's part to conciliate.

"I have no regard for a married couple if they have no regard for the Sabbath, and therefore I should advise them to have a place in God's house. They must not tease John if he would not attend a place of worship, but try persuasion, and if they went the right way about it they would succeed. I also advise the reading of the Scriptures in the house.

"This brings me now to the last part of my subject, 'Mothers.' It is the most important part, and I confess I never approach it but with some diffidence. It is no small matter to advise in regard to the training of children; in some families we find character so dissimilar. What would break the heart of one would scarcely effect the heart of another. What judgment, what wisdom, what firmness is required! If there is anyone on the face of the earth that needs God's help, it is the mother of a family of children. And what a sound, too, there is in the word mother! The three words—mother, home, heaven—what a blessed sound they give! No nation ever rises above its mothers. Every nation is what its mothers make it. God has planted a depth of love in your heart, Mary, next only to His own; He has given you a power that can never be told.

"When a child is put into your arms, from your mouth drop words into that little immortal soul that will influence it for good or bad for time and eternity. Lamartine said, 'The hand that rocks the cradle rules the world,' and it does. Never brawl to your child. Some people make the training of their children a perfect misery. But there are others who make the training of their children a real pleasure. Their quiet mode of speaking, along with their imperative firmness, bring out of their children a deep affection for them. Never give an order to a child that you don't intend to have carried out. Many thousands of mothers are the cause of their children's own disobedience. They give orders which they never enforce, and then when they want their children to do something, they turn refractory, and won't.

"Oh, the power of a mother; and the tormenting disposition of some! There are some mothers who are always scolding their children. If a child is rough, they call it naughty, and threaten to kill it. God made the kitten to run round after its tail; and why should not children amuse themselves? Let them play. They need it. And when you give an order, just make up your mind before you give it that it must be done, and when that order is given in a mild, kind, firm spirit, whatever the consequence may be, have it done. If it takes the whole day to have the question settled, take that whole day, and you will then have won. O the mighty responsibility resting upon mothers."

"YOUNG MEN, HUSBANDS, AND FATHERS."

"My subject to-night is 'Young Men, Husbands, and Fathers,' and if the subject of the previous night was of importance, I am sure the one on hand is of equal importance, inasmuch as men and women, by associating and mingling together in joys or sorrows, cannot possibly separate their interests, for the interest of one is the interest of the other.

"In looking at a young man, I would review him at home. Men can put on appearances outside such as they would have others to regard them, but their true character is developed at the fireside. There is an old maxim, and a very true one, 'If you want to know what a man is, live with him.' I will look at a young man first with regard to his conduct to his parents, for that is an unmistakable manifestation of the moral character of a young man. 'Honour thy father and thy mother, that thy days may be long in the land which the Lord thy God giveth thee,' was not written for nothing. I believe that all scriptures were written by the inspiration of God, but when we remember that the ten commandments were engraved by the Almighty's own fingers on the tables of stones, and that He Himself wrote that very commandment, 'Honour thy father and thy mother,' how great should be the importance attached to it. The commandment did not say, 'Honour thy father and thy mother if they are good fathers and mothers'; it made no distinctions.

"Some boys disobey their parents, quarrel with their brothers and sisters, and bring sorrow every time they cross the threshold. I never knew a young man prosper who disobeyed his parents. I would say to every one present who have almost caused their mothers' hearts to break through their misconduct, get that state of things right as soon as you can, and try whenever you enter your homes to go in such a manner as to draw out a welcome from all.

"I would also look at a youth out of doors. A correct estimate of a youth's character can generally be formed by looking at his companions. If I wanted to tell a lad's character I would say, 'Bring me his companions'; for 'he that walketh with wise men shall be wise; but the companions of fools shall be destroyed.' If a young man thinks his character worth anything, he will be very careful in the selection of his companions. Young men of respectable moral characters will not stand at the corners of streets in groups, with short pipes, or cigars. Either a cigar or a pipe shows that there is something radically wrong in a young man, because any young man with any regard for self respect will not use them. I once got a youth a situation as a draughtsman in a firm, after very great difficulty, and on the day but one before he should have commenced work the master came to my house, and said, 'Mr. Ashworth, I will not take that lad. I just called at the watchmaker's for my watch, and the young monkey came to the window with a pipe in his mouth. I would not have him about my place.' Through that one single act the youth lost prospects worth thousands of pounds. Youths may form bad habits, but it is not easy to get rid of them. The wisest course is not to smoke at all, or wait until your beards have grown grey, and then you will never begin.

"I wish to say a word about pigeon flying. That is one remove from the cruel bull-baiting and cock-fighting, but it shows what a miserable low state of mental capacity those who indulge in it have got to. The pigeon flyers have a very appropriate name for the betters, whom they call 'blacklegs.' A better wants something which is not his own without working for it, and I hope no young man present will ever disgrace himself by having anything to do with betting or pigeon flying. Some young men swear. What an indication of depravity is that. It is a terrible illustration of a man's vicious heart. God has said, 'Thou shalt not take the name of the Lord Thy God in vain, for the Lord will not hold him guiltless that taketh His name in vain.'

"We will suppose that John has arrived at a period of life to take his position in the world. If he wished to take a respectable position he would have no time to stand at street corners idling his time away, if he would fight the battle of life against the world manfully. If a young man only took the right course he would win. There was no position in England that a man could not obtain if he proved himself to be the fittest man for that post. The road was open even for a poor young man to become prime minister some day. If a young man must obtain a position it would have to be the result of early application. Therefore he would advise young men to have very few companions for they wasted time which should be spent in mental improvement and cultivation. If they looked at a building in course of erection and saw the men carrying the bricks up three or four storeys high, and who did the most laborious work in the place for about eighteen shillings a week, and look at the man with a fine coat on and bright shoes, whose services could not be purchased for five pounds a week, they would find that the only difference between the two was that one had taken advantage of early intellectual training whilst the other had not. A young man of to-day could have books exceedingly cheap, in fact he could purchase a small library for twenty shillings, which Queen Elizabeth could not have purchased with her crown. Works on any department of science or art could be purchased for a few shillings, and they might purchase books for twenty shillings which would make them the masters of thousands around them. And as a young man now rose in the world he would look to his level for a wife.

"I have often thought I could tell a fortune out of a class book, by looking at the number of times a scholar attended his class in the Sunday school during the year. When Mr. Kershaw, the late member of parliament for Stockport, visited the school in which he was a scholar, he asked for the class book used at the time he went to the school. The book was produced, and it was found that during a period of seven years he had never missed once.

I am not at all surprised at such a man becoming a member of parliament.

"I would next go to John's history, when he was getting a wife. One of the greatest blessings to a man is a good wife, and one of the greatest curses is a bad wife. I would advise John to be honourable at such time. Some young men thought it was a great honour to be flirting with two or three at a time, but there was no young woman worth a straw who would be one of the three. A young woman had to depend a great deal upon a young man's honour, and I would say to John, 'Never be guilty of a single act towards a young confiding female, which could not be set before God Almighty, and which you could not tell to your dearest friend.' You will never repent taking my advice if you only follow it out. It was John's business to provide a home for Mary and himself, and I would strongly urge every young man to begin housekeeping out of debt, so that they could call all their own. I also very earnestly advise John never to go into a public-house, for if he did he could bid farewell to every grand and noble prospect in this world. I knew a man who, after a night's debauchery, went to the alehouse the following morning, and said to the landlord, 'Will you trust me a pint?' but he would not, and a Milly who had a mop, cleaning the lobby, threatened to mop him out if he did not go. With this the man went to a pump adjoining, and said, 'Pump, let me sup.' He got hold of the handle and pumped until the clear crystal spring issued forth, and he drank to his heart's content. He then said to the pump, 'Thank thee, pump. I'll never touch another drop of drink, so help me God, and pump, thou art a witness.' Saying thus he went away and kept his promise. That man was then a poor man, but he has since become a manufacturer, and of such importance that when a member of parliament was required for Rochdale, he had to be consulted on the subject. I would urge John to save up his spare pence against a rainy day, or against he got married.

"I would now look at John as the husband of Mary. In the first place John should not call at a public-house with his wages, for nobody was so big a fool as a drunken man. I am a tetotaller, and believe I am respected by the landlords of Rochdale as much as any drunkard in the town.

I would suppose John had a good wife, and would advise them not to give up courting after marriage. Love never grows old, and they might court each other as long as they lived. They might have their cottage as happy a spot as any on earth. If there was not love in the cottage, it was not the fault of the cottage, but of the inmates. When John's wife tried to please him he should be pleased, and when she did anything clever he should praise her, for women liked nothing better than praise. He should speak kindly to her, and try to encourage her when she did her best. John should always remember that it took two to quarrel, and if one would not quarrel the other could not. John had no need to quarrel with his wife, and if he was a sensible man he would not. When John came home he should always try to bring a smile with him. Some men had a smile for everybody's wife, and a pat for every child's cheek, but their own, and nothing went on wrong anywhere but at home. There were many scores of men who were as insignificant as an old slipper outside, but when they got home the very demon seemed to have taken possession of them, and the sound of their feet was a signal for sorrow for everybody in the house. The wife was afraid he would say something which would grieve her, for he was too big a man to be pleased. He was a contemptible wretch outside, but he was a master inside, and he made everybody feel it, for he was a great tyrant, and every tyrant was a coward.

"Another man comes home from his work, and the moment his feet are heard the children are in high glee, and his wife pricks up her ears at the sound of his voice. The children kiss and caress him, and show him all their possessions, and the father is happy; and the wife thinks they are the happiest group in Christendom, when the children are climbing up their father's knee, and up his chair. When he returns to his work the children kiss him, and each kiss is worth sixpence to that hard-working man, but the wife's kiss is worth a shilling, and he goes to his workshop with a light and happy heart. John should always take a smile home; and if he is out of temper, and will only look at himself through the looking-glass, keeping his face in the same position, he will never be bad tempered again. Fireside happiness is possible in every home in the kingdom. Whatever crosses a wise man meets with outside, he will always have one happy corner to go to. John must bear and forbear, not get into debt, but limit the expenditure to the income. I urge family prayer, and the use of the Bible at least once a day, for the thought that a man's prayer is heard is a great stimulus to him. No home can be perfectly happy without practical religion, and the necessity of fireside piety is very evident to all good men.

"In conclusion, I will look at John as a father, and would advise him always to encourage his children by praising them whenever he can. By saying to little Johnny, upon his showing you some work, 'Well, now, that is clever,' or to little Mary, 'That is first-rate,' a fire is put into their little hearts which will some day bless them. You should speak kindly, mildly, but firmly to your children, and never give an order which you do not intend to be obeyed. You should be careful what commands you give, but insist upon them being carried out at any risk, and your children will bless you some day. You should never speak unkindly to a drunkard's child, for it is not their own fault that they are in such a condition. I would urge upon all fathers to attend to the education of their children."

As a Preacher, Mr. Ashworth's style was direct, forcible, easy, unaffected, conversational, and homely. His addresses were not sermons, in the ordinary sense of the word; while thoroughly scriptural in tone, he adapted his pulpit ministrations to the common affairs of every-day life, and enforced practical duties rather than doctrinal dogmas. He aimed to show the beauty of goodness, and the importance of self-control. Gifted with a rare faculty for narrative and illustration, and well acquainted with "the art of putting things," his addresses charmed by their vivacity and freshness.

The following sketch is from the *Christian World, when he* preached in Bayswater chapel, London, in *1869*:—

"His manner was that of a friend arguing with a friend. His sermon was of an experimental and practical character—of the power of prayer, of how the effectual fervent prayer of a righteous man availeth much. It was a subject of which the preacher evidently had his heart full, and if only the power of utterance had been in proportion to what he thought and felt, the effect would have been very great. He was struggling with emotion; he was full of his theme—how Moses prayed, how Joshua prayed, how Elijah prayed, how Hezekiah prayed, how Mr. Müller had built a palace at Bristol by prayer, and filled it with orphans whom he maintained by prayer. Nations and individuals had all benefited by prayer. He then spoke of that upper room prayer meeting, and of the Pentecostal outpouring when Peter preached to the men of Judea, when three thousand souls were added to the church. Certainly as an original preacher of charity sermons Mr. Ashworth must be considered to bear away the palm."

His great *forte* in preaching was that the *common people* not only heard him gladly, but could understand what he said. One of his congregation, who found Christ at the Destitute, and is now in heaven, came into the town seven years ago, out of Yorkshire, and went from one place to another without meeting with a preacher that was intelligible to her. It came into her mind she would go to the place they called the "Chapel for the Destitute," and the first evening after service she said, "Aye, bless God; this is the place for me. I can understand every word he says."

The only sermon we find written out at any length amongst his MSS is his trial sermon, preached in the school-room of Baillie-street chapel on the 8th October, 1837, from Isaiah xxviii. 16. It has a lengthy introduction, giving an account of the origin and history of the Jewish people, with the three following divisions: "I.—The Foundation.

II.—The immovable security of them that build on this Foundation. III.—The inevitable destruction of those that build on any other foundation."

As a rule, he had nothing more written than the heads of his sermons, of which there were generally three, with their sub-divisions. The best of them he lost a few years ago, with his portmanteau, at Bradford station.

The reader will be able to judge of the style from the few selected.

"Mark v. 19. 'Go home to thy friends,' &c.

I.—The man here mentioned had a devil in him.

II.—He came to Christ to have it taken out.

III.—Christ cast out the devil, and sent the man to tell his friends about it.

IV.—Christ can still cast out devils, if we will come to Him.

"There were swearing devils, drinking devils, lying devils, thieving devils, filthy devils, Sabbath-breaking devils, and idle devils. When Christ cast the devils out, He did not cast them out one at a time, but all at once. This man got rid of these devils by coming to Christ, &c."

"Numbers xxxii. 23. 'And be sure your sin will find you out.'

I.—As a rule these words are true in regard to this world.

1. Sin is the transgression of the law, by a word, thought, or action, a duty omitted.
2. Sin is retributive; it comes back again sooner or later. Adam, Cain, Achan, Haman, David, Ananias, and Sapphira; prisons, hulks, penal settlements, ruined homes, constitution, character, guilty conscience, life of misery.

II.—They are absolutely true as regards the world to come.

1. The great assize. Everything revealed that day.
2. Every sin has its just recompence. All is found out.

III.—There is but one way of escaping its consequences.
1. Mercy flies on wings of love. Receive mercy and pardon.
2. Justice follows after, if mercy be rejected."

"Ezekiel xxxvii. 3. 'And he said unto the Son of man, Can these bones live?'

I.—The valley of dry bones.
1. Moral and spiritual condition of the Jews; forsaken God; idolatry.
2. The Jews a type of all mankind; all dead.

II.—Ezekiel's order respecting the bones.
1. Means to be used; preach or prophesy to them.
2. How utterly useless to preach to dry bones. Various sorts of preaching—polemical, logical, sectarian.
3. Preach God's word.

III.—The power that gave new life to these dry bones.
1. God's Spirit in His own word: Jonah, Nathan, Peter, Paul.
2. Bones clothed; lived; stood up. God's Spirit did it.
3. The conscious new life."

"Romans xii. 2. 'And be not conformed to this world,' &c.

I.—Worldly comformity. What is it?
Lust of the flesh: rich man, prosperous farmer.
Lust of the eye: Achan, Gehazi, deceitfulness of riches.
Pride of life: Haman, Nebuchadnezzar. Lust of other things.

II.—What are its effects?
Service of God a secondary matter. Our Lord's injunction reversed; a sad illustration; *collier*.
Soul's welfare neglected; no union with the church. Prayer-meetings distasteful, class-meetings objectionable, Bible not read, spiritual death.

III.—What is a transformed or renewed mind?
A mind or heart renewed by divine grace: a new man in Christ Jesus.
A mind conformed to the will of God. Above the

pomps and vanities of the world. Walking with God, talking with God, dwelling in Him, and with Him hereafter."

"Hebrews ii. 3. 'How shall we escape?' &c.

I.—Salvation is provided and offered.

1. Provided by God Himself.
2. Foretold by the prophets.
3. Announced by angels.
4. Secured by Christ.
5. Preached by the apostles.

II.—We may neglect this great salvation.

1. By careless indifference; no worship; no Bible.
2. By wilful ignorance.
3. By worldly-mindedness.

III.—If we neglect it, how shall we escape?

1. Escape is impossible. No other salvation, God's offer rejected.
2. Neglect has brought destruction. Boat on the 'Falls'; man in business.
3. We only need neglect, and all is lost; damned in hell, neglected; no hope in death."

"1 Peter xi. 21. 'Leaving us an example,' &c.

Christ was the world's Teacher of truth. The world's example of purity and holiness. The world's Redeemer by His death and resurrection. Our purpose, for the present, is to look at Christ as our example.

I.—In works of mercy.

1. In feeding the hungry; 5,000 with bread.
2. Comforting the mourner; mother, child; father, son.

II.—In humility.

1. Mingling with the poor; fishermen.
2. Sharing in their sorrows; Martha and Mary.
3. Washing the feet of His disciples.

III.—In prayer.

1. Rose up before day.
2. Went into the wilderness.
3. He went on to the mountain all night."

CHAPTER XIX.

1874.

"THURSDAY, Jan. 1, 1874. The last moments of the old year and the first moments of the new, I was on my knees in Castlemere chapel, and felt how solemn a time it was to be reviewing past days, and thinking of days approaching. Oh how good God has been to me this past year; what countless mercies by sea and land, guarding and protecting me when travelling in foreign climes. I would praise and bless Him for this. During the year now past and gone, I have had many failings and conscious defects, and trust this year I may live nearer to my God, be more holy in my life, more useful in my labours, and more earnest in trying to point sinners to Jesus. Willingly do I afresh consecrate myself to Thee, my Father and my God; humbly yet cheerfully do I surrender all into Thy hands. Oh bless me; still continue to bless me, and make me more than ever an instrument of good to others. Guide my pen and tongue, so that all I write, or speak, may be to Thy glory. Give me strong health, and peace at home. Bless my now only son Harold, my wife, my grandchildren, and all my relations. Lord, accept of this dedication, this new consecration to Thy service, for Christ's sake. Amen."

"Jan. 4. Administered the Sacrament at the Destitute.

"Jan. 8. Spoke at Mr. Shaw's widow's tea meeting; five hundred present.

"Jan. 12. Our children in School-lane Sunday-school had their annual tea meeting at the Chapel for the Destitute; unmistakable evidences of good being done. Two hundred present, including twenty-five old scholars formerly attending Brickfield Branch school. One boy and three girls recited 'St. John the Aged' exceedingly well, and each received five shillings, the gift of Captain Freeman, late of the S.S. *Minnesota;* fourteen learned the first Psalm at my request.

"Jan. 25. Preached Mrs. Wilson's funeral sermon, Cornholme; seven sons present."

Mrs. Wilson was a dear and respected friend of Mr. Ashworth's. She was the wife of Lawrence Wilson, and the mother of eight sons, all members of a Christian church. She was converted at fourteen, was a class-leader forty-eight years, visited the sick, was kind and hospitable to her neighbours, and died a triumphant death. The memory of the just is blessed.

"Feb. 9. Attended and spoke at the annual meeting of the Rochdale Town Mission, held in the Baptist schoolroom, West-street. Mr. James Ashworth in the chair."

This being the last Rochdale Town Mission meeting Mr. Ashworth attended, the following report of his address on that occasion will no doubt be acceptable, and show his views on the great question of "how to reach the masses."

"He said he regarded such organisations as that of missions being an absolute necessity, and such as every Christian community ought to possess, inasmuch as by their arrangements they were admirably adapted to reach a class that otherwise would not be reached by any other influence or agency. Manchester had ninety missionaries, though at one time he believed they had one hundred, and the mission there was perhaps one of the best regulated organisations in the city. It was surprising to find the number of cottage meetings held by these ninety men weekly, and the vast number of visits to the sick, and the dying, and to persons that never would be seen or visited but for this agency. What was the result? Why every street in Manchester, however low, however degraded, however wretched, had these men going to and fro as angels of mercy, visiting homes the most wretched, and scattering the seed of the kingdom of faith in Christ. The effect of this was, that many of these districts were in a state of moral elevation that would have been impossible without this agency. He contrasted Manchester with Sheffield, where there were only seven missionaries, and there had been a tremendous effort to raise these seven. Compared with Manchester, as to population, Sheffield ought to have forty-five such missionaries. The consequence was that there were streets in Sheffield where the people were in the utmost moral degradation, and not a single soul attended a place of worship, and not a single child entered the Sunday school. In other respects he contrasted Sheffield unfavourably with Manchester. To show the change in Manchester he pointed to the Hall of Science, Campfield, once the very temple of infidelity, but now used as a Free Public Library. There was only one room in Manchester (if indeed there was a single one, for a short time ago there was not) where these men (Atheists) could meet; that was, they were not sufficiently organised to meet amongst themselves. They formerly had a railway arch, but now even that had been converted into a mission station, and was used as a preaching place. If they had ninety missionaries in Sheffield, the condition of that town would be very different to what it was now. He wanted ten in Rochdale, and he always had advocated that number. He appealed to the ladies to do their utmost to get subscriptions for the mission, and subsequently gave some very forcible, and, in many respects, rather amusing exemplifications of the character of mission work in the back slums."

Mr. Ashworth also lectured in the Public Hall on behalf of the Town Mission on the 17th of March, the chair being occupied by the mayor, Mr.

Charles Whittaker. On which occasion he gave his "Rambles in the New World."

He also continued his labours at home and elsewhere without any interruption or serious apprehension till towards the end of July, although for several months he was far from well, and had frequently monitory symptoms that there was something wrong. So early as February 23rd he says, "Feel not quite well to-day, a swelling of the liver, and cough." To an unskilled person he looked comparatively well, but when on a visit to London in May, the keen eye of Mr. Spurgeon could detect it at once, and looking him in the face, said, "Brother, you are not well; you want rest." One day he felt so overpowered with heaviness and exhaustion that he could almost have lain down in the street. Being near St. Paul's cathedral at the time, and finding the doors open and service being held, he went in, sat down in a corner as much out of sight as possible, and fell into a sound sleep.

On his return from London he records,—

"May 16. I find my London labours have been rather too heavy. Not well. Letters, letters, letters; all calling out for help.

"May 26. Feel low and sleepy; the heavy work (Halifax) on Sunday was too much for me.

"May 28. Not well; most of the day on the sofa.

"May 30. Not well, and very idle; no wish to read, write, or think; weary, very weary."

This was evidently the beginning of the struggle; the strong man was reluctant to yield, and he called it idleness and weariness.

"June 2. Not well to-day; took a walk amongst the fields. Oh, how glorious are the works of God; manifest all around. Truly all His works do praise Him. Spoke to a group of young men on religion and temperance."

Referring to the latter, it was Mr. Ashworth's invariable practise, when he went into the country, either on weekdays or Sundays, to endeavour to get into conversation with the various groups of men he met on his way, especially on the Sabbath. He carried with him small slips of paper, containing a text of Scripture, which he distributed amongst them, such as—

THOU
GOD SEEST
ME.

Genesis xvi. 13.

BE SURE
YOUR SIN WILL FIND
YOU OUT.

Numbers xxxii. 23.

Some of our readers will remember, that on the occasion of his visit to poor James Burrows, when under sentence of death in Manchester prison (Narrative 33), Burrows said to him, "Do you remember one Sunday speaking to me and some other young men, who were pigeon-flying near Thornham lane, and telling us that Sabbath-breaking, dog-running, and pigeon-flying must come to a bad end?"

"I think I do; for I have often spoken to young men on the road from Rochdale to Middleton," Mr. Ashworth replied.

"Yes, you did," said Burrows, "but we only laughed at you when you were gone, for we were a bad lot. Like and like go together; and wicked companions have brought me to this. Living at an alehouse, going to alehouses, and bad company have done it all; and it will do it for more beside me. Oh! I wish I had taken warning in time."

When comparatively a young man, one Sunday, being planned at Hartley, a preaching station in the neighbourhood of Rochdale (during the chartist agitation), he was going through Stoneyfields, when he saw before him a number of men, some of them without hats, and others without coats; and as he overtook them he found they were discussing the chartist and land schemes; that they were denouncing all parsons and chapel-going people. He walked at their speed, and it was some time before they were aware of his presence. As soon as he was discovered they made way for him to pass on, but he declined, and then they began to interrogate the stranger as to who and what he was.

"Who art thou?"

"A working man."

"Art thou a chartist?"

"I am a radical."

"Art thou a member of the land scheme?"

"No."

"Does thou take the *Northern Star?*"

"No."

At which one said, "I thought thou wert a queer radical; thy clothes on thy back are too fine."

"Yes," replied Mr. Ashworth, "just put your hand on my coat sleeve and feel how smooth it is."

The man did so, and said, "It is fine enough for a parson."

"A working chap!" said another, "I should like to know how thou gets clothes like thou has."

"Well, I'll tell you; but just allow me to ask you two questions first. Do any of you go to church or chapel?"

"No," was the reply, "except to weddings or buryings."

"Well, how is it that those who regularly attend a place of worship, and take notice of what parsons say, have better clothes, better homes, and are more respected than those that never go?

"Now," said Mr. Ashworth, "I am a working man. I work six days in the week as hard as any man; I go to chapel on the Sunday, and take notice of what parsons say; and these are the reasons why I am able to have such fine smooth clothes as you see me have. 'Godliness is profitable unto all things, having the promise of the life that now is, as well as of that which is to come.'"

"That's a parson," said one; "That's no working chap," said another.

On arriving at Hartley, Mr. Ashworth turned round and told them his errand, gave them a pressing invitation to go in to the service, which with much persuasion they did.

In after years, when he became better known, the young men, when they saw him approaching, would prepare themselves for a short speech, for they knew he would never pass them without a word of advice for their good. His constant motto was, "In the morning sow thy seed, and in the evening withhold not thy hand." The writer never knew him spend an idle or useless hour.

After conducting services at Scarborough and Bridlington, Mr. Ashworth went to Bramham, near Tadcaster, on July 8, where, on behalf of the Wesleyans, he preached in a large marquée, erected for the purpose, in the afternoon, from James v. 16, "The effectual fervent prayer," &c., and lectured in the evening on "Young Women," &c. The country people came for many miles round. It is said he preached a most powerful and impressive sermon on prayer, and that it was a day that will be long remembered.

On Saturday, July 11th, he went to Bacup, spoke at a temperance meeting, conducted three services on the following Sabbath, and walked home seven and a-half miles at the close.

On Monday, July 13th, he left home for Sandbach in Cheshire, where he preached in the afternoon and lectured in the evening, making in all fifteen services in eight days.

His last Sabbath services were on July 19th, at Greenhill in the morning, Destitute in the evening, and out of doors, in the Butts, at eight o'clock, The last week-day service was at the Chapel for the Destitute, on Thursday, July 23. The following day he records,—

"July 24. Fairly broke down.

"July 27. Feel very much prostrated, but very happy. I know in whom I have believed. Oh, how precious Christ is to my soul; nothing but Christ.

"August 5. Fallen from the ranks. This to me is a new experience, but my Captain is with me.

"August 8. Living or dying my prospects are bright.

"August 12. Days and nights of weakness and pain, yet all is well.

"August 19. 'Set thine house in order,' so said Isaiah to Hezekiah. How beautiful are the words of Hezekiah after he had been sick. Isaiah xxxviii. 9."

The morning he had been reading about Hezekiah he said, "I seem to live amongst these grand Old Testament worthies, but I have been thinking what a foolish thing Hezekiah did after the Lord had spared his life fifteen years (Isaiah xxxix), and that perhaps the Lord thinks it best to take me now, in case I might live to do some foolish thing."

Mr. Ashworth went to the Hydropathic establishment at Matlock Bank, in the hope that he would receive benefit as on former occasions, but returned, after a stay of six weeks, without any improvement. While there he writes,—

"Sept. 10. Thursday. I remember and pray for my poor dear people at the Destitute. For fifteen years weekly have I stood before them on this evening, reading and expounding the word of God.

"Sept. 17. Notice that those persons who play cards, seldom or never attend the morning or evening service.

"Sept 28. The people all anxious about me, and show great kindness.

"Oct. 1. A great trial not being able to write the tale for annual report, but I feel I cannot, so great is my mental prostration.

"Oct. 3. My dear wife returned home to-day; feel the parting."

In the preface to the Annual Report of the Chapel for the Destitute, issued October 1st, Mr. Ashworth writes,—

"I regret to state, that for several months, I have felt my health giving way, and been obliged to give up all work, and it being still so precarious, I am under the necessity of issuing this year's report without the usual narrative, which I have not been able to write. I am sorry for this, knowing that so many of our friends expect it, but they will bear with me under the circumstances.

"My fellow-labourer, Mr. Calman, is conducting our operations, and I am hoping that, through the blessing of God on the means employed for restoration, I may be able soon to resume my much-beloved work in my Master's vineyard."

For the first time for sixteen years, Mr. Ashworth was unable to be present and conduct the anniversary service of the Chapel for the Destitute, held on the first Sunday in October, his place being supplied by Mr. John Harley.

Mr. Ashworth wrote the following letter to his congregation:—

"Matlock, Oct. 2nd, 1874.

"My dear Friends,

"I did hope to have been with you on the day of our sixteenth anniversary, but I feel I must not, for my health is still precarious, and I cannot undertake anything that requires effort, or thought, or that produces excitement; and I find it the best to be passive and quiet, using the means and praying that God will bless them.

"I am pleased and thankful to tell you that I have constant peace, through my Lord and Saviour, Jesus Christ, which I have preached to you and others; and I have always found, and still find it, a source of true consolation. I think my greatest joy would be to have health and strength again; to be able, as an instrument, to lead perishing souls to Jesus: this is the grandest of all work. I am much indebted to my fellow-workers for their constant care over the chapel and school; and also to Mr. Harley, and those ministers who have helped to supply my place.

"The Lord bless you all, and the children and the teachers at the school. I know you pray for me, and for this I thank you. I am in good Hands, and quite able to say, 'Thy will be done.'

"Yours very affectionately,

"JOHN ASHWORTH."

"Oct. 16. Matlock; weary, very weary; long for home. Lord, give me resignation to Thy will; severe vomiting.

"Oct. 17. Returned home; thank God.

"Oct. 27. Went to consult Dr. William Roberts, of Mosley-street, Manchester.

"Oct. 30. I am now trying to set my house in order.

"Nov. 9. Humanly speaking, my case is hopeless. Lord, undertake for me.

"Nov. 13. Prayers are offered up for me in the churches and social means, and many are making my case the subject of special prayer; how kind and good. Lord, bless them for their sympathy.

"Nov. 14. I think our hymns are sweeter to me than ever. What sublime thoughts, what glorious conceptions, what grand ideas; surely many of them are inspired.

"Nov. 23. Mr. John Bright called to see me; remained about an hour; anxious I should have the best medical advice. Mrs. Bright brought prescriptions for liquid food.

"Nov. 28. Our old vicar, Dr. Molesworth, called to see me to-day; a pastoral visit.

"Nov. 29. Sunday. It is a sweet thought to me, that thousands will be happy in the service of the Lord to-day.

"Dec. 7. At the earnest request of my medical adviser and many friends, I reluctantly went to London to consult Dr. Pavey, Grosvenor-street; a night of vomiting."

With this visit to London the entries in his diary cease. There was no longer any doubt as to the malignant nature of the disease; and from the symptoms, which became more and more apparent as it progressed, it was evident that *cancer* had fastened its fatal fangs on his system, and although everything was done to arrest its course that medical skill could suggest, it steadily increased, till at last the passage to the stomach was entirely closed, and even liquid food rejected; and he who had so often "fed the hungry," was now doomed to "starve in the midst of plenty." He quietly and calmly resigned himself into the hands of his Heavenly Father, and could say,—

"The hour of my departure's come,
I hear the voice that calls me home."

The annual tea meeting was held at the Chapel for the Destitute on Christmas Day, when the following letter was read, the last Mr. Ashworth wrote with his own hand:—

"My dear People,

"I now write to you from my bed of increased sickness and pain, but I write with no diminished confidence in the goodness of that God whose servant I am. You are this day gathered together to a social tea, commemorating Christ Jesus coming into the world to save sinners—to save them to lives of peace and holiness here, and to eternal joy hereafter. Some of you can testify of the power of Christ to save, and are happy, because you have peace with God; and my prayer is that you may every one realise this unspeakable blessing; this, by faith in Christ, you may have. His own precious words are, 'Come unto me, and I will give you rest.' For many years, as your minister, I have presided over this, your annual meeting, but now all active labour in the vineyard of my Lord seems to be ended; the Master calls: I bow in submission to His will. On the day of my departure, if I shall not be able to say with Elisha, 'The chariot of Israel and the horsemen thereof,' I shall be able to say with Paul, 'There is laid up for me a crown, and not for me only, but for all that love his appearing.'

"I commend to you Mr. Calman, long my fellow-labourer amongst you, and now my successor; him receive in the spirit of charity and love, and may the smile of heaven, more and more, rest upon the Chapel and School for the Destitute.

"Yours in heavy affliction,

"JOHN ASHWORTH."

The cause of the malady was a mystery, and to no one more mysterious than to Mr. Ashworth. He was very abstemious and regular in his habits, and used to say he could not accuse himself of having done anything to injure his body, that would induce such a complaint, unless it was over exertion. He was naturally a remarkably strong man, with a healthy, vigorous constitution, which he said "was difficult to kill"; and, humanly speaking, he might have been expected to live twenty years longer. But the hour had come; his work on earth done; and what we know not now, we shall know hereafter. One symptom peculiar to the disease is great mental depression. Mr. Ashworth was not exempt from this, and having a vivid imagination, was very susceptible and easily wrought upon. On reading to him, as he lay in bed, the proof of "The Top Room" (the last of "Strange Tales"), when I came to the paragraph,—"If there be anything that brings heaven down to earth, that fills and thrills the soul with extatic emotions, and gilds the path of life with perpetual sunshine, it is treading in the footsteps of Him who went about doing good; to carry words of sympathy to the disconsolate, bread to the hungry, counsel to the wayward; to stretch forth a helping hand to the sinking and fallen, and point the lost to a Saviour," he wept and sobbed like a child.

There was no singing of hymns, no extatic emotion, but there was inward settled peace through faith in Christ; and when some of his friends in their letters of kind sympathy were disposed to flatter him, he would say,—

"'Nothing in my hands I bring,
Simply to Thy cross I cling.'"

His faith in the atonement of Christ was strong, fixed, and firm.

His sufferings at times were most intense and excruciating, and he "longed to be at rest." In speaking to a dear friend who had called to see him, when asked what his views of heaven were, he said, "Wherever it is, to be with Christ will be heaven, and that will be glorious."

Saturday, January 16th, 1875, he was suffering great pain, and hoped, if it were the Lord's will, he "might be in heaven to-morrow," but added, "The Lord knows all about it. The Lord help me. I have had living grace, and I shall have dying grace." After reading the morning's letters to him, several of them from dear friends expressing their deep sympathy with him in his sufferings, he was moved to tears, and said, "How kind my friends are to think of me, how good they are," and then repeated a quotation from one of the letters,—"Thanks be unto God, who giveth us the victory, through our Lord Jesus Christ."

"Committee Room, Stockport Sunday School,
"My dear Sir, "17th January, 1875.

"The committee and visitors of the Stockport Sunday-school, desire me to acknowledge the receipt of your kind message, and are exceedingly grateful for your kind remembrance of them and their work, especially in a season of suffering, such as you are now passing through.

"On their part, they thankfully acknowledge the valuable services you have rendered at Stockport, not to the school only, but also to the population at large. They believe that many a home has been made happier through your wise counsel, and that many of our townspeople, to whom you have pointed out the way of life, are now walking therein.

"They trust that even in your painful affliction you find the Lord's grace sufficient for you, and that you find strength and victory in the promise, 'When thou passest through the waters I will be with thee, and through the rivers they shall not overflow thee.'

"With great personal regard and much sympathy,

"I remain, my dear Sir, Yours most sincerely,

"WILLIAM LEIGH,

"Mr. John Ashworth, Rochdale." "Hon. Sec.

"Maldon, 21, 1, 1875.

"My dear Friend, John Ashworth,

"A letter received this morning from our mutually dear friend E. Thwaite, conveyed the touching information of thy present state, and I longed to express my very near sympathy with thee, and how thankful I feel for the sense vouchsafed thee; that the everlasting arms are underneath for thy support in this time of physical suffering. We are told to 'rejoice with them that do rejoice, and weep with them that weep'; and whilst I *do* thus feel for thy suffering state, I don't know that the *rejoicing* does not predominate. Thou *hast* loved, and served thy dear Lord, and He will, I verily believe, grant that an entrance shall be ministered unto thee *abundantly*, into the everlasting kingdom of our Lord and Saviour, Jesus Christ; where it will be thy joy to cast thy crown, decked with jewels, (souls, which it has been thy blessed privilege to gather from the highways to the marriage supper of the Lamb) at the feet of *thy Redeemer*.

"Perhaps I have said enough to be read to thee in thy weak state; but I am so reminded of what *Hopeful*, in the 'Pilgrim's Progress," said to his friend *Christian*, when passing through the river, 'Be of good cheer, my brother; I feel the bottom, and it is good'; and though no 'ringing of bells' will announce the glad welcome on thy arrival, I doubt not it will be with joy unspeakable and full of glory—*seeing Jesus face to face*—in blest communion with the 'general assembly and church of the first-born,' &c.

"Farewell, dear friend and brother! and may an entrance be granted me also, through 'wondrous Mercy gate.'

"I thought of *thee* as entering by the gate *Beautiful;* but doubtless it is the *same* and *only gate;* and a beautiful gate it is—the love of God in Christ Jesus to His redeemed children.

"From thy affectionate friend,

"CHRISTIANA ALSOP."

During an attack of vomiting, and while leaning over the side of the bed, he said,—"'Safe in the arms of Jesus'; thank God, 'Safe in the arms of Jesus'"; then spoke tenderly to his dear wife, "hoped the Lord would give her grace and patience for all he had to go through, be with her all her life, and bless her."

Thursday, Jan. 21, the Doctor said the beginning of the end was come, *i.e.*, the last stage of the disease.

Sunday morning, January 24th, I called on my way to school. On going to his bed side, with deep emotion he grasped my hand, and with a "Bless you, my brother," I will never forget, "The Lord bless you, and bless the teachers and the dear children; and God bless my poor people at the Destitute." These were the last words I heard from his lips, and on Tuesday morning, January 26th, at forty-five minutes past ten, the Master said, "Come up higher," and he calmly fell asleep in Jesus.

As I looked on the dear familiar face and placid brow, now calm with the peace of death, I felt I had indeed lost a friend. "As a son with the father" I had "served with him in the gospel."

I need offer no word of eulogy. The brief narrative in this memoir of the life and labours of John Ashworth, though imperfectly given, will speak for itself. Thousands who have felt his kindly hand, listened to his wise counsels and touching words, will echo his praises, and treasure up his memory in their hearts with loving thoughts and tender recollections of all in him that was noble, houourable and good. "A good name," it is written, "is better than precious ointment, and the day of death than the day of one's birth."

CHAPTER XX.

FUNERAL.

MR. ASHWORTH left specific instructions with regard to his funeral, the following report of which is from the *Rochdale Observer*.

FUNERAL OF MR. JOHN ASHWORTH.

"THE mortal remains of the late Mr. John Ashworth, of Broadfield, were interred at the Rochdale Cemetery on Saturday last, and never since the lamented decease of a gentleman who also bore the honoured name of Ashworth has there been witnessed a more general demonstration of affection and esteem in Rochdale for one of its foremost citizens, for such the late Mr. John Ashworth may be truly called. While leaving to others the regulation of the sanitary and other affairs of the town, Mr. Ashworth was sedulously and affectionately engaged in a sanitary work—if it may be so called—of a very different kind, and of equal, nay, greater, importance—the purifying and uplifting of the souls of the outcast, forsaken, and criminal classes. Nor were his labours confined to his native town, for many places throughout the kingdom had the benefit of his occasional presence, and profited by his influence. Thousands who knew him not personally yet came within the reach of his influence, for his 'Strange Tales' circulated far and wide, and it is impossible to estimate the good which those eloquent and pathetic stories have been the means of accomplishing. Not only, therefore, did the inhabitants of Rochdale assemble in large numbers to pay their last tribute of respect to one who has done a work the value of which cannot be estimated, and one who has helped to make Rochdale famous, but many came from distant parts of the country to take part in the sad ceremony of consigning to the grave the honoured remains of a friend who had been most dear to them. The Right Hon. John Bright, between whom and Mr. Ashworth a long friendship had existed, and who had frequently visited him during his severe illness, returned from Birmingham so as to be present at the interment. Mrs. Sturge, widow of the well-known Mr. Joseph Sturge, of Birmingham, and an intimate friend of Mr. Ashworth's, being unable to be present herself, sent Mr. J. W. Kirton to represent her. The great Sunday school at Stockport, where he was personally well known, sent its representatives. Mr. J. H. Raper, the Parliamentary agent of the Alliance, also attended the funeral. Ministers of every Dissenting denomination in the town were present, and large numbers also from Manchester, Bury, Bacup, Haslingden, Burnley, and other Lancashire towns. Many persons came from Bradford and Sheffield, and from towns much more distant. The funeral cortège was arranged to start from the deceased's late residence in Broadfield at eleven o'clock on Saturday morning. Around which a great crowd assembled to witness its departure.

"The procession was headed by the congregation attending the Chapel for the Destitute, and the teachers and scholars from the Mission-room. Large numbers of people congregated along the route, and most of the shops and other places of business, both in the line of route and in the other parts of the town, were closed for a time. A very large number of people also went to the cemetery to witness the interment. When the coffin was taken from the hearse to be borne into the chapel, there were placed upon it three wreaths of flowers. The largest was composed of camellias, white roses, and lilies. It was sent by the teachers and scholars of Stockport Sunday School. Of the other wreaths, one was given by Mrs. James Petrie, of Rochdale, and the other by Mrs. John Ashworth, of Nissi Villa, Rochdale. The coffin was of polished oak, with raised lid and brass handles. The shield was of brass, engraved with the following inscription:—'John Ashworth, died January 26, 1875, aged 61.' The chapel was crowded during the impressive service, which was conducted by the Rev. W. R. Brown, minister of the United Methodist Free Church, Baillie-street, assisted by the Revs. T. W. Townend and T. B. Saul.

"During the service, the Rev. T. W. Townend offered up an impassioned and deeply impressive prayer. At the conclusion of the service in the chapel, a procession was formed to the newly-made grave or vault, which is close to the gravelled walk leading from the main entrance of the cemetery to the chapel, and on the left-hand side going from the entrance to the chapel, nearly half way between the two. As the coffin was being lowered into the grave many of the deceased's late congregation were unable to restrain their feelings and burst into tears, their example affecting even the little ones from the Mission-room, who could hardly be expected to realise the loss they had sustained. Amid the most reverent silence, broken only by occasional sobs, the remaining portion of the burial service was gone through. According to Mr. Ashworth's wish, the following hymn was sung at his funeral:

"Heaven is a place of rest from sin,
  But all who hope to enter there
Must here that only course begin
  Which shall their souls for rest prepare.

Clean hearts, O God, in us create,
  Right spirits, Lord, in us renew;
Commence we now that higher state,
  Now do Thy will as angels do.

A life in heaven!—O what is this?
  The sum of all that faith believed;
Fulness of joy and depth of bliss,
  Unseen, unfathomed, unconceived.

While thrones, dominions, princedoms, powers,
  And saints made perfect, triumph thus,
A goodly heritage is ours,
  There is a heaven on earth for us.

The Church of Christ, the school of grace,
  The Spirit teaching by the Word;—
In *those* our Saviour's steps we trace,—
  By *this* His living voice is heard.

Firm in His footsteps may we tread,
  Learn every lesson of His love,
And be from grace to glory led,
  From heaven below to heaven above.

At the conclusion of the service the teachers and Sunday-school children sang the following appropriate hymn;—

I have heard of a place over there,
  Where Jesus, my Saviour, doth reign:
There will be no more death over there,
  Neither sighing, nor sorrow, nor pain.

Chorus.—Oh! I've a home over there, over there,
    Where Jesus, my Saviour, doth reign—
  'Tis a beautiful place over there,
    Over there, over there.

I have friends that have gone over there,
  And I hope to rejoin them again;
How delightful to meet over there,
  And with loved ones for ever remain.

There are angels that sing over there,
  How pleasant their singing must be;
There are crowns for the faithful to wear,
  And I trust there's a bright one for me.

There are mansions for all over there,
  For the poor and the homeless below;
There is room for the world over there,
  And my Saviour invites all to go.

"No funeral oration was delivered at the grave, but the benediction having been pronounced, many crowded to take a last look at the coffin containing the remains of him whose memory will ever be fresh in their hearts, and whose influence, widely felt in the present generation, will continue through generations to come. Mr. Ashworth did not reach the allotted span of life, but to him the words of the poet are applicable—

> 'We live in deeds, not words; in thoughts, not breaths;
> In feelings, not in figures on a dial.'

If he did not live so long as many, he lived more, and usefulness is the measure of life. That useful life is now closed, but of him it cannot be said that 'the good' he has done is 'interred with his bones.' 'He being dead, yet speaketh.'"

The following is the inscription he has left for his tomb-stone:—

JOHN ASHWORTH,
AUTHOR OF
"STRANGE TALES," "WALKS IN CANAAN,' &c.,
BORN
JULY 8TH, 1813,
BORN AGAIN OF THE SPIRIT
OCTOBER 3RD, 1836,
LEFT THE KINGDOM OF GRACE,
FOR THE KINGDOM OF GLORY,
(JANUARY 26TH, 1875.)

One of his last dying bequests was, that all the children of the Sunday-school in School Lane should have a pair of new clogs and a pair of new stockings, which wish was carried out on the Wednesday following, in the presence of Mrs. Ashworth and the other executors, when one hundred and twenty-nine children received the dying gift of their benefactor and friend.

Since his decease his widow has been the recipient of many kind expressions of sympathy in her bereavement. The Baillie-street (U.M.F.C.) Leaders' Meeting sent the following letter of condolence, containing also a graceful tribute to the memory of her late husband:—

"Dear Mrs. Ashworth,—In accordance with a resolution adopted by the Baillie-street leaders' meeting, on Monday evening, Feb. 1st, we desire to express to you their deep sense of the great loss the church has sustained in the death of your husband, and also their sincere sympathy with you in your present painful bereavement.

"During thirty-five years Mr. Ashworth discharged his duties as one of the leaders of the Baillie-street society with exemplary diligence and fidelity, and, besides ministering to the comfort and edification of the members of his own class, as a frequent attender at the leaders' meeting he has rendered important service in the management of the affairs of the church. Apart from his great usefulness as a preacher, philanthropist, and author, the worth of his labours as an adviser and helper of those who have been intimately associated with him in Christian fellowship is such as calls for grateful acknowledgments to Almighty God. For the grace bestowed on him in life, and for his entrance into everlasting rest, we would offer praise unto the Lord. And we earnestly pray that the richest consolations of that gospel he delighted to proclaim may be plentifully granted you in the heavy grief that has befallen you. Many hearts have joined in fervent petitions that divine support may be given you, and we rejoice to believe that the God to whom these supplications have ascended will be your strength and comforter. 'Our light afflictions, which are but for a moment, work for us a far more exceeding and eternal weight of glory.'

"On behalf of the Baillie-street leaders' meeting we remain

Yours faithfully,

JOHN TURNER,
HENRY BUTTERWORTH, } Society Stewards.

"Baillie-street Leaders' Meeting, February 3rd, 1875."

A similar expression of sympathy was received from the Committee of Baillie-street Sunday-school, which stated that Mr. Ashworth became a teacher in December, 1840, was general superintendent in 1848-49, and retained his connection with the school as a teacher till his death.

Sometimes deeds speak more forcibly than words. At the Christian church, Bury (Rev. F. Howarth's), Mr. Ashworth had for several years been accustomed to conduct the morning service at the Sunday-school anniversary; and on that occasion in March last (1875), as the teachers and scholars came in attired in the habiliments of mourning, their pastor thought how many of them must have lost friends, and on enquiring, a teacher whispered, "John Ashworth." As soon as the gallery was filled, all rose, and sang the hymn "Over There." Many were in tears. The scene and the service were said to be most affecting and impressive.

I can only select one other tribute of affection from amongst many, showing the estimation in which the subject of this memoir was held, and that is from an intimate friend Mrs. Bagshawe, of Ford Hall in Derbyshire, whose discernment and appreciation of Mr. Ashworth's character is endorsed by all.

"Ford Hall, Chapel-en-le-Frith,
"January 27th, 1875.

"Dear Mr. Calman,

"I can scarcely tell you with what mingled feelings we received your telegram. Dear John Ashworth! I cannot believe that we shall see his face no more in this world. We are feeling true grief and sorrow for ourselves. To none, excepting his own family, will his loss be greater than to us; but he has died in harness, which would be a less trial to a mind like his, than if he had lingered on to helpless old age. I had often thought how bitter it would be for him when far advanced in years and unable to work for his Master, to feel that his active mission on earth was ended, and that nothing but a merely passive existence lay before him. God's grace can support us under all circumstances; but such a life would have been slow torture to John Ashworth.

"What a wonderful union of fine qualities of heart and mind our dear friend possessed; his intense pathos, his droll, quiet humour, his enjoyment of everything beautiful, his grand common sense and practical judgment, and the rarest gift of all—the power of seeing a question in its different bearings; all these made him such a many-sided man. It is seldom that one character combines so much variety. He had, too, the tenderest sympathy with suffering of any man I ever saw. Poverty and misery attracted him like a magnet. He did not speak to the poor and wretched because he ought, but because he could not help it. . . . And now that he is gone from us, and his ever welcome visits have become only a pleasant memory, those who enjoyed them would thankfully acknowledge that of the helps heavenward, with which our Father has cheered and strengthened them, one that will be cherished till life's latest hours, is the friendship of John Ashworth."

Sermons, having special reference to the death of Mr. Ashworth, and by way of improvement, were preached not only in Rochdale, but in Bury, Bradford, Birmingham, Sheffield, Leeds, Hull, and many other places where he was well known and his services much valued, showing from the various labours of the deceased what can be done by the power of a consecrated life, even under the most adverse circumstances, and as a stimulus to others to go and do likewise.

At his own Chapel for the Destitute Mr. John Harley preached to his sorrowing flock from Rev. xix. 13, "Blessed are the dead which die in the Lord," &c., and administered the Lord's Supper at the close; both services were deeply impressive and solemn.

At Baillie-street chapel, where the deceased has been for many years a member, Sunday-school teacher, and local preacher, the funeral sermon was preached by the Rev. T. W. Townend, the following condensed report of which, from the *Rochdale Observer*, is a manly and truthful outline of the various prominent traits in the life and character of the departed.

THE LATE JOHN ASHWORTH, OF BROADFIELD.

"On Sunday evening last, in the Baillie-street United Methodist Free Church, which was crowded on the occasion, the Rev. T. W. Townend delivered a discourse on the Christian life and labours of the late Mr. John Ashworth, of Broadfield. The preacher selected as his text, Acts xiii, 25: 'As John fulfilled his course.'

"Extravagant eulogies of departed friends were in any place unseemly, and in connection with God's worship they would be abominable. A temple erected for the honour of God's name should never be desecrated by the burning of incense to the glory of man. Where heathen nations were accustomed to deify illustrious men after their death and pay to them divine honours, they might expect excessive laudation to be commonly bestowed on the dead; but we who professed to believe that we had all sinned and come short of the glory of God should hold such a practice in detestation. It was, however, quite consistent with Christian teaching to make such reference to deceased servants of God as were likely to lead men to copy their virtues.

"Death had recently struck down one who was a leader and standard-bearer in the army of the living God, and his departure from us was so impressive and admonitory an event that it ought not to be unimproved. The name of John Ashworth, the author of 'Strange Tales,' and the founder of the Chapel for the Destitute, had occupied so large a space in the attention of the religious public of this and other lands that he could not be allowed to pass from us without some notice being directed to his life and labours, and to the great lessons which they taught, especially in the chapel where he had been so long a worshipper, and in connection with whicn he had for many years been an important office-bearer. It was with a view of making some remarks suitable to the occasion that he selected the text which he had read.

"THE WORDS OF THE TEXT MIGHT BE REGARDED IN THE FIRST PLACE AS INDICATING PERFECT INDIVIDUALITY OF CHARACTER.

"John the Baptist had a course and character of his own; he stood out from the rest of mankind as a striking example of moral courage and independence. Though John the Baptist had an extraordinary work, and passed through an extraordinary course of events, and was in many respects an extraordinary man, so that we could not presume to rank ourselves with him, it was quite certain that each of us as we passed through life would have both opportunity and necessity for the assertion of individuality of character. There would be times and circumstances in which they would have to act on their own personal convictions, irrespective of the sayings and doings of other people. There ought to be in them so much loyalty of conscience that they should be prepared to pursue the way of duty at all hazards and at all cost. They might be true to their convictions without claiming for themselves infallible wisdom. While not shrinking to avow their own religious belief they might still grant the same privilege to others whose belief might be different. But they must not try to repress a sense of duty. They must not stifle the voice of conscience for the sake of pleasing others. Instead of walking according to the course of this world, they must mark out for themselves a course which would be in conformity with the teachings of divine law. The determination to abide by what he believed to be truth and right made its possessor mightier than opposing orces. He who lived in the fear of God was not likely to be moved by the power of men. Conscious of the sincerity of his purpose to do God's will, his soul was fortfied against ll the scorn and cruelty of evil men.

"It was to persons of this character that they must look

for the finest examples of fortitude; fortitude more daring and heroic than ought ever exhibited in the most renowned exploits of chivalry; a fortitude which no difficulties could crush; a fortitude which, though single-handed in the conflict, would, through God, maintain its position against any number of human or infernal adversaries. Their late friend John Ashworth might be associated with men of that class. On great moral and religious questions he had an opinion and belief of his own, from which he would not swerve. While he had so much catholicity and charity as willingly to serve various sections of the church in any good enterprise, he would never make any compromise of religious principle.

"On some subjects he had sentiments which were contrary to popular views and feelings, but this did not prevent him giving expression to his opinions. He would sooner incur public disapprobation and censure; he would sooner suffer the spoiling of his goods and be bereft of all earthly possessions than do violence to his own convictions on matters relating to man's highest interests and future destiny. The courage that lived in the martyrs was not wanting in him, and had his lot been cast in the days of violent persecution he would have been willing to die in a dungeon or to have been burnt at the stake for the sake of the truth. Moral elasticity, that would either stretch or contract to suit itself to varying times and places, was a thing he abhorred. His mind was of too Puritanic an order; he was too much impressed with the solemnity and importance of Christian duty to allow of any trimming, time-serving policy in the affairs of religion.

"Some of his doings as a philanthropist, which indicated great tenderness of spirit, also indicated great moral strength. He had not only a heart to feel for others' woes, but he had the bravery to institute means for their relief in the face of formidable obstacles. His Chapel for the Destitute was not opened without some severe mental struggles, and unless he had been a man of great moral firmness and decision—a firmness and decision strengthened by divine influence, he never would have opened it. He besought God's help for the task, and that help was afforded. And there they saw the secret of his power; he was strong in God. 'I prayed earnestly,' he said, 'that He would give grace and firmness of purpose, to endure any amount of ridicule, abuse, misrepresentation, opposition, or imposition; that He would take money matters entirely into His own hands, and send us pecuniary help as it might be required. Believing that God would bless the undertaking, I determined not to consult any human being, but go at once to work, dependent upon God's help and blessing.' That resolution showed the noble make of the man. He had the intrepidity to go on without consulting any human being, believing that the enterprise would have the divine sanction and blessing. Such marked independence and perfect individuality of character manifested in the pursuit of great and good objects were rarely to be found. It was to men of that stamp that the world was indebted for its greatest reforms and improvements, and its most beneficial moral and religious agencies.

"'JOHN FULFILLED HIS COURSE.' THOSE WORDS SUGGESTED THAT EVERY MAN HAD A COURSE TO FULFIL, AND A WORK TO DO IN THIS WORLD.

"Diversified as were the conditions of human life, there was no state in life where they might not find some sphere of usefulness. Having eloquently dilated upon this theme, showing that all might live for some wise and noble end, the preacher said that an anxious desire to accomplish the work which Providence had assigned him was a prominent character of their brother whose death they that evening lamented. His was no aimless life, a simple getting through the world and nothing more. He lived as one who had a solemn charge laid upon him, as one intent upon doing his Master's will. In his intercourse with Mr. Ashworth he had been deeply impressed with the intense earnestness with which he prosecuted works of usefulness. He never suffered the grass to grow under his feet. There was no danger that he would rust for want of exercise. His powers never seemed to tire of his much-loved work of doing good. He was never weary of talking on topics that stood directly related to his work. His career furnished one of the most noteworthy instances to be found in the present age of earnest Christian enterprise and effort, commenced under inauspicious circumstances, becoming crowned with signal success. Had he been a visionary, or an idler, or a misanthropist, or a miser, or a spendthrift, or a drunkard, how different would have been the associations that gathered round his name. The eminence he acquired he acquired by the faithful discharge of what he felt to be his duty. It was while he was engaged in Christian and philanthropic labours that he collected many of the incidents recorded in the books that raised him into celebrity. Had he made an ambitious attempt to rise to some position for which he had no fitness, failure would have been the result, but by availing himself of the means of usefulness within his reach he produced most wonderful effects.

"Many had marvelled at the consequences of his labours, but perhaps no person in the world was more surprised than Mr. Ashworth himself. By fulfilling his course, not by stepping out of it, he wrought the deeds that made him illustrious. It would be interesting and instructive to enter into a full and careful consideration of the influences which contributed to the formation of his character, and which served to develop the qualities by which he became so conspicuous in the service of the Saviour. Amongst the most powerful of these influences, so far as human instrumentality was concerned, must be numbered the godly example, the tender affection, the fervent prayers, and the patient endurance of his pious mother, or as he himself expressed it, 'her quiet, steady, Christian conduct.' She did not forget her children in her prayers at the throne of grace ; one by one they were named by her in her supplications. Mr. Ashworth related how one morning, when he had risen early and was not aware that anyone else in the house had risen before him, he was creeping softly down the stairs, when he heard a low voice. Sitting down on the steps, he heard his mother praying for himself, as well as his brothers and sisters. 'Lord help John,' she said, 'and keep him from bad company, and make him a good and useful man.' 'Her words went to my young heart,' said Mr. Ashworth, 'and they are ringing in my ears to this hour. That short prayer uttered by my mother, when she thought no one heard her but God, to me has been a precious legacy.'

"Having dilated upon the subject of the influence of a Christian mother upon her children, the preacher said that Sunday-school instruction had an important place in the formation of the character of their deceased brother. In his tale entitled 'My Mother,' Mr. Ashworth remarked: 'From the first day I went, to the day I am writing this narrative, I have never left the Sunday-school, and I have had tens of thousands of blessings as a consequence. The Sunday-school has been a blessing to millions, but to none more than to myself. A mother's prayers and the Sunday-school have been my safeguard and blessing.'

"While a scholar in the Sunday-school he gave signs of youthful promise. They were all familiar with the touching story of him standing on the platform, before all the congregation, without shoes and stockings, at a certain Whit Friday school festival, when he received the highest prize for the year. On the principle that childhood showed the man, as morning showed the day, it might on that occasion have been easily anticipated that the barefooted lad who carried away the first prize, would at some future period make his mark in the world. The struggles and privations of his early life, painful though they were, were of great service to him in inuring him to hardship and toil. They taught him patience, and self-reliance, and sympathy for the sufferings of others. He would probably never have become the strong, large-hearted, heroic man he did, but for his early trials.

"In boyhood he had a fondness for books, and displayed that aptitude for relating narratives for which he was afterwards distinguished. One who had ample means of verifying the truth of the statement said: 'Whilst yet a ragged urchin he used to gather his sisters round him and read to them 'The Tales of the Covenanters.' They thought him a king while he turned John Brown into verse in those early days.'

"From other sources, he (the preacher) had learnt that at that time his power of story telling was remarkable, and sometimes produced most powerful impressions upon his boyish companions. In this, as in some other things, the child was father to the man. He could not relate all the circumstances which led to Mr. Ashworth's conversion to God, but he had himself left a record of the day.

"Speaking of the various kinds of conversion, he said that Mr. Ashworth's conversion was sudden. As described by himself, his deliverance from the terrors of guilt occurred opposite the cemetery where his remains now lay interred, on the 3rd October, 1836. Previously there had been some change in his outward mode of life in relation to religion, but it was on that day he became sensible of being a new creature in Christ Jesus. This blessed spiritual change lay at the foundation of his future Christian usefulness. Having himself become a participator in the blessedness of the Christian life, he was soon engaged in efforts for the spiritual enlightenment of others. His labours in the Sunday-school were prosecuted with new interest and vigour. After a while he became a recognised office bearer in the church. His name first appeared on the circuit preachers' plan in 1838; and during thirty-five years he sustained the office of leader in the church worshipping in that (Baillie-street) chapel. As years advanced his public labours and his influence widened. Retirement from business enabled him to extend his exertions as a philanthropist, preacher, and author. Though no hand of a mitred ecclesiastical dignitary had been laid upon him, he had received the God-given ordination. A divine appointment to the ministry was granted him, and he was in the true apostolic succession. He never troubled himself in preaching about nice metaphysical distinctions, but talked to men in a plain, pointed, practical, homely, hearty fashion. His utterances had the ring of genuineness and sincerity. He proclaimed the gospel as one who himself felt its quickening influence, and as one who himself believed it would meet the spiritual wants of his hearers.

"Having referred to his visits to many parts of the country, by which he travelled thousands of miles on what might be designated errands of mercy, and also to the most hearty reception he everywhere met with, the preacher said that deeds of philanthropy were Mr. Ashworth's delight; to advise the perplexed, to convert the scornful, to relieve the necessitous, was his loved employ. No small amount of his time was spent in counselling and helping those who by misfortune or their own folly and sins had been reduced to want and wretchedness. His house, to use his own words, was a 'moral hospital.' Many sad tales of woe were poured into his ears, and though in some instances his kindness was doubtless abused, in many more his genial, generous sympathy was rewarded with gratitude. He had too much shrewdness and discrimination to deal with all alike who sought his advice and aid. He could and did administer faithful warning and reproof to the wayward and prodigal, but he could never remain insensible to their suffering.

"While labouring as a preacher and philanthropist, he was also diligent as an author. His productions were public property, and public opinion had pronounced its verdict upon them. If success were any proof of merit, his writings had it in an uncommon degree. Through them his name was known and loved in every quarter of the globe. In varied languages, and amongst millions of diversified nationality, they were a source of incalculable spiritual benefit, and it was not unlikely they would yield greater moral benefits after his death than during his life.

"THAT IT IS BY DOING OUR DUTY AND FULFILLING OUR COURSE THAT THE TRUE DIGNITY AND BLESSEDNESS OF LIFE IS TO BE FOUND.

"Having eloquently discoursed upon this theme in its general application, the preacher said that the blessedness of doing the will of the Lord was in a great measure given to their deceased brother. His religion was emphatically a religion of doing. While he founded all his hope of acceptance with God on the atoning sacrifice of the Redeemer, he gave evidence of his faith by his works. He did what all might do. He became 'rich in good works.'

"Having referred to Mr. Ashworth's zealous labours amongst the despised, the neglected, and the outcast, taking hold of every opportunity to sow the seeds of truth and kindness, the preacher said that a record of all that Mr. Ashworth saw and heard while engaged in his benevolent pursuits would form a marvellous book, and would furnish most painful revelations of the moral and spiritual desolation of many of the people. His life had many lessons—lessons worthy the study of everyone; and this, among the rest, it most emphatically taught, *viz.*, that the church ought to show a more watchful care towards the spiritual wants of the indigent and immoral portion of the community.

"THE TEXT REMINDED THEM THAT THERE WAS A TERMINATION TO MAN'S EARTHLY COURSE.

"The most useful as well as the most useless life must have an end. Wise men and fools, the basest and the best, alike die. That was a trite truth, but what grave and perplexing questions were suggested by it! Why should the good be taken away from us? Why should one so beloved, and honoured, and useful as John Ashworth be removed from us when to all appearance he was little beyond the prime of manhood. His bodily strength had suffered scarcely any abatement when he was seized by the affliction which cut short his days; and his mental powers were never more vigorous and active. He was reaping the advantages of experience to a degree he had never done before, and in some important respects he was never so well fitted to give spiritual counsel, and to wield the pen, which in his hand was so mighty an instrument, with skill and efficiency. Why, then, should he have disappeared? To us short-sighted creatures, so slow to read and understand the acts of Infinite Wisdom, it did seem strange and mysterious, and were there no hereafter for man, no prospect of entering into a state where the most painful problems of the present order of things shall be solved, we might in the agony of despair exclaim, 'Wherefore hast Thou made all men in vain?' Taught by Divine revelation that our times are in the unerring hands of the Almighty it was our privilege to believe that His saints died neither too soon nor too late. When their course was finished and the great purposes of their existence on earth were answered, He called them to join the spirits of just men made perfect. No one amongst his hearers had a firmer reliance on the truth that 'God doeth all things well' than John Ashworth.

"When spoken to by friends during his illness as to whether there was any probability that he would recover, he had more than once replied to the effect that unless his work in this world was done God would not remove him to another. Though not unwilling to live—though, in fact, desirous to live, if God should be pleased to prolong his days, for he had plans of labour which were but partially executed—yet he was quite prepared to leave the issue with the Lord.

"As they beheld his fine athletic frame enfeebled and racked with disease, and heard him say, 'I have fed the hungry, and now myself am starving whilst there is plenty around me'—alluding to the fact that he was unable to swallow solid food—there was enough to make them deeply sad. He (the preacher) said to him about a fortnight before his death, 'The struggle is hard.' 'Yes, it is,' he answered, 'I cannot tell you how hard it is, but the will of the Lord be done.'

"Addressing him (the preacher) in the same interview, Mr. Ashworth said, 'Preach the gospel;' emphasising these words, 'the gospel, preach the gospel.' 'I thank God,' continued he, 'I have not only tried to preach the gospel, but I have believed it.' Yes, he believed it, and in his last hours, when earth's scenes were fast fading from his view, he found that he that believeth shall not make haste. The ground on which he built his confidence did not fail him when his tabernacle of clay was beginning to dissolve; he rested upon immovable rock. There were no heart-quakings in the final conflict. He went down to the vale of death as one who knew he was going home to his Father in heaven. Such utterances as these fell from his lips during the closing moments of his life, 'I want to be at rest, I want to be at rest;' 'Oh, it is glorious, it is glorious; all glorious, all glorious.' 'Bless the Lord, bless the Lord, bless the Lord for ever and ever.' Now he had gone to swell the chorus of blessing and thanksgiving which angels and redeemed men give to God and the Lamb for ever."

As the hope of Mr. Ashworth's recovery grew fainter, he naturally turned his thoughts with some anxiety to the Chapel for the Destitute, and prepared the following circular letter, addressed to all subscribers and friends, upon whose continued sympathy and support he seemed confident.

BROADFIELD, ROCHDALE,

December 29th, 1874.

Dear Friend,

Feeling that my health is gradually giving way, and having an impression that my work is done, I most sincerely thank you for the sympathy and support you have given to the "CHAPEL FOR THE DESTITUTE," and all our operations in connection therewith: and I have now great pleasure in recommending to you, as my successor, Mr. ANDREW L. CALMAN, who has been my fellow-labourer in the work for upwards of ten years, and has kindly undertaken, with the help of God, the responsibility of carrying it on, and who will, I have no doubt, act as a faithful steward of all moneys that may henceforth be entrusted into his hands. Farewell!

Yours in Christ,

JOHN ASHWORTH.

Witnesses:

Hannah Ashworth, his Wife.
John Ashworth, Nissi Villa, Rochdale, his Nephew, and an Executor.

CHAPEL FOR THE DESTITUTE.

BAILLIE-STREET, ROCHDALE.

PUBLIC SERVICE every Sabbath Evening, at Six o'clock: and on Thursday at 7-30.

EXPERIENCE MEETING on Tuesday, at 7-30.

MOTHERS' MEETING on Wednesday at 2.

ADULT SCHOOL for Men and Women of any age, anxious to learn Reading and Writing, on Sabbath Afternoon, in the same place, at 2-30.

In the MISSION ROOM, No. 1 Court, School Lane:—

SABBATH SCHOOL in the Morning at Ten, and Afternoon at Two o'clock.

PUBLIC SERVICE every Sabbath Evening at Six.

TUESDAY, ENQUIRERS' MEETING at 7-30.

WEDNESDAY, MOTHERS' MEETING at Two o'clock.

WEDNESDAY, GIRLS' SEWING CLASS at 7-30.

FRIDAY, BOYS' CLASS at 7-30.

BAND OF HOPE MEETING on the First Wednesday of every Month at 7-30.

Ye houseless, homeless, friendless, penniless outcasts, Come!
In rags and tatters, ... Come!
Ye poor, and maimed, and halt, and blind, ... Come!
Of whatever colour or nation; creed or no creed, ... Come!

Jesus loves you,
And died to save you.

Come then, to Him, all ye wretched,
Lost and ruin'd by the fall;
If you tarry till you're better,
You will never come at all.

NO COLLECTION.

All we seek is your welfare, both body and soul.
Come, poor Sinners; come, and welcome.

WORKS BY JOHN ASHWORTH.

SECOND SERIES.

14.	Mothers ...	81,000
15.	Twenty Pounds; or, The Little Prayer	97,000
16.	All is Well	106,000
17.	My Uncle; or, Johnny's Box	59,000
48.	Old Adam	54,000
19.	Ellen Williams ...	54,000
20.	Trials	53,000
21.	Answered at Last	48,000
22.	Priscilla...	56,000
23.	Julia; or, The First Wrong Step	57,000
24.	No Cotton	50,000
25.	My Young Ragged Friends	48,000

Nos. 14 to 25 in Packets at 1/-.

THIRD SERIES.

26.	The Lost Curl ...	47,000
27.	Emmot	57,000
28.	The Widow	42,000
29.	Sarah; or, I Will Have Him ...	66,000
30.	My Sick Friends. Part 1.	43,000
31.	My Sick Friends. Part 2.	38,000
32.	George ...	46,000
33.	James Burrows	86,000
34.	John and Mary	43,000
35.	A Sad Story	67,000
36.	Lucy's Legacy ...	43,000
37.	Edmund	39,000

Nos. 26 to 37 in Packets at 1/-.

FOURTH SERIES.

38.	The Golden Wedding ...	43,000
39.	William the Tutor	36,000
40.	Fathers	37,000
41.	Little Susan	35,000
42.	Old Matthew	45,000
43.	Old Ab'	32,000
44.	Milly ...	30,000
45.	The Fog Bell	29,000
46.	Mrs. Bowden	26,000
47.	Happy Ned	41,000
48.	Harry ...	30,000
49.	A Dancer	29,000

Nos. 38 to 49 in Packets at 1/-.

FIFTH SERIES.

50.	The Old Deacon	15,000
51.	The Red Lamp. Part 1.	32,000
52.	Billy Bray	25,000
53.	Job Morley	27,000
54.	The Bible Woman	15,000
55.	My Blind Friends	13,000
56.	The Red Lamp. Part 2.	15,000
57.	The Wanderers	10,000
58.	Fathers' Sins	10,000
59.	"Penny it Shillin'."	15,000
60.	The Old Exchange	8,000
61.	The Top Room	11,000

Nos. 50 *to* 61 *in Packets at* 1/-.

The following are issued in Welsh, and may be had One Penny each.

Rhif 1. Joseph, neu y Gongl Ddystaw.
„ 2. Niff a'i Gwn.
„ 3. Fy Mam.
„ 4. Sanderson ac Alice Fechan.
„ 5. Yr Awr Dywell.

Ereill i ganlyn.

"If any man may take to himself the proud thought that he has been instrumental for God in the generation in which he lived, the man who wrote 'Strange Tales,' who had seen three million copies of these 'Strange Tales' circulated in his lifetime, may at least go out of the world with the conscience that he had lifted up his voice for what was true, what was pure, what was lovely, and what was of good report."—*Bishop of Manchester.*

"Mr. Ashworth's Tales and Books are above my praise; they are circulated, I believe, not by thousands, but by millions, and the result is that the name of John Ashworth is a Household word, not only in the lordly halls, but in the lowly homes of England."—*Dr. Guthrie.*

Walks in Canaan.

With 7 full-page Illustrations and Map. Cloth, 2s. 6d.; extra cloth, gilt edges, 3s. 6d. Thirty-second thousand.

Back from Canaan.

(A Sequel to Walks in Canaan.)

With 7 full-page Illustrations and Map. Cloth, 2s. 6d.; extra cloth, gilt edges, 3s. 6d.

WORKS BY JOHN ASHWORTH.

Carte of John Ashworth,

Copied from the last Photograph taken in New York. Price 6d.

Simple Records.

FIRST SERIES. CLOTH, 1/6.

ALSO FIRST AND SECOND SERIES BOUND TOGETHER, 3/-.

In Packets, as Tracts, 9d. Also in separate Tracts, 8 pages One Halfpenny; 16 pages, One Penny Each. 24 pages, 1½d.

	PAGES.
Little Sandy	8
New Eyes	8
The Three Sisters	8
The New Mound	8
A Troublesome Halfpenny / The Three Truant Boys	8
The New Shawl / I'm too Big Now	8
Where's my Jacket? / Shall we Expel Him? ...	8
The Brothers / Edward's Grave / The White Frock	16
Kate / Willy / Lucy Smith	16
A Mistake	8
Old Thomas / Rachel Riley / Philip	16
A Broken Promise	8
"Let me pat Turk"	8
Rose	8
My First Book	16
The Contest	8

SECOND SERIES. CLOTH, 1/6.

	PAGES.
"Proud of my Father" ..	8
The Little Church	16
The Two Monuments ...	8
The Young Disciples... ...	8
Fellow Labourers	8
No Whip	16
Annie Waddington	16
The Children's Verdict ...	8
Newgate	8
Happy To-day	8
A Covenanter's Grave / Charms and Witches ...	24
A Spree	8
All is Right	8
All Wrong	8
Power of Mothers	8

Tubbs & Brook, Printers, Manchester.

Lightning Source UK Ltd.
Milton Keynes UK
UKHW012346070119
335173UK00008B/744/P